North Atlantic PANORAMA
1900-1976
P Ransome-Wallis

Anchor Line SS CITY OF ROME of 1881, a single-screw ship of 8415tG. She was one of the most beautiful ships of her time /NMM

North Atlantic
PANORAMA
1900-1976
P Ransome-Wallis

Queen Elizabeth 2

Wesleyan University Press
Middletown, Connecticut

Library of Congress Catalog Card Number: 77-74564
ISBN 0-8195-5016-7
First edition

CONTENTS

Introduction 6
Author's Notes 10
Acknowledgements 10
1897–1973 11
Appendix 1 176
Appendix 2 177
Appendix 3 179
Appendix 4 181
Appendix 5 184
Appendix 6 189
Appendix 7 189
Bibliography 190
Index 191

INTRODUCTION

The twentieth century has seen the transatlantic passenger liner provide a standard of travel which for opulence, comfort and luxury has never been equalled, let alone surpassed, in any other field of transportation.

At the turn of the century the modern liner was beginning to take shape. Elegant clipper-bowed ships, often carrying sails as reserve 'power', were still in service but the introduction of such ships as the *Hamburg-Amerika* FÜRST BISMARCK of 1890 and the *White Star* MAJESTIC of the same date showed the North Atlantic liner in a form which was to be familiar for the next fifty years. With the building of the *Norddeutscher Lloyd* KAISER WILHELM DER GROSSE in 1897 the transatlantic liner achieved completely new standards of speed and luxury, and with its inherent possibilities for use as a commerce raider in time of war provided a challenge to which other nations, especially Great Britain, were bound to respond.

Soon, however, the North Atlantic passenger trade developed two distinct trends, which were to be followed for the next sixty years. *Cunard* and *Norddeutscher Lloyd* became the principal advocates of the high speed luxury ship, and were eventually challenged by *Compagnie Générale Transatlantique* and *Italia*, and much later by *United States Lines*. Other companies, notably *White Star* and *Hamburg-Amerika*, provided very large ships of moderate speed but even greater luxury. All companies built smaller but still very comfortable ships for their 'secondary' services.

In the technical development of great ships, the twentieth century has seen enormous strides forward.

The rivetted hull with knife-edge bow and counter stern has given way to the largely pre-fabricated welded hull with bulbous bow and cruiser stern. Aluminium alloy superstructures have replaced heavy steel upperworks and funnels have become fewer in number and developed strange shapes.

In accommodation, wood has been largely replaced by non-inflammable synthetic materials and the lofty dignity of the public rooms of the Atlantic liners of the prewar years has generally given way to lower deck-heads and modern 'sophisticated' décor. Air conditioning, stabilisation, cabin telephones and even television are now standard passenger comforts.

Safety at sea has not lagged behind in the general development, and modern navigational aids, including radar, position- and direction-finding devices and many other electronic and sonic instruments, have become standard equipment.

Passenger liners built specifically for North Atlantic service remained predominantly steamships and few motor ships were built for the Western Ocean. The turn of the century saw triple- and quadruple-expansion reciprocating engines firmly established and able to provide speeds in excess of 20 knots. The courageous decision to equip the *Allan* liners VICTORIAN and VIRGINIAN with direct drive steam turbines in 1905 was a great step forward, and a large number of important ships followed using this form of propulsion.

Hamburg-Amerika SS FÜRST BISMARCK, 8430tG was a twin-screw ship with triple expansion engines and a speed of 19 knots. Her appearance is very much more like that of the transatlantic liner of the twenties and thirties and seems a long way removed from the clipper-bowed CITY OF ROME of only nine years earlier / NMM

In 1909 the *White Star* LAURENTIC, for which high speed was not required, set new standards of economy by introducing a low pressure turbine powered by steam already expanded in quadruple-expansion engines. The turbine drove a third, centrally placed, shaft. This arrangement, a brainchild of the Harland and Wolff yard, became quite widely used and was very successful.

It soon became obvious that turbine efficiency could be greatly improved by the use of reduction gearing between the turbine and the shaft. A simple form of single-reduction helical gearing was first used in commercial service in 1911 and this was followed seven years later by the introduction of a lay shaft between the turbine gear wheel and that of the shaft, that is, double-reduction-gearing.

The successful application of the greatly increased power output of these forms of turbine drive would not have been possible with the old type of multiple collar thrust-block. With the introduction to merchant ships of the famous Michell thrust in 1914, however, the problem was completely overcome and the direct drive turbine for ship propulsion gave way entirely to geared turbine drive.

Another fascinating development of steam propulsion was the greatly improved efficiency of boilers. Although experiments with oil-firing had taken place as long ago as 1870, it was not until the early 1920s that it became widely adopted in North Atlantic liners, and coal-fired boilers were then converted on a large scale to burn oil. Steam pressures were increased, but there were a number of setbacks and it was not until after the end of World War II that pressures in excess of 400psi were regarded as generally acceptable.

It is of interest to compare the numbers of boilers required in the largest liners; the following table, referring to ships of *Cunard Line*, shows the progress in boiler efficiency.

Date	Ship	Number of main boilers	Pressure (psi)	Output of turbines (shp at service speed)	Service speed (knots)
1907	MAURETANIA	25	165	68000	25
1912	BERENGARIA	46	235	62000	23
1914	AQUITANIA	21	195	60000	23
1935	QUEEN MARY	24	400*	160000	28
1940	QUEEN ELIZABETH	12	450*	160000	28
1968	QUEEN ELIZABETH 2	3	850†	110000	28

* 700°F *of superheat*
† 950°F *of superheat*

Seven major events have influenced the fortunes of North Atlantic shipping in the twentieth century.

1. During the first decade, the great exodus of people from Europe to North America. This resulted in ships being built to carry large numbers of emigrants in third class accommodation, often of dormitory type, and at the cheapest possible rate.
2. World War I, which nearly wiped out the fleets of some companies but which resulted in boom conditions on the North Atlantic for the decade following the Armistice of 1918. Except that—
3. The passing of the United States laws of 1924 limiting immigration dramatically altered the pattern of North Atlantic shipping and put some companies out of business.

White Star SS MAJESTIC, 9965tG, was similar in dimensions, propulsion and speed to FÜRST BISMARCK but her appearance and silhouette were very different. Many *White Star* liners of much later years were not dissimilar in appearance /NMM

The first class dining room of *Cunard* SS AQUITANIA shows the rather ornate but superb elegance of the great North Atlantic liners at the height of their fame /NMM

4. The great Depression of the early 1930s caused more financial failures in the shipping world than perhaps any other single cause.

5. World War II caused losses in merchant shipping so great that at times it was doubtful if they could be sustained. A number of large North Atlantic ships were lost, and others were converted permanently for other duties. Once again, there was a postwar boom during most of the decade following 1945.

6. After World War II transatlantic air travel rapidly increased in facility and popularity and, despite the improvements and developments in sea travel, more and more passengers travelled by air. In the year 1957 approximately one million passengers were carried by air across the North Atlantic and about an equal number went by sea. In 1962 all the North Atlantic lines together carried only 42000 passengers on scheduled voyages.

7. The ever-increasing popularity of pleasure cruising in ocean liners, especially in the United States, has to some extent compensated for the loss of passenger trade on scheduled services, and by providing work for ships and men, especially during the winter, has been the saving of some companies.

Cruising has also resulted in the construction of a new type of liner, the 'dual-purpose' ship, providing private facilities and, being fully air-conditioned and stabilised, equally at home in bitter North Atlantic weather and the calm heat of tropical seas.

Since 1968 there have been no regular sailings during the winter months between the United Kingdom and North America, and even during the summer there are comparatively few, though a considerable number of crossings, both eastward and westward, are included in cruising itineraries. *Cunard*'s QUEEN ELIZABETH 2 and the *CGT* liner FRANCE provided the most regular and frequent summer service, but FRANCE was not economic and was withdrawn late in 1974. Until late 1972 *Italia* operated MICHELANGELO, RAFFAELLO, LEONARDO DA VINCI and CRISTOFORO COLOMBO on a regular service between Genoa, Naples and New York, with calls at other Mediterranean ports, and this area was the best served in Europe. Now the first two have been sold as accommodation ships and the last two operate between Genoa and South America, but are also used for cruising. The same is true of the *Greek Line*, which no longer operates QUEEN ANNA MARIA (ex EMPRESS OF BRITAIN) on the service between Haifa, Piraeus and New York. The *Spanish Line* ships COVADONGA and GUADALUPE were withdrawn and scrapped in April 1973 and the Barcelona, Puerto Rica and New York service discontinued.

The ending of so many of the North Atlantic passenger services has resulted in a large number of transfers and sales of ships. Many famous transatlantic liners now sail with new names and often with considerable alteration to their appearance. The shipyards of Italy and Greece particularly have much expertise and experience in passenger ship reconstruction and rebuilding, and comparatively few of the world's cruising ships have been built new for the present owners.

While it is sometimes difficult to identify all of these rebuilt and renamed ships it is often far more difficult to unravel the complicated and devious structures of many of the owning companies. Not only is the ownership of the ship often obscure, but the 'ownership of the owners' can be far more so. Add to the puzzle the operating of ships under 'flags of convenience' and the whole business becomes incredibly complex.

The purpose of this book is to describe and to illustrate the development of the North Atlantic passenger liner in the twentieth century. During this period many shipping companies participated in the North Atlantic passenger trade and a large number of ships was built.

The term 'North Atlantic passenger liner' refers to those ships which have traded between Europe and the Eastern seaboard of the United States and Canada. Ships trading to Central and South America and to the Caribbean are not included. No attempt is made to list *all* North Atlantic ships. This has already been done by N. R. P. Bonsor in his *North Atlantic Seaway*.

The decision as to what to include and what to leave out of the book has been very difficult but throughout four principles have been followed:

1. To describe all of the very important giant express liners and to illustrate each with one or more photographs.
2. To include descriptions and photographs of a representative selection of the smaller and often less well-known liners which sailed the 'Western Ocean'; also to include some of the ships whose service in this sphere was only temporary.
3. To show some of the ships as they appeared in wartime service—this perhaps as a small tribute to the immense contribution made by these ships during two world wars.
4. To illustrate and describe the ships in chronological order, the relevant dates being shown at the head of each page.

The great liner fleets of *Cunard, Canadian Pacific, Hamburg-Amerika* and many others, have gone forever. It is hoped that some memories of them may be awakened in the pages of this book.

January 1977   P R-W

The modern furnishing and decor of *Cunard* QUEEN ELIZABETH 2 contrasts strongly with that of AQUITANIA. While the rather odd-looking chairs are no doubt very comfortable the rough and apparently badly fitted carpet would certainly not have been acceptable fifty years ago /*Cunard*

AUTHOR'S NOTES

The ships illustrated and described herein are presented in chronological order and the relevant dates are shown at the head of each page.

A single date thus: 1922, indicates that the ship entered service on the North Atlantic in that year.

Two dates separated by an oblique thus: 1907/1920, indicates that the ship was completed during the first year and worked elsewhere. The second date is the year in which that ship commenced North Atlantic service.

Two dates separated by a hyphen thus: 1956-1961, show the period during which two or more ships of the same class, entered North Atlantic service.

Abbreviations have been kept to a minimum. The following are used:

bhp = brake horsepower
ihp = indicated horsepower
shp = shaft horsepower
rpm = revolutions per minute
psi = pounds per square inch (steam pressure)
oa = overall (length or breadth)
pp = between perpendiculars (length)
tG = tons gross
tN = tons nett
tD = tons displacement
tdw = tons deadweight.

Note on Tonnage

Gross tonnage is a measurement of space not of weight and indicates the total permanently enclosed space of a ship—her internal volume. One ton gross is equivalent to 100 cubic feet.

Nett tonnage is the gross tonnage *less* the space occupied by engines, boilers, bunkers, crew quarters and all other space which, though essential for the working of the ship, is 'non-earning'. The net tonnage therefore indicates how much revenue earning space there is in the ship.

Tons displacement is the actual weight of the ship in long tons (2240 pounds avoirdupois), as determined by the equivalent weight of water displaced by the ship when afloat.

Tons deadweight is the total weight of cargo, fuel, stores, crew and all items which are not actually a part of the ship, but which the ship can carry when she is floating down to her load marks.

In this book the size of the ships illustrated is expressed in tons gross. This is the usual (and rational) measurement employed for passenger liners. The figures given are usually those relevant to the ship when built. Quite minor structural alterations can obviously alter the gross tonnage figures and these are not recorded. Where extensive reconstruction has resulted in a major shift of the figures, these are given when known.

Note on Speed

The unit of speed at sea is the knot. *One knot is the rate of one nautical mile per hour.* It is not a distance, and therefore to talk about 'knots per hour' is rubbish. A nautical mile is equivalent to 6080ft, or 800ft more than the land mile of 5280ft.

Note on Dimensions

In order to avoid an excess of figures in the text, the length and breadth of ships are given in Appendix 1 at the end of this book.

Note on Passenger Accommodation

Nearly always this will vary during the life of the ship and the numbers of passengers carried in each class may be altered considerably. Unless otherwise indicated, the figures given are those appertaining to the ship as she first went into service.

ACKNOWLEDGEMENTS

I am very grateful to the many famous shipping companies who have so generously supplied information about their companies and their ships and who have also provided many excellent photographs.

Beken of Cowes, Real Photographs of Broadstairs and Skyfotos of Ashford Airport have been most helpful in their endeavours to find for me views of particular ships.

To G. A. Osbon Esq of the National Maritime Museum, Greenwich, go my very sincere thanks for his unfailing and cheerful efforts to find for me so many of the rare photographs which are now presented in this book.

Credits are given beneath each photograph and for the most part these are self-evident. However, the initials 'NMM' are used to indicate National Maritime Museum, while the credit 'P R-W' indicates that the photograph was taken by the author.

1897-1907

KAISER WILHELM DER GROSSE was built for *Norddeutscher Lloyd* (*NDL*) by the Vulkan Yard at Stettin in 1897. Strictly, she does not come within the scope of this book, but her influence on North Atlantic shipping was so great that there is every justification for her inclusion.

In the 1890s, *NDL* had only a number of comparatively small and slow ships with which to maintain their North Atlantic services. Competition, mainly from Britain, but also from the German *Hamburg-Amerika Line*, was fierce and *NDL* therefore decided to invest in a new ship, more luxurious, larger and faster than anything then in existence. The builders were required to guarantee not only that the ship achieved her designed speed of 21 knots on trials, but that she should at least achieve this speed as an average on her first eastward and westward Atlantic crossings. KAISER WILHELM DER GROSSE fulfilled her contract, averaging 21·39 knots outwards and 21·91 knots homeward. Furthermore, her performance steadily improved and in March 1898 she gained the Atlantic Blue Riband with speeds of 22·31 knots westbound and 22·35 knots eastbound. She thus gained for Germany a record which until that time had been almost exclusively British and the result paid off handsomely in the great increase of passenger traffic which was gained by *NDL*.

Strangely enough the first successful challenge to this speed supremacy came from Germany when in 1900 *Hamburg-Amerika Line*, who had never shown much interest in North Atlantic speed records, gained the Blue Riband in July 1900 with their new ship DEUTSCHLAND, which also was built by the Vulkan yard at Stettin. However, this venture proved unprofitable and no 'running mate' was built for DEUTSCHLAND. *Hamburg-Amerika*, like the British

White Star Line, in future concentrated on large comfortable ships of moderate speed.

Norddeutscher Lloyd however built three more ships each of which was faster than those of any other company except DEUTSCHLAND and there was considerable competition between this ship and the *NDL* ship KRONPRINZ WILHELM of 1901, KAISER WILHELM II of 1903 and her sister ship KRONPRINZESSIN CECILIE of 1907. Each of these ships was an improvement and, in the case of the last two, a considerable enlargement of the basic design of KAISER WILHELM DER GROSSE. All were very beautiful four-funnelled liners, all could exceed 23 knots and all had reciprocating engines driving twin screws. The German Admiralty was interested in their wartime potential as commerce raiders and so they presented more than simply a commercial challenge to Britain. The far reaching result of *NDL*'s bold experiment of 1897 was the government-subsidised construction of *Cunard*'s MAURETANIA and LUSITANIA and the exciting, if delayed, events which followed.

SS KAISER WILHELM DER GROSSE of *NDL* was of 14349tG. She had twin screws driven by two four-cylinder triple-expansion engines each of 14000ihp. She was very well subdivided into watertight compartments. Her regular service was between Bremen and New York, calling at Southampton outward and Plymouth homeward. She could carry 332 first class passengers, 343 second class and no fewer than 1074 in third class between decks.

She became an armed merchant cruiser on the outbreak of World War I but during the first month

SS KAISER WILHELM DER GROSSE of NDL /Real Photographs

of the war she was sunk by the old British cruiser HIGHFLYER while she was bunkering (illegally) in Spanish territorial waters at Rio de Oro.

It is of interest that this ship was the first passenger liner in the world to be equipped with wireless telegraphy. Operating on the Marconi system, experimental transmissions were made between KAISER WILHELM DER GROSSE and a German lightship in 1899.

The first ever ship-to-shore transmissions were, however, made by Marconi himself when he was a passenger in the *American Line* SS ST PAUL of 1895. Using short-range equipment he was able to transmit messages to a receiving station previously established at The Needles, Isle of Wight, on November 15th, 1899.

SS KRONPRINZ WILHELM, 14908tG went into service between Bremen, Southampton and New York in 1901. She was only slightly larger than KAISER WILHELM DER GROSSE but considerably more powerful; her two four-cylinder triple-expansion engines were each of 16500ihp. Her contract speed was 23 knots and she exceeded this regularly in service. Her appearance was almost identical with that of her predecessor and her passenger disposition remained almost the same. She carried 367 first class, 340 second class and 1054 in the third class between decks.

She was a popular and successful ship and made at least three crossings at record speed. At the outbreak of World War I she was in New York, but managed to get away before the enforcement of the internment laws and she obtained some armament in the West Indies from the German cruiser KARLSRUHE. As a commerce raider, she did little harm to the Allies and eventually the problems of maintaining, supplying and bunkering a single ship so far from her home waters proved to be insuperable. KRONPRINZ WILHELM therefore returned to the United States and internment at Newport News in April 1915.

When the United States came into the war in 1917 the ship was repaired and used as a troop transport, being renamed VON STEUBEN. She never returned to commercial ownership and was scrapped in 1923.

SS KRONPRINZESSIN CECILIE, 19503tG was the last of the *NDL* quartet of express liners and was built by the Vulkan yard, Stettin, being completed in 1907. She was a sister ship of KAISER WILHELM II of 1903 and the machinery in both ships was almost identical in design. However, that of KRONPRINZESSIN CECILIE was more powerful; her twin screws were driven by reciprocating engines which aggregated 45000ihp against 38000 in KAISER WILHELM II. Her contract speed was 23·5 knots, about ½ knot more than her sister.

The engines of these two ships were unique and represented the ultimate development of the steam reciprocating engine for marine use. Two quadruple-expansion engines used in series, one ahead and in line with the other, powered each shaft. Each engine had only three cranks, the high-pressure cylinder being mounted above the intermediate-pressure and in tandem with it, there being a common piston rod for the two cylinders. These two cylinders were in the centre of each engine, the two low-pressure being at the extremities. Transverse and fore and aft bulkheads divided the engine room into four water-

SS KRONPRINZ WILHELM /NMM

tight compartments, each containing an engine. The overall height of each engine was 49·75m, which has probably been equalled only by stationary installations in mills and pumping stations. Nineteen boilers supplied steam at 16kg/cm² and burned 690 tonnes of coal per day at 23 knots.

The ships were luxurious in their appointments; in each the first class dining saloon was of magnificent proportions, capable of seating 500 passengers at a time. The passenger complement of KRONPRINZESSIN CECILIE was 617 first class, 326 second class and 798 third class in the 'tween decks, and these numbers were similar in her older sister ship.

With her three 'running mates' she gave splendid service on the North Atlantic until the outbreak of World War I, but the sensational introduction of the record-breaking MAURETANIA and LUSITANIA in 1907 robbed the German service of much of its glamour.

All the German ships had strengthened positions for gun mountings and it was intended that they should be used as heavily armed commerce raiders but on the outbreak of World War I KAISER WILHELM II was in New York and, with many other German ships, was interned. KRONPRINZESSIN CECILIE was homeward bound carrying £2m in gold. Rather than risk capture by the Royal Navy, she returned hurriedly to Bar Harbor, Maine and was later interned at Boston, Mass.

In 1917, with the entry of the United States into the war, both ships were refitted by the Americans and used as fast transports, first to take US troops to Europe and later to bring them back again. KAISER WILHELM II was renamed AGAMEMNON and later MONTICELLO, and KRONPRINZESSIN CECILIE was renamed MOUNT VERNON. In 1918 she was torpedoed

by a German submarine but her magnificent subdivision saved her and she was repaired at Brest.

After the war both ships were found to be in such poor condition that the United States Shipping Board was unwilling to provide the huge sum of money needed to rehabilitate them. After being moored in the Chesapeake river for sixteen years, both ships were sold for scrap in 1940.

SS DEUTSCHLAND, 16502tG was built by the Vulkan Yard, Stettin, for *Hamburg-Amerika Line* (*HAPAG*) and went into service in 1900. She had twin screws driven by two sets of six-cylinder quadruple-expansion engines of 33000ihp, which gave her a service speed of 23 knots. She was the first and only *HAPAG* record breaker. She took the Blue Riband from the *NDL* KAISER WILHELM DER GROSSE and then fought a ding-dong battle for this supremacy with the *NDL* quartet over the next seven years, until MAURETANIA and LUSITANIA put the record beyond the reach of any of them.

DEUTSCHLAND suffered badly from vibration at high speeds and her accommodation for 700 first class, 300 second class and 280 third class passengers was seldom fully booked. She was however an elegant and beautifully proportioned ship and in 1911 she was taken off the North Atlantic and converted to become a luxury cruising 'yacht' with a maximum speed of 18 knots, which certainly cured the vibration. Her name was changed to VICTORIA LUISE.

At the outbreak of World War I the ship was in Hamburg and remained there throughout the war. At the end of hostilities she was considered by the

SS KRONPRINZESSIN CECILIE /NMM

SS DEUTSCHLAND /NMM

Reparations Commission to be in too bad a condition to be worth refitting. She was then left in the possession of *HAPAG* who, being desperately short of ships, repaired her, removed two of her funnels and renamed her HANSA.

In 1920 *HAPAG* made a twenty-year agreement with *United American Lines* for the reintroduction on an equal share basis of *HAPAG*'s prewar services and it was for this joint company that HANSA made many crossings between Hamburg and New York during the period 1922-1924. At the end of that time a new DEUTSCHLAND (sister ship of ALBERT BALLIN) went into service and the old record breaker was withdrawn and scrapped in 1925.

1900

The *Cunard* sister ships, SS IVERNIA, 14058tG, and SS SAXONIA, 14381tG, were completed for service in 1900, the former built by Swan Hunter, the latter by John Brown. They were elegant ships, each with four masts and a single very tall funnel. They had twin screws driven by two quadruple-expansion engines which gave them a service speed of 15 knots. In addition to their generous passenger capacity (each ship carried 164 first class, 200 second, and 1600 third class passengers) they could carry a large quantity of cargo. They soon gained a reputation as excellent and steady sea-boats and became very popular on the North Atlantic.

IVERNIA and SAXONIA were built for the Liverpool–Boston service of the company but as a result of the Boer War IVERNIA first ran to New York, deputising for the six *Cunard* mail steamers which had been hurriedly requisitioned for trooping. In 1912 both ships were transferred to the Trieste–New

Cunard SS IVERNIA, the first ship to carry the name /
Cunard

Cunard SS SAXONIA /*Cunard*

York service, carrying emigrants from Europe to America.

During World War I the two ships were requisitioned as troopships and in 1917 IVERNIA was torpedoed and sunk off Cape Matapan by a German submarine.

SAXONIA survived the war and, after being extensively refitted and having her funnel made shorter, she sailed between London and New York, usually with a call at Cherbourg, and later on the emigrant trade between Hamburg and North American ports. With the passing of the United States immigration laws, she became redundant and was scrapped in Holland in 1925.

SS STOCKHOLM, 12976tG, of the *Swedish-American Line* was a twin-screw ship powered by two triple-expansion engines which gave her a speed of 15 knots. When new, her funnel was heightened to improve the steaming of her boilers.

STOCKHOLM was built by Blöhm and Voss, Hamburg, as POTSDAM and she went into service for the *Holland-America Line* in 1900. With two sister ships, RYNDAM and NOORDAM (and later with other ships) she maintained the Rotterdam–New York passenger and mail services for that company until 1915. By then, as a result of World War I, this trade was greatly reduced and POTSDAM was sold for a high price to the newly formed *Swedish-American Line* for their Gothenburg–New York service.

For a 13000-ton ship her passenger capacity was enormous; she carried 282 first class passengers, 210 second class and no fewer than 1800 in the third class.

It is of interest to note that her sister ship NOORDAM was chartered by *Swedish-American Line* for the two years 1923-1924 and during this period sailed as KUNGSHOLM.

Despite the difficulties of wartime sea transportation, this Scandinavian company prospered greatly and, during her first year of service for her new owners, in seven two-way Atlantic crossings STOCKHOLM carried more than 7500 passengers and 53000 tons of cargo. She continued to give profitable service to the *Swedish-American Line* until 1929, when she was sold to Norwegian owners to become a whaling fleet depot ship and her name was changed to SOLGLIMT. Her career came to an end in 1944 when she was sunk by the Germans at Cherbourg.

SS LAKE CHAMPLAIN, 7392tG, was a four-masted twin-screw steamship with two triple-expansion engines which gave her a speed of 13 knots. She could carry 100 first class, 80 second class and 500 third class passengers. She was built by Barclay Curle for *Elder Dempster*'s Liverpool–Canada service and she made her maiden voyage in June 1900.

Elder Dempster had taken over *Beaver Line*'s ships and services in 1899; the original *Beaver Line* went bankrupt in 1894 but D. and C. MacIver were running the company as managers of Beaver Line

Above: SS STOCKHOLM /*Swedish American*

Below: SS LAKE CHAMPLAIN /NMM

Associated Steamers until they too, went into liquidation.

The new ship's service with *Elder Dempster* was of short duration, though during her time with them she obtained the distinction of being the first British ship to be equipped with wireless telegraphy. The Marconi equipment was housed in a cupboard 4·5ft × 3·5ft erected on her deck. In 1903 *Elder Dempster*

sold their entire Canadian fleet to *Canadian Pacific Railway* and LAKE CHAMPLAIN inaugurated the Liverpool–Canada service of her new owners in April 1903. In 1906 she and the other *Elder Dempster-Beaver Line* ships were relegated to intermediate services with the introduction of the first 'Empress' steamers, EMPRESS OF BRITAIN and EMPRESS OF IRELAND (qv). Soon after, LAKE CHAMPLAIN was carrying only cabin class and third class passengers.

When in 1913 *Canadian Pacific Railway* made an agreement with Austrian State Railways to carry Central European emigrants from Trieste to Canada, LAKE CHAMPLAIN was one of the two ships so employed, being renamed RUTHENIA for the purpose.

At the outbreak of World War I she came home after being used for three months to take the BEF to France; she was then taken over by the Admiralty and rebuilt with a wood superstructure to imitate the battleship KING GEORGE V. There is no record that the Germans were ever deceived by this disguise and in 1915 she was stripped of her woodwork and KING GEORGE V (acting) once again became RUTHENIA, an Admiralty store-ship and water carrier at Scapa Flow.

Her next conversion was to an RFA fleet oiler and she was sent out to Hong Kong and then Singapore as an oil storage hulk, where she was captured by the Japanese in 1942. Her oil tanks were removed and she was used to take prisoners of war from Singapore to Bangkok and possibly elsewhere. She was named CHORAN MARU by the Japanese and was captured and used, also for the transportation of prisoners of war, by British forces when they recaptured Singapore in 1945. In 1949 the old ship was towed home to the Clyde and scrapped by W. H. Arnott, Young & Company at Dalmuir.

1900-1901

In 1895 *Hamburg-Amerika Line* scheduled their express liners sailing from Hamburg to New York to make a call at Cherbourg as well as Southampton. This service, which was augmented by fast boat trains between Paris and Cherbourg, quickly became very popular and it was obvious to the French *Compagnie Générale Transatlantique (CGT)* that new fast and luxurious ships would be required if their services between le Havre and New York were to remain viable.

CGT, which was state-aided, requested a subsidy from the French Government to finance the building of three 20 knot ships for the North Atlantic service. After five years of uncertainty and political wrangling

and upon renewal of the mail contract with the company in 1898, a substantial subsidy, to start in 1901, was agreed for the construction of four ships over the ensuing ten years, subject to certain conditions. The two most important of these conditions stipulated, first, that the ships should be capable of a speed of 22 knots and, second, that they should be so constructed as to be easily and quickly convertible to armed merchant cruisers in time of war.

SS LA LORRAINE /L. Dunn

The first two ships were laid down in 1898 at the St Nazaire yard of *CGT* and, in August 1900, LA LORRAINE, 11146tG, sailed from le Havre on her maiden voyage to New York. She was followed, eight months later, by her sister ship LA SAVOIE, 11168tG. These ships were splendid in appearance and good sea boats; much of their accommodation was quite luxurious. LA LORRAINE carried 68 passengers in 'de luxe' first class, 378 in ordinary first class, 116 in second class and 552 in third or steerage accommodation. LA SAVOIE carried about 150 fewer third class passengers, but otherwise her passenger complement was nearly identical with that of her sister ship. Both ships had considerable cargo space.

The ships each had twin screws driven by two four-cylinder triple expansion engines, which developed 22000ihp, and which received steam from 18 coal-fired boilers. In service, they maintained a speed of

SS LA SAVOIE /L. Dunn

20 knots but on trial each ship attained slightly less than 22 knots.

Soon after the outbreak of World War I in 1914, both ships were commissioned as armed merchant cruisers each carrying a main armament of seven 5·5in guns. LA LORRAINE was renamed LORRAINE II but LA SAVOIE retained this name. Both ships survived the war and during 1918-1919 were refitted and returned to their 'civilian' duties; LORRAINE II resumed her prewar name, but lasted only three more years before being sold and scrapped at St Nazaire in 1922. LA SAVOIE remained in service until 1927, when she was sold and scrapped at Dunkirk the next year. During the last four years of her life she carried only cabin and third class passengers.

1901

The *American Line* SS HAVERFORD, 11635tG, was built by John Brown. She was a twin-screw ship powered by two triple-expansion engines and had a speed of 14 knots. Her passenger capacity was 150 second class and 1700 third class.

SS HAVERFORD /NMM

She entered the company's service between Liverpool and Philadelphia in 1901 and, apart from a short period during which she sailed between Southampton and New York, she remained on this route until the outbreak of World War I in 1914.

During her war service on the North Atlantic she was torpedoed, but managed to remain afloat, and

she was repaired and put back on the Liverpool–Philadelphia service in 1919. The *American Line* was owned by the International Mercantile Marine Company (IMM) and HAVERFORD was operated under the British flag. In 1921, the ship was transferred to the *White Star Line*, also an IMM company, though she retained her name and also remained on the Liverpool–Philadelphia service. In 1924 the service was withdrawn and the next year HAVERFORD was scrapped. During 1923 the *American Line* ceased to exist and its services were all either terminated or taken over by other IMM companies.

1901-1907

T. H. Ismay bought the *White Star Line* as a broken and bankrupt company in 1867 and during the next thirty years he built it into one of the greatest and most prosperous shipping companies the world has ever seen. Before his death in 1899 the North Atlantic policy for the company had been established, a policy which once and for all took the company out of the 'express liner race' and concentrated on very large comfortable ships of moderate speed.

This approach was splendidly illustrated by the introduction of the so-called Big Four ships, CELTIC, CEDRIC, BALTIC and ADRIATIC, which were built by Harland and Wolff and went into service in 1901, 1903, 1904 and 1907 respectively. Each of these ships measured more than 20000 tons Gross and on this basis each was in turn the 'largest ship in the world' at its introduction. Each had twin screws powered by quadruple-expansion reciprocating steam engines, supplied with steam at 210psi from eight double-ended coal-burning boilers. The first three ships had a service speed of 16 knots, but ADRIATIC had 17 knots.

Their appearance differed in detail, but each of the four had two funnels and four masts and was flush-decked, with a straight stem and a counter stern.

They were very successful ships, their profitability coming not only from the large number of passengers carried but also from their great cargo capacity. They were excellent sea-boats and became very popular despite their slow speed.

The four ships were intended for a weekly inter-mediate service between Liverpool and New York but ADRIATIC, after making her maiden voyage from Liverpool, sailed on the *White Star* mail service from Southampton which she inaugurated. With the coming of OLYMPIC and TITANIC four years later she returned to the Liverpool service with the other three ships of the 'Big Four'.

To accommodate the new *White Star* mail service on its transfer from Liverpool, a new dock was constructed at Southampton and first used by ADRIATIC in 1907. This was known as the White Star Dock, a name it retained until 1922 when, as other companies (notably *Cunard*) were making increasing use of the port, the name was changed to the Ocean Dock.

SS CELTIC, 20904tG, the first of the 'Big Four' was the second *White Star* ship to carry the name. Soon after her entry into service she made a Mediterranean cruise from New York. On the North Atlantic she carried 347 first class, 260 second class and 2342 third class passengers in accommodation which ranged from extreme luxury to extreme sparseness. She carried 486 officers and crew.

In 1914 she became an armed merchant cruiser and later a troopship. She was damaged by a mine in 1917 and was torpedoed in 1918 but each time she reached port and was repaired. She returned to the Liverpool–New York trade in December 1918. Ten years later she was converted to a 'cabin class' ship but in December that year she was stranded on rocks outside Queenstown (Cobh) harbour and became a total loss.

SS CELTIC /NMM

SS CEDRIC, 21035tG, was a sister ship to CELTIC. She had, however, greatly improved accommodation for the same number of passengers. Her career in World War I and afterwards was similar to that of CELTIC and she became a 'cabin class' ship for 1223 passengers in 1928. In 1931 she was broken up.

SS BALTIC, 23876tG, was the third of the 'Big Four' and an enlargement of the original two ships, being longer by 28ft and having 1ft more beam. Her machinery was however the same as that in the earlier ships and at times she had difficulty in maintaining her service speed of 16 knots.

She had accommodation for 425 first class, 500 second class and 1900 third class passengers but in

Top: SS CEDRIC /NMM

Above: SS BALTIC /NMM

1927 she was altered to a 'cabin class' liner and carried a total of 1670 passengers and a crew of 557.

During the whole of World War I she maintained, with ADRIATIC, the Liverpool–New York service, carrying many troops as passengers.

The only recorded major incident in the career of the BALTIC occurred on January 23rd, 1909, when she answered a wireless call for assistance made by the *White Star* SS REPUBLIC (ex-*Dominion Line* COLUMBUS of 1903). In dense fog, 180 miles east of the Ambrose Light, the Lloyd Italiano SS FLORIDA had collided with REPUBLIC, which was so badly damaged that she sank twenty-four hours later. Although the locating of the two ships by BALTIC was very difficult in the prevailing conditions, after some eleven hours she arrived on the scene and all the 1260 passengers from both ships were safely transferred without loss of life. This was the first occasion that wireless telegraphy had proved its value in saving life at sea. The FLORIDA reached New York under her own steam.

BALTIC was laid up in 1932 and sold for scrap to Japanese shipbreakers the next year.

SS ADRIATIC, 24541tG, was the last and largest of the 'Big Four'. The reason for her delayed appearance, more than three years after BALTIC entered service, is not clear. According to some authorities, precedence was given to the construction of SS AMERIKA, which occupied the building berth intended for ADRIATIC.

In hull dimensions she was identical with BALTIC and carried the same number of passengers and crew. Her engines, however, were enlarged and she developed a total of 17000shp against the 14000shp of the other three ships. This gave her a service speed of 17·5 knots and she was thus able to work with the older but faster ships, TEUTONIC, OCEANIC and MAJESTIC, on the Southampton–New York mail service until the arrival of OLYMPIC in 1911. After that most of her sailings were between Liverpool and New York, a service which, with BALTIC, she maintained throughout World War I, carrying many troops and thousands of tons of munitions.

She was converted to a 'cabin class' ship in 1928 and in 1933 was taken off her regular North Atlantic route to go cruising.

ADRIATIC was sold for scrap in 1934, soon after the *Cunard-White Star* merger.

SS ADRIATIC /Real Photographs

1900/1903

Norddeutscher Lloyd (*NDL*) SS PRINZESS IRENE, 10881tG, was a twin-screw ship powered by two quadruple-expansion engines and with a speed of 15 knots. She was completed by Vulkan, Stettin, in 1900 for *NDL* Far East services but in 1903 was transferred to the North Atlantic, running between Mediterranean ports and New York. She carried 398 cabin class passengers and 940 in the third class.

She ran regularly on the North Atlantic until the outbreak of World War I in 1914, which found her in

New York. Here she was interned until the entry of the United States into the war in 1917 when she was commandeered as a US Government transport and renamed POCAHONTAS.

In 1920 she was sold to the *United States Mail Steamship Company*, and early in 1921 inaugurated their service from New York to Genoa. This company was, however, financially unsound and ceased to exist after the end of 1921.

POCAHONTAS was then, in 1922, sold back to her original owners, *Norddeutscher Lloyd*, now desperately short of tonnage after the German defeat in the war. The ship was completely refitted, renamed BREMEN, and for the next ten years ran fairly consistently between Bremen and New York. In 1928 she was again renamed to become KARLSRUHE, her

SS PRINZESS IRENE /Real Photographs

previous name being required for the new liner BREMEN which became the holder of the Atlantic Blue Riband.

KARLSRUHE sailed regularly until 1932 when she was withdrawn from service and broken up.

1903

SS CARPATHIA, 13555tG, was built for *Cunard* by Swan Hunter but her completion was delayed by strikes and she did not join the similar ships IVERNIA and SAXONIA (qv) on the profitable Liverpool–Boston service until May 1903. She was slightly smaller and slower than her two predecessors and two quadruple-expansion engines driving twin screws gave her only 14 knots in service.

She carried a great deal of cargo and her passenger accommodation was for 200 second and 1500 third class only, the former now being designated 'cabin class'. She was a very popular and profitable ship and

became well known for the part she played in rescuing survivors from TITANIC in 1912. She took part, as required, in the Trieste–New York emigrant service. She was requisitioned as a troopship during World War I and her end came in July 1918 when she was torpedoed and sunk by a German U-boat in the North Atlantic.

SS CARPATHIA /Real Photographs

1905

The *Allan Line* was one of the oldest and most important shipping companies in the North Atlantic trade between Canada and the United Kingdom. The line began operating in 1853 under the name *Montreal Ocean Steamship Company* and, although always referred to by the name of its founder, it was only officially the *Allan Line* after 1897, when the company was reorganised.

In 1902, however, the supremacy of the company in the Canadian trade suffered a setback when the *Dominion Line*, which had run in close conjunction with the Grand Trunk Railway, was taken over by *International Mercantile Marine*. A further serious challenge arose the next year when *Canadian Pacific Railway* took over *Elder Dempster*'s Canadian (*Beaver Line*) service, with its fifteen ships.

As a reaction to this competition, *Allan Line* ordered two fast and well appointed twin-screw steamers from Workman, Clark of Belfast. Originally the ships were to have reciprocating engines and a speed of 16 knots, but soon after work on the first ship had started the decision was made to instal triple-screw turbine drive and the construction of the ships was transferred to Alexander Stephen of Linthouse, Glasgow. Up to that time turbines had only been used for merchant ship propulsion in a few steamers on short sea and Clyde services, so the *Allan Line* decision was a particularly bold one. In the event, the ships VICTORIAN and VIRGINIAN proved to be two of the most successful vessels ever built, and both paid for themselves many times over.

They had Parsons direct-drive turbines, the high pressure turbine driving the centre shaft and two low pressure turbines drove the wing shafts. They had three-bladed screw propellers which, when turning at 264rpm absorbed about 15400shp for a speed of 19 knots.

They were exceptionally handsome ships, with the best passenger accommodation to be found in the Canadian services at the time. They each carried 426 first class, 280 second class and 940 third class passengers, and much of their popularity stemmed from the fact that, in spite of their high speed, they were singularly free from vibration in all parts of the ship.

SS VICTORIAN, 10687tG, was the first ship on the North Atlantic to be turbine driven and at the time of her introduction was one of the fastest ships in being. Her usual run was between Liverpool and Canadian ports and, with her sister ship VIRGINIAN, she maintained a fast and regular passenger and mail service between the United Kingdom and Canada.

In 1914 she became an armed merchant cruiser in the famous 10th Cruiser Squadron and served in this capacity until the end of hostilities.

Allan Line was taken over by the *Canadian Pacific Railway* in 1909 but no announcement to that effect was made until 1915, when the name of the latter company's marine interests was changed to *Canadian Pacific Ocean Services*.

On her return to civilian life VICTORIAN was put to work on the Glasgow–St John (New Brunswick) service and her name was changed to MARLOCH in the Canadian Pacific Fleet. She was scrapped in 1929.

Allan Line SS VICTORIAN when new /NMM

SS VIRGINIAN, 10757tG, followed the career of her sister ship VICTORIAN, in peace and war, until her war service ended and she was returned to *Canadian Pacific Ocean Services*, in 1920. She was then laid up for a short time but in the same year was sold to *Swedish-American Line* as their second ship, being renamed DROTTNINGHOLM. (She is as such seen here.) After working hard for her new owners between Gothenburg and New York in the prosperous postwar years, she was withdrawn for two years to be virtually rebuilt and re-engined with single-reduction-geared turbines and oil-fired boilers. As rebuilt her gross tonnage became 11143. During her absence the Netherlands ship NOORDAM was chartered (page 122).

She worked with GRIPSHOLM and KUNGSHOLM (qv) until the outbreak of World War II. During the war years she worked for the International Red Cross, repatriating civilians and wounded soldiers all over the world. After the war the old ship went back on the Gothenburg–New York service and in 1948 she was sold again, this time to *Panamanian Home Lines*, in which *Swedish-American Line* is a majority shareholder. She was now named BRASIL and sailed for a time between Genoa and South America. She was then renamed yet again, and as HOMELAND was transferred to the Hamburg–New York and later the Genoa–New York services.

Swedish-American SS DROTTNINGHOLM 1920 ex VIRGINIAN 1905 /*Swedish-American*

In 1955, just fifty years after her début, this gallant old ship was sold for scrapping at Trieste.

After their unsuccessful venture into the North Atlantic express passenger trade with their liner DEUTSCHLAND (qv), *Hamburg-Amerika Line* (*HAPAG*) decided on a policy of providing a reliable and regular North Atlantic passenger service with very large well-equipped ships of moderate speed. In this they followed the British *White Star Line*, and the first two *HAPAG* ships to implement the new policy were very similar in design to *White Star* liners of the period.

The first of the new ships to go into service, in 1905, was SS AMERIKA, 22225tG, built by Harland and Wolff of Belfast and very similar to the successful *White Star* ships CEDRIC and CELTIC (qv). The German ship did not however have the island bridge characteristic of the *White Star* ships and the arrangement of her decks was different.

The second *HAPAG* liner was named KAISERIN AUGUST VICTORIA, and though similar to AMERIKA was not a sister ship. She was built by Vulkan, Stettin, and later became EMPRESS OF SCOTLAND (qv).

AMERIKA was a twin-screw steamship with quadruple-expansion engines which developed 14800shp for a speed of 17·5 knots. Her appointments were on a luxurious scale and she had accommodation for 386 first class, 150 second class and 1972 third class passengers. She was noteworthy in being the first North Atlantic liner to serve à la carte meals in her first class dining saloon. On her completion she was the largest ship in the world.

She entered the Hamburg–Dover–New York service, later calling at Southampton instead of Dover, and in 1914 was transferred to the Hamburg–Boston service after IMPERATOR replaced her on the New York run. She experienced a number of incidents during her first nine years in service, the most sensational being a jewel robbery on board in 1910 and the most tragic when she rammed and sank the British submarine B-2 in the Straits of Dover, with the loss of fifteen lives. The German ship was held by the court of inquiry to have been to blame for this accident.

At the outbreak of World War I AMERIKA was in Boston, Mass and was interned until 1917, when the United States became a belligerent. She was then taken over as a US naval transport and was quite heavily armed. However, just before she left Hoboken Pier on her first trooping voyage, she sank at her berth, it was generally believed as a result of being scuttled by pro-German ratings. She was raised and refitted, and was used for repatriation work during 1919 and 1920, being managed by the United States Shipping Board, who renamed her AMERICA. After completing these duties, she was refitted for civilian passenger service and chartered to the *United States Mail Steamship Company* which soon got into financial difficulties and was in 1922 reconstituted as *United States Lines*. AMERICA ran successfully for both companies as a 'first and third class only' ship between Bremen and New York.

SS AMERIKA /NMM

In 1926 the ship was very badly damaged by fire and was not able to sail again until the following year. During the years 1931-1940 she was laid up as a reserve US Navy transport and in 1940 became first a barracks ship for the US Army and then a troopship, sailing under the name EDMUND B. ALEXANDER. However, in 1942 the United States Army had her completely rebuilt; she was fitted for oil-burning and her two funnels were replaced by one much wider funnel. By 1943, therefore, she was a sound and modernised 17-knot troopship with accommodation for 5000 men. After the war she repatriated many US servicemen and took occupation troops and families back to Europe. She was then laid up and ultimately scrapped in 1957, after a long life of fifty-two years.

The third *Anchor Line* ship to carry the name CALEDONIA was a steamship of 9223tG, built by Henderson for the Glasgow–New York service of the company. She was completed in 1905 and had only two funnels, although she was a larger ship than her immediate predecessor, the three-funnelled SS COLUMBIA of 1902, which was of 8292tG.

CALEDONIA had twin screws driven by two triple-expansion engines and her speed was 16 knots in service. Nearly all her commercial life was spent on the Glasgow–New York service. She was requisitioned as a troopship on the outbreak of World War I and was torpedoed and sunk in the Mediterranean in 1916.

The year 1905 saw the introduction on the North Atlantic of two of the most beautiful ships ever to sail for *Cunard Line*. These were the 'pretty sisters' CARONIA, 19594tG, and CARMANIA, 19524tG, both built by John Brown for the Liverpool–New York

express service. Each ship could accommodate 300 first class, 350 second and 1100 third class passengers, as well as a large amount of cargo. They each had a speed of 18 knots in service but, whereas CARONIA had quadruple-expansion engines driving twin screws, CARMANIA was a triple-screw ship powered by direct-drive steam turbines which developed 21000shp at 18 knots. The reason for making this difference between the two ships was to determine which form of propulsion would prove the more suitable to power the two projected 'giant' liners LUSITANIA and MAURETANIA. The decision was easily made in favour of the direct-drive turbine, though both CARONIA and CARMANIA handsomely exceeded their contract speeds on trials.

CARONIA had a long, profitable and comparatively trouble-free life, sailing regularly until she served first, as an armed merchant cruiser, and then as a

Above: SS CALEDONIA /NMM

Below: SS CARONIA /Cunard

troopship during World War I. After the war she went back on the Liverpool–New York run, but occasionally worked from Hamburg. In 1923 she was extensively refitted and converted to burn oil fuel. She then carried 425 cabin, 365 tourist and 650 third class passengers on the *Cunard* Canadian service between Liverpool and Quebec. In 1926, with CARMANIA, LANCASTRIA and TUSCANIA, she began a weekly service between London, Southampton, le Havre and New York until the slump five years later brought her career to an end. CARONIA was sold to Japan, from whence she sailed in 1932 as TAISEIYO MARU, to be scrapped a year later.

CARMANIA was one of the most distinguished of all *Cunard* liners and she had a truly eventful career. In 1912 her adventures began with a serious fire on board, and the next year she saved many survivors from the emigrant ship VOLTURNO, which had caught fire in very heavy seas in mid-Atlantic.

At the commencement of World War I CARMANIA was taken over by the Admiralty as an armed merchant cruiser, being armed with twelve 4·7in guns. While patrolling in the South Atlantic she encountered the German liner CAP TRAFALGAR of the *Hamburg South America Line*, also serving as an armed merchant cruiser. In the ensuing vigorous and gallant action both vessels were damaged and set on fire and the German ship sank. CARMANIA ultimately reached Gibraltar and was then refitted for passenger service, re-entering the wartime Liverpool–New York service in 1917.

After the war her career closely followed that of her sister ship CARONIA and her conversion to oil-burning and to a 'cabin class' liner also took place in 1923. She was scrapped at Blyth in 1932.

SS CARMANIA /*Cunard*

1906

SS NIEUW AMSTERDAM, 17149tG, was built for *Holland-America Line* by Harland and Wolff and entered the Rotterdam–New York service in 1906. She was the first ship to carry the name and was a typical product of the Belfast builders, with four masts and a single funnel. Two quadruple-expansion engines of 10800ihp drove twin screws to give her a speed of 16 knots. She also carried sails, which could have been used in an emergency but never were.

She was a large and comfortable ship for the 417 first class and 390 second class passengers, but the dormitory conditions for her 2300 third class passengers must, to say the least, have been very cramped. Her cargo capacity was about 14800tdw.

For the first two years after the outbreak of World War I the neutral *Holland-America Line* reaped great profit from its North Atlantic services. However, the increase of unrestricted U-boat warfare caused the company to withdraw all its passenger ships from the Western Ocean except NIEUW AMSTERDAM, which continued for most of the war to earn large amounts for her owners from both cargo and passenger trade. After the war she was completely refitted and became a 'cabin-class only' ship for 480 passengers, running

SS NIEUW AMSTERDAM /Holland-America

between Rotterdam, Boulogne, Southampton and New York.

NIEUW AMSTERDAM continued to give good service on the North Atlantic until 1932 when she was scrapped in Japan.

Canadian Pacific SS EMPRESS OF SCOTLAND, 25037tG, was a twin-screw 17-knot ship driven by two quadruple-expansion reciprocating engines. She was completed in 1906 by Vulkan Werke, Stettin, for *Hamburg-Amerika Line (HAPAG)* as KAISERIN AUGUST VICTORIA, in honour of the German Empress, her name being changed from EUROPA at her launch. With the very similar SS AMERIKA, which was built in 1905 by Harland and Wolff, she operated the Hamburg–Dover–New York service before World War I. She was also similar in appearance to contemporary *White Star* liners, and provided luxurious accommodation and excellent facilities while maintaining a moderate speed. At the time of her introduction she was the largest ship in the world, with a gross tonnage of 24581, slightly less than in her later days. She had accommodation for 472 first class passengers, 174 second class and 1820 in the third class, mostly in dormitories.

After the Armistice of 1918 she was first used for the repatriation of American troops from Europe, and then sailed under charter to *Cunard Line* between Europe and the United States. In 1921 she was bought by *Canadian Pacific Steamships*, who renamed her EMPRESS OF SCOTLAND and sent her to Hamburg for a complete refit and for the conversion of her boilers from coal to oil fuel. She made her first

voyage for her new owners in 1922 on the Southampton–Quebec service, but subsequently spent much of her time cruising, her Mediterranean cruises from New York being particularly well patronised.

December 1930 saw the end of her service with *Canadian Pacific*. She was sold for scrapping but before this was completed she caught fire and broke her back in the shipbreakers' yard at Blythe. October 1931 saw her final demolition.

The *Canadian Pacific Railway* SS EMPRESS OF IRELAND, 14191tG was built by Fairfield and with her sister ship, SS EMPRESS OF BRITAIN, 14188tG, went into service between Liverpool and Montreal in 1906. These two were the first of *Canadian Pacific Railway*'s Atlantic ships, and were the largest and most luxurious vessels on the Canadian–UK service at that time. They were twin-screw ships, each with two quadruple-expansion engines giving them a speed of 18 knots. Each vessel could carry 310 first class, 350 second class and 800 third class passengers.

EMPRESS OF BRITAIN became an armed merchant cruiser during World War I and returned to commercial duties in 1919. She was later rebuilt, renamed MONTROYAL, and eventually scrapped in 1930.

EMPRESS OF IRELAND had a comparatively short life. On the night of May 29th, 1914, while in the St Lawrence soon after leaving Quebec, she met thick fog. She collided with the Norwegian collier STORSTAD and sank within fifteen minutes, with the loss of 1053 lives. This was *Canadian Pacific*'s worst ever tragedy.

The third of the *CGT* liners to be built under the terms of the 1901 government subsidy (page 17) was LA PROVENCE, a twin-screw ship which went into transatlantic service from the Penhoët yard in 1906. With a gross tonnage of 13753 she was larger than LA LORRAINE and LA SAVOIE and her two four-cylinder triple-expansion engines developed some 5000ihp more than those of the earlier ships. Her service speed was 21 knots and she exceeded 23 knots on trial. For her size her passenger capacity was not excessive, with accommodation for 422 first class, 132 second class and 808 third class passengers.

Above: SS EMPRESS OF SCOTLAND, the photograph shows her as KAISERIN AUGUST VICTORIA /NMM

Below: SS EMPRESS OF IRELAND /NMM

The entry into service of LA PROVENCE put *CGT* very much in the forefront of transatlantic passenger traffic. Not only was she their largest-ever North Atlantic passenger liner but also the fastest. With her 21 knots in service she could compete with and better the performance of most of the express liners of the day. Strangely, it was not until the entry into service of the 23666-ton, 24-knot FRANCE (qv) in 1912 that LA PROVENCE was exceeded in size and speed by a *CGT* liner.

In 1914 the ship was taken over by the French Navy and became PROVENCE II, an armed merchant cruiser, but she was also used as an armed troop transport. She was thus engaged when her career ended in February 1916 when she was torpedoed and sunk by a German submarine in the Aegean with an extraordinarily heavy loss of life, no fewer than 830 men being lost.

SS LA PROVENCE /Real Photographs

1907

The *Allan Line* SS CORSICAN, 11419tG, was built by Barclay Curle and went into service in 1907 between Liverpool and St John, NB. She was a twin-screw ship with two sets of triple-expansion engines, which gave her a speed of 16 knots. She carried 208 first class passengers, 298 second class and 1000 third class.

She collided with an iceberg in 1912 but escaped serious damage and continued working between United Kingdom and Canadian ports.

CORSICAN became a troopship four days after the commencement of World War I and served as such until December 1918. She was taken over in 1916 by *Canadian Pacific Ocean Steamship Company* with the fifteen other *Allan Line* vessels but her name was not changed to MARVALE until 1922, when she was converted to a 'cabin class' ship. In 1923 she was wrecked on the Freel Rock off Newfoundland and became a total loss, though there was no loss of life.

1907

Cunard Line SS LUSITANIA and MAURETANIA

The three *Norddeutscher Lloyd (NDL)* record-breaking liners, KAISER WILHELM DER GROSSE, KRONPRINZ WILHELM and KAISER WILHELM II, and the *Hamburg-Amerika* liner DEUTSCHLAND had created new standards of luxury and speed on the North Atlantic at the turn of the century. These ships, together with the *NDL* KRONPRINZESSIN CECILIE of 1907, presented a considerable threat to CUNARD, whose prestige on the North Atlantic had always

been supreme. Furthermore, British pride as a seagoing island people had received a considerable setback by the large purchases of British shipping interests by the American *International Mercantile Marine Company* (page 189). Probably the most important factor of all, however, concerned national

Above: SS CORSICAN /NMM

Below: SS LUSITANIA at sea

security. All the German ships could readily be converted to fast armed merchant cruisers and used as 'commerce raiders' in time of war so, when the suggestion was made by the *Cunard Company* that it should build two ships larger, faster and more luxurious than any then in existence, the British Government of the day agreed reluctantly to subsidise their construction with a £2½m loan and to contribute a substantial annual subsidy for their upkeep, subject to certain stipulations regarding speed, the use of the ships in time of war and an undertaking that *Cunard Line* should remain a British-owned company.

Such was the background to the placing of contracts in 1904 for two sister ships, with John Brown to build LUSITANIA and Swan Hunter to build MAURETANIA. Both ships were launched in 1906 and both were completed the next year, LUSITANIA sailing on her maiden voyage from Liverpool to New York on September 17th, 1907, and MAURETANIA on November 16th.

Each ship had accommodation for 2335 passengers, 560 in the first class, 475 in the second and 1300 in the third class. First class public rooms were elegantly magnificent, though the décor differed between the two ships. Both had, however, the most beautiful carved wood panelling in dining saloons, smoke-rooms and lounges, which must have presented a tremendous fire hazard. Second class passengers had solid comfort and adequate space, rather than elegant luxury, while the third class accommodation was perhaps the most spacious and best ventilated of any contemporary ships. Officers and crew in each ship totalled 938, of whom 394 worked in the engine and boiler rooms, 204 being stokers.

LUSITANIA and MAURETANIA were built as coal burners; each ship had 22 double-ended and 2 single-ended boilers supplying steam at 195psi. The boilers were divided into four groups, each group working under forced draught in a watertight compartment. Each of the four funnels was an uptake for one group of boilers. At full speed MAURETANIA burned more than 900 tons of coal in 24 hours, and LUSITANIA slightly less.

Each ship had quadruple three-bladed screw propellers driven directly by steam turbines of 68000ihp, the high-pressure turbines driving the two wing shafts and the low-pressure turbines the inboard shafts. Astern turbines were fitted only to the two inboard shafts. Maximum revolutions were 230rpm but this was apparently never reached, and maximum speeds of 27 knots were attained with 195rpm. Great care was taken by the designers to guard against excessive vibration. Like many direct-drive turbine ships, the two Cunarders gave little trouble in this respect, though in MAURETANIA's later years passengers said she could be most uncomfortable when being driven hard in a moderate sea.

In appearance, the ships were beautiful, with knife-edge bows and counter sterns. It was said of

SS LUSITANIA at New York soon after her introduction / *Cunard*

SS MAURETANIA as she appeared on the North Atlantic / NMM

MAURETANIA that 'there was hardly a straight plate in her'. Masts and funnels were raked at just the correct angle to provide a sense of urgency and speed. MAURETANIA had an array of large cowl-type ventilators ranged along each side of her funnels, while LUSITANIA's ventilators were of the hinged-flap type and much less conspicuous. These features provided a ready means of distinguishing between the two ships.

MAURETANIA ultimately proved herself the faster of the two ships, though it was LUSITANIA which first regained the Blue Riband for Britain. There was considerable rivalry between the two ships, but MAURETANIA eventually won the Blue Riband in 1908 and remained the fastest passenger liner in the world for the next twenty-two years, a unique record.

Both ships were given new four-bladed screw propellers in 1909 and this greatly improved their performances. They regularly averaged more than 25 knots both eastward and westward across the Atlantic and so provided a fast and reliable service between Liverpool and New York until the outbreak of World War I.

After the commencement of hostilities LUSITANIA continued for nine months in her peacetime service, it appears with an unfortunate disregard for the hazards of war.

Early on May 6th, 1915 the Admiral Commanding, Queenstown, sent out a general signal to all shipping warning of U-boat activity off the south coast of Ireland. Later in the morning of the same day he warned LUSITANIA, homeward bound from New York, that submarines had been sighted in the southern part of the Irish Channel and at 1300 hours he repeated to her that a submarine had been seen five miles south of Cape Clear. All these signals were received by the ship and as a result all LUSITANIA's

lifeboats were swung out and all watertight doors closed. Speed was also increased, but only to 18 knots, and the ship did not steer a zig-zag course.

The next day, off the Old Head of Kinsale, two torpedoes fired by Unterseeboot-20 (Kapitan-Leutnant Schwieger) hit the ship. No warning was given by the submarine, although it was known that LUSITANIA was unarmed and was making an Atlantic crossing in commercial passenger service; Germany's signature to the Hague Convention was thus shown to be of no value.

LUSITANIA sank surprisingly quickly, going down by the head twenty minutes after the torpedoes had struck. The loss of life was heavy, 1198 persons being drowned, 124 of them American. The incident was hailed in Germany as a triumph, but elsewhere in the world it was received with horror. It had a tremendous effect in helping to turn the United States away from isolationism and towards involvement in events in Europe.

MAURETANIA and LUSITANIA had been specifically earmarked for service as armed merchant cruisers in time of war. The idea was never practical, as was clearly demonstrated by the sinking of the German KAISER WILHELM DER GROSSE (qv). Although MAURETANIA was requisitioned by the Admiralty soon after the outbreak of World War I, the futility of operating such large, fast, coal-burning ships in this role was soon recognised and the ship spent eight months laid up in the Mersey. She was then converted to a troopship, leaving on her first voyage to the Dardanelles only five days after the sinking of LUSITANIA. After three return voyages, MAURETANIA

was fitted out very comprehensively as a hospital ship, working between Mudros and the United Kingdom. After only four return trips, she had all her expensive hospital fittings removed and once again became a troopship, before being laid up in the Clyde during the whole of 1917.

As a result of the entry of America into the war and of the great shortage of shipping, in 1918 MAURETANIA was fitted out as a bizarrely camouflaged armed troopship and, flying the White Ensign, was renamed HMS TUBER ROSE. She left for the Clyde in March 1918 and spent the rest of the war bringing American troops to France and, after the Armistice, taking them home again. She was returned to her

owners in May 1919 and in March of the next year began her postwar commercial service, working from Southampton to New York.

Between 1921 and 1922 she was completely refitted, her accommodation brought up to contemporary standards and the numbers of each class of passenger carried modified to meet the requirements of the time. Her boilers were altered to burn oil fuel and this brought about a further improvement in her

Above: SS MAURETANIA as a troopship in World War I / *Cunard*

Below: SS MAURETANIA as a cruise liner in 1931 /PR-W

speed and performance. For the next eight years, with AQUITANIA and BERENGARIA, she maintained the Southampton–New York service with wonderful regularity. During 1927 she steamed 77500 miles at an average speed of 25·5 knots and frequently improved on her own best performances.

In 1929 the new German ships BREMEN and EUROPA easily beat MAURETANIA's long-held Atlantic records. Accepting the challenge, in August 1929 the old ship made her fastest-ever crossings—26·85 knots westward and 27·22 knots eastward—a most gallant effort but not good enough to regain the Blue Riband.

MAURETANIA sailed on her first Mediterranean cruise from New York in 1923, and made one each year until 1931. From then until her withdrawal in 1935 she was engaged almost exclusively on cruising. Although it was out of character with her great days on the North Atlantic, her appearance was most beautiful and elegant, with a white hull contrasting vividly with her red funnels.

It was reported that, even on her last voyage to the shipbreakers at Inverkeithing, MAURETANIA would keep increasing her speed over that intended, and when the breakers came to demolish her turbines they were found to be 'as good as the day they were built'.

There never has been, and probably never will be, a ship so nationally well loved as the old MAURETANIA:

The *Hamburg-Amerika Line* (*HAPAG*) SS PRESIDENT GRANT, 18072tG, was laid down at Harland and Wolff's Belfast yard in 1903 as SERVIA for *Wilson's and Furness-Leyland Line*. This line had been taken over by the *American International Navigation Company* (later *International Mercantile Marine*) in 1901. The order for the ship was cancelled in 1904 but two years later *HAPAG* bought her (and a sister ship SCOTIAN, which became their PRESIDENT LINCOLN) and she was completed as PRESIDENT GRANT in 1907.

She and her sister ship entered the *HAPAG* Hamburg–Plymouth–New York service in 1907. PRESIDENT GRANT had enormous passenger capacity, carrying 200 first class, 150 second class and no fewer than 3006 third class passengers, mostly emigrants. She was a 14-knot twin-screw ship powered by two quadruple-expansion engines. Her appearance, and also that of PRESIDENT LINCOLN, was unique on the North Atlantic, for she had six masts, one funnel and an island bridge.

PRESIDENT GRANT was interned at New York on the outbreak of World War I but when America entered the war in 1917 she was seized by the US Government and put into service as a troopship, retaining her old name. In 1923 she was sold to the United States Shipping Board and after a complete refit, during which she lost two of her masts, she became the 'cabin class' ship REPUBLIC sailing between New York and Hamburg or Bremen.

On the outbreak of World War II, she was once again taken over by the US Government as a troopship, her large passenger capacity making her ideal

1907

SS PRESIDENT GRANT /NMM

Above: PRINZ FRIEDRICH WILHELM as built /NMM

Right: Canadian Pacific SS MONTNAIRN ex PRINZ FRIEDRICH WILHELM, as she appeared towards the end of her twenty-two years of service, during which she carried six different names /NMM

for this purpose. She never returned to commercial service and was scrapped in 1952 after forty-five years of hard work.

PRINZ FRIEDRICH WILHELM, 17082tG, was built by Tecklenborg AG at Geestemunde in 1907 for *Norddeutscher Lloyd.* She was a coal-burning twin-screw steamship, her reciprocating quadruple-expansion engines giving her a service speed of 17 knots. She was built for the Bremen–Southampton New York intermediate service and provided a very high standard of comfortable accommodation at moderate cost. She had a capacity of 416 first class, 338 second class and 1726 third class passengers. She was a near-sister to the company's BERLIN, which later became the *White Star* ARABIC.

After World War I she made several voyages between Liverpool and Quebec, being chartered from the Reparations Commission by *Canadian Pacific Ocean Services*, who in 1921 bought the ship for their trans-Pacific services and renamed her EMPRESS OF CHINA, although she never sailed with that name. Two months later her name was changed to EMPRESS OF INDIA and she was used on the Liverpool–Canada service before sailing between Liverpool and New

York on charter to *Cunard*. Then she was refitted as a 'cabin and third class only' ship and sailed between Liverpool and Canada as MONTLAURIER. In 1925 she was transferred to the Glasgow–Montreal service and lastly she worked between Antwerp, Southampton and Quebec. Her name was again changed, first to MONTEITH and then to MONTNAIRN, a name which she finally kept until she was sold to Italy for scrapping in December 1929.

1908

SS ROTTERDAM, 24149tG, the fourth ship to carry the name for *Holland-America Line*, went into service between Rotterdam and New York in 1908. She was a twin-screw ship driven by two quadruple-expansion engines of 16760ihp, which gave her a service speed of 17 knots. Harland and Wolff built her at their Belfast yard and she took her place as one of the great transatlantic liners. She was converted to burn oil fuel in 1923.

At the time of her construction, European emigration to North America formed the most valuable section of transatlantic traffic. This is reflected in the disposition of ROTTERDAM's passenger accommodation, which provided for 520 first class, 550 second class and no fewer than 2500 third (or emigrant) class. The changing pattern of sea travel may be seen in the fact that, at the end of her service, she was scheduled to carry 540 first class and 670 tourist class passengers only.

The ship was laid up in Rotterdam during most of World War I and in the postwar years she spent much of her time cruising. She was always kept in beautiful condition and was at all times a popular ship.

ROTTERDAM was sold for scrapping in 1940 and thus escaped capture by the invading Germans.

SS ROTTERDAM in harbour at Rotterdam in 1930 /PR-W

1909

SS LAPLAND, 17540tG, was completed by Harland and Wolff for *Red Star Line* in 1909. She was a twin-screw ship powered by two quadruple-expansion engines which developed 16000shp and gave her a speed of 16 knots in service. She had a straight stem and a counter stern and soon had a reputation for comfort and steadiness on the North Atlantic. Her passenger capacity was 450 first class, 400 second class and 1500 third class. She sailed under the Belgian flag between Antwerp and New York.

The *Red Star Line* was one of the constituent companies of the American-owned *International Mercantile Marine Company (IMM)* (page 189) and so, when the Germans occupied Antwerp in World War I, LAPLAND was transferred to the fleet of *White Star Line*, another *IMM* company, under the British flag. Between 1914 and 1920 she ran between Liverpool or Southampton and New York, carrying passengers, troops, munitions and food. In 1920 she returned to the *Red Star Line* Antwerp–New York service but remained under the British flag, and for a time London was her terminal European port. At about this time she was converted to burn oil fuel.

The depression of the early 1930s brought the *Red Star* transatlantic service to an end and LAPLAND was for a time employed in cruising to the Mediterranean from London. Despite the many such cruises she made, it became uneconomic to run her and she was sold for scrapping in 1933.

The *White Star Line* SS LAURENTIC, 14892tG, was laid down at Harland and Wolff's yard late in 1907 as ALBERTA for the *Dominion Line* which, like *White Star*, was owned by *International Mercantile Marine (IMM)*. While still on the stocks the ship's name was changed and she was completed in 1909 for the *White Star Line*. This was yet another example of the frequent transfers of ships between the constituent companies of the *IMM* group.

LAURENTIC was a coal-burning triple-screw ship, the two wing shafts each being driven by a four-cylinder triple-expansion engine which exhausted into a low-pressure turbine driving the centre shaft. She had a service speed of 16 knots and she entered service in 1909 between Liverpool, Quebec and Montreal. Her passenger complement was 230 first class, 430 second class, 1000 third class, and she carried 387 officers and crew.

She proved to be a reliable and popular ship which during the winter made cruises to the Mediterranean and the West Indies.

She was taken over as a troopship in 1914 but a year later became an armed merchant cruiser in the 10th Cruiser Squadron. In January 1917 she was on 'special duty', carrying £5m of gold bullion from the British Government to Canada, when, off Lough Swilly, she struck two mines and sank in twenty fathoms of water.

SS LAPLAND /Real Photographs

Top: SS LAURENTIC /NMM

Above: SS MEGANTIC /NMM

Then began one of the most difficult salvage operations which had ever been attempted up to that time. It was possible to work on the wreck only during the summer months and the ship rapidly broke up under the stress of currents and swell. Despite the great problems involved, during the next seven years the naval diving team salvaged all but £41,000 of the £5m bullion. The cost of the operation was only 2¾ per cent of the value of the salvaged gold.

The *White Star Line* SS MEGANTIC, 14878tG, was a very similar ship to LAURENTIC, with the same hull dimensions and passenger capacity. She was laid down at Harland and Wolff's yard as the *Dominion Line* ALBANY and transferred to *White Star* while still under construction on the stocks.

She was a twin-screw coal-burning ship with a service speed of 16 knots and powered by two quadruple-expansion engines, the intention being to run her against the triple-screw LAURENTIC (qv) so that the most suitable and economic form of propulsion for the projected giant liners (OLYMPIC, TITANIC, BRITANNIC) could be determined. The final decision was to adopt the triple-screw reciprocating and turbine arrangement of LAURENTIC for the new ships.

MEGANTIC entered the Liverpool–Quebec–Montreal service in 1909, two months after LAURENTIC. She served as a troopship during World War I and, after returning to commercial service in December 1918, made some voyages to New York and once to Australia and New Zealand. She became a 'cabin class' ship in 1928 and for three years sailed from London to Canadian ports. She was consistently used for cruising during the winter months. She was sold to Japan for scrapping in 1934.

The *Atlantic Transport Line* (*ATL*) was founded in 1882 to operate a cargo service between Baltimore and London. In 1892 it began operating passenger ships between New York and London. The *ATL* ships were registered in London and sailed under the British flag, though the company was predominantly American owned. In 1898 the *Atlantic Transport*

Company of West Virginia was formed and this all-American company took over the ships and assets of *ATL*. The ships, however, still sailed under the British flag. In 1902 the *International Navigation Company* bought the *Atlantic Transport Company* as well as several other North Atlantic shipping lines, and changed its name to *International Mercantile Marine (IMM)*. Among its companies *IMM* owned *White Star Line* and *Red Star Line*, and so a number of transfers of ships occurred between *ATL* and these and other companies of the group.

SS MINNEWASKA, 14317tG, was built for *Atlantic Transport Line* by Harland and Wolff and she went into the London–New York service in 1909. She was the third of the company's ships to carry the name.

MINNEWASKA was a twin-screw ship, powered by two quadruple-expansion engines which gave her a speed of 16 knots. She carried 340 first class passengers and a large quantity of cargo.

In 1915 the ship was taken over by the British Government as a military transport. The next year she struck a mine in Suda Bay and, after being beached, was abandoned as a constructive total loss.

SS CINCINATTI, 16339tG, was built by Schichau and completed for *Hamburg-Amerika Line (HAPAG)* in 1909. She was a twin-screw ship with two quadruple-expansion engines which gave her a speed of 16 knots. She could carry 243 first class passengers, 210 second class and 2305 in third class dormitories.

Above: SS MINNEWASKA /NMM

Below: SS CINCINATTI /NMM

CINCINATTI first went into the Hamburg–New York service, with calls at Boulogne and Southampton. In 1913 she worked into Boston instead of New York, a service on which she had AMERIKA and CLEVELAND as 'running mates'. She was in Boston on the outbreak of World War I and was interned.

When the United States came into the war in 1917 CINCINATTI was seized and became the US troopship COVINGTON. While serving in this capacity she was torpedoed and sunk by a German submarine in 1918.

1907/1910

SS ROYAL EDWARD, 11117tG, was a triple-screw ship powered by direct-drive steam turbines. She was a fast ship and though her contract speed was 19 knots she frequently exceeded 20 knots in service.

SS ROYAL EDWARD and her sister ship, ROYAL GEORGE, 11146tG, were built by Fairfield as CAIRO and HELIOPOLIS respectively. They went into service in 1907 for the British-owned *Egyptian Mail Steamship Company*, inaugurating an express service between Marseilles and Alexandria. The company failed and the two ships were purchased by the Canadian Northern Railway's new company *Canadian Northern Steamships* (The 'Royal Line'). They were partly reconstructed to make them suit-able for the North Atlantic, their names were changed and in 1910 they began a fast fortnightly service between Avonmouth and Montreal in sum-mer and Halifax, NS, in winter. They became well known on the North Atlantic for their tendency to roll excessively.

Soon after the outbreak of World War I both ships were taken over as troopships, and ROYAL EDWARD was torpedoed and sunk in the Aegean Sea by a German submarine in August 1915. She had 1472 troops on board, of whom 200 were lost.

ROYAL GEORGE was sold to *Cunard Line* in 1916 and survived the war. She ran between Liverpool or Southampton and New York until 1920, when she was withdrawn as not being up to *Cunard* standards. She was scrapped in 1922.

SS ROYAL EDWARD /NMM

1911

One of the most interesting *CGT* ships to be put into service during the early years of the century was ROCHAMBEAU, which was built at Penhoët and entered North Atlantic service between le Havre and New York in 1911. A steamship of 12678tG, she was the first French liner to have four screws. The inner two screws were driven by two four-cylinder triple-expansion engines, while the outer two were each powered by a low pressure turbine. Her speed in service was 15 knots, but she achieved nearly 18 knots on trials.

Designed as an emigrant and secondary service ship, she had no first class accommodation but carried over 600 passengers in the second class and nearly 1300 in the third. In 1915 the company, fearing that the advancing Germans might capture the Channel Ports, transferred their transatlantic terminal from le Havre to Bordeaux, whence ROCHAMBEAU sailed until 1918.

She remained in merchant service for the whole of the war but was used for the repatriation of American troops during 1919. Her last North Atlantic crossing was made in 1932, after which she was laid up for two years at le Havre before being sold for scrapping at Dunkirk in 1934.

SS ROCHAMBEAU /L. Dunn

1911-1915
The Three White Star Line Sisters

Following their policy of maintaining a weekly mail service between Southampton and New York with very large luxury liners of moderate speed, the *White Star Line* planned three such ships, to be named OLYMPIC, TITANIC and (possibly) GIGANTIC. Under the leadership of J. Bruce Ismay, the company placed orders for the first two ships with Harland and Wolff of Belfast. OLYMPIC was first to be laid down, in December 1908, and TITANIC followed five months afterwards. The third ship was, however, ordered later and was not laid down until November 1911.

Each of these three great ships was driven by triple screws, two four-cylinder triple-expansion engines driving the wing shafts, while an exhaust steam turbine drove the centre shaft. Twenty-nine boilers provided steam at 215psi. Each ship had four funnels, the after funnel being a dummy. All three were designed for a speed of 21·5 knots, their engines being of 50000ihp. OLYMPIC frequently exceeded this speed in service. The maxima for the other two ships were never determined.

There were several differences between the ships: for example, the passenger accommodation in OLYMPIC was 735 first class, 675 second class and 1030 third class, whereas TITANIC carried 905 first class, 564 second class and 1134 third class passengers. The third ship was designed to carry up to 2570 passengers and 950 crew, but she never entered commercial service.

Top: SS OLYMPIC showing her elegant lines /*Cunard*

Above: An unusual view of OLYMPIC. She was a graceful ship from whatever angle she was viewed /NMM

Left: SS TITANIC at Southampton before leaving on her maiden voyage /NMM

This trio of great liners was dogged by the worst ill-luck ever to befall three sister ships.

OLYMPIC, 45324tG, sailed on her maiden voyage from Southampton to New York in June 1911. Three months later she was in collision with the cruiser HMS HAWKE and sustained serious damage. She was held to be to blame for the accident but the correctness of this decision is still very much open to doubt.

TITANIC, 46329tG, left Southampton on her maiden voyage on April 10th, 1912, and four days later collided with an iceberg, which ripped open her starboard side below the waterline for 300ft, flooding too many of her watertight compartments to enable her to remain afloat. She sank with the loss of 1503 lives, there being only 750 survivors.

As a result of this disaster OLYMPIC was extensively reconstructed by her builders, at a cost of over £½m, and she was out of service for six months. Her gross tonnage was raised to 46493 and the number of her lifeboats was increased.

Work on the new ship which had been laid down in November 1911 was stopped and large scale alterations were made to her design, including a considerable extension of her 'double skin'. As a result her beam was increased by 1·5ft to 94ft, and in consequence it was that much greater than that of OLYMPIC and TITANIC. The name GIGANTIC, which it had been thought the ship would carry, was now no longer considered suitable and she was launched as BRITANNIC on February 20th, 1914.

At the outbreak of World War I the ship was far from being finished, and her completion as a luxury liner was first delayed and then cancelled. She was instead completed as a well-equipped hospital ship, being requisitioned for service in the Gallipoli

SS BRITANNIC as a hospital ship in October 1916. One of the few known photographs of this ship. /NMM

campaign in December 1915. Her gross tonnage was 48158, the greatest of the three ships of the *White Star* trio.

HMHS BRITANNIC, once intended to be Britain's largest liner, ended her short career of eleven months by striking a mine in the Aegean Sea and sinking, with the loss of twenty-one lives.

The lone survivor of the trio, OLYMPIC, survived the war, during which she acted as a troopship, on one voyage in, May 1918, ramming and sinking the German submarine U-103. She returned to her commercial duties on the Southampton–New York run in June 1920, having first been completely refitted and converted for burning oil fuel. Even her postwar career was marred by accident. She was in collision with the liner FORT ST GEORGE in New York harbour in March 1924, and ten years later she collided in fog with the Nantucket lightship, as a result of which the lightship sank with the loss of seven lives. Despite these tragic episodes OLYMPIC remained a popular and comfortable ship, but on the takeover of the *White Star* assets by *Cunard* in 1934 she became surplus to requirements and was withdrawn and scrapped in 1935. Thus came to an end the adventurous life of the only survivor of three tragic ships.

1907/1912

In spite of the considerable interest and influence of France in Eastern Canada, French shipping services to Canada were not very frequent during the first years of the twentieth century. In 1912, however, cargo and emigrant services were improved by the introduction to the le Havre–Quebec (or Halifax) route of the four ships LA TOURAINE (1891), FLORIDE (1907), NIAGARA (built 1908 as CORSE) and CAROLINE (1908).

CAROLINE was a twin-screw steamship powered by two three-cylinder triple-expansion engines which gave her a speed of 14 knots. Her gross tonnage was 6693 and she carried 50 second and 106 third class passengers as well as a large amount of cargo. With a similar gross tonnage, FLORIDE carried 51 first class and 785 (!) passengers in the third class while the remaining two ships on the Canadian service were much larger.

In 1929 CAROLINE was transferred to the le Havre–New York secondary service, being renamed JACQUES CARTIER. On some voyages her terminal port in France was Bordeaux or Dunkirk. Transatlantic trade, however, was very depressed during the next two years and JACQUES CARTIER was laid up at the end of 1931. She never sailed again and was scrapped in 1934.

SS CAROLINE /L. Dunn

1912

SS FRANCE, 23769tG was built at Penhoët for the *Cie Générale Transatlantique (CGT)* and was the fourth and last ship of the subsidy contract (agreed in 1901) with French Government (page 17). She went into service between le Havre and New York in 1912.

She was the second *CGT* ship to carry the name and by far the largest ever built for the company. FRANCE was the first French turbine-driven liner and had Parsons turbines coupled directly to four screw shafts; a total of 42000shp was developed, giving a speed of 24 knots. Her speed on the North Atlantic was second only to the *Cunard* MAURETANIA and LUSITANIA and her accommodation was believed by

many travellers to be the most comfortable and luxurious of any ship afloat. Her appearance was sleek; the four funnels were smaller and placed further forward than those of the *Cunard* and *White Star* ships, and they appeared to be more widely spaced.

The policy of *CGT* to provide a large proportion of luxury accommodation, despite the demand for cheap emigrant passages, is seen in the fact that the numbers of passengers which could be carried in first and second class cabins exceeded those in the third class, there being room for 555 first class, 440 second class and 950 third class passengers.

FRANCE was the first of the three great liners projected by *CGT* for the North Atlantic luxury express services. As a result of World War I the second ship, PARIS, did not enter the service until 1921, while ILE DE FRANCE was delayed until 1927, by which time FRANCE was at least 'middle-aged'.

During World War I FRANCE served first as a naval transport, being named FRANCE IV, then as a hospital ship, reverting again to transport duties at the end of the war. She was 'demobilised' and resumed her original name in 1919, and after a refit, during which an explosion on board killed nine men, she resumed

SS FRANCE /Beken

her North Atlantic duties. During 1923-1924 she was again given a thorough overhaul, her accommodation being completely reconstructed and her boilers converted to burn oil fuel.

By 1928 she was becoming uneconomic as a high speed liner, and was used for long periods as a cruise ship. In 1932 FRANCE was laid up, and after a fire on board had caused serious damage she was sold for scrap in 1934.

1913

SS KRISTIANIAFJORD, 10669tG, was the first ship of the *Norwegian America Line* (*Den Norske Amerikalinje*), which was founded in 1910. She was built by Cammell Laird and was a twin-screw ship powered by two quadruple expansion engines, giving her a speed of 15 knots.

Her maiden voyage in 1913 established for the

company a passenger service between Christiania (now called Oslo), Bergen and New York. Later the same year she was joined by SS BERGENSFJORD, 11015tG, which had been completed by the same builder.

SS KRISTIANIAFJORD /*Norwegian-America*

On the outbreak of World War I, after many difficulties the neutral *Norwegian America Line* became a most important and profitable link between Norway and New York and the two ships carried many passengers from the belligerent countries as well as neutrals. They also brought much-needed cargoes to Norway.

In 1917 KRISTIANIAFJORD was stranded off Cape Race, Newfoundland, and became a total loss.

BERGENSFJORD was joined in 1918 by STAVANGER-FJORD (qv) and for nearly twenty years these ships maintained the Norway–America services of the com-

SS BERGENSFJORD /*Norwegian-America*

pany. In 1932 BERGENSFJORD was completely refitted and re-engined, being provided with low-pressure turbines in addition to her reciprocating engines, the turbines being connected to the two shafts through hydraulic couplings.

In 1940 BERGENSFJORD became a troopship and, surviving the war, was sold in 1946 to *Home Lines*, becoming their SS ARGENTINA. She later became JERUSALEM of the *Israeli Zim Lines*.

1913-1916

In the years immediately before the outbreak of World War I *Cunard Line* ordered three new ships for its service between United Kingdom ports and Canada. These ships were ANDANIA, 13405tG, ALAUNIA, 13405tG, both built by Scotts, and AURANIA, 13400tG, built by Swan Hunter. The first two were identical sister ships and entered the London–Southampton–Quebec–Montreal service in 1913. They were twin-screw ships powered by quadruple-expansion engines and their speed in service was 15 knots. They each carried 520 cabin class passengers and 1540 in the third class.

ANDANIA became a troopship during World War I and she was torpedoed and sunk by a German submarine off the north-west coast of Ireland in January 1918.

ALAUNIA had an even shorter life, for in October 1916 she struck a mine and sank in the English Channel, soon after having landed her passengers at Falmouth.

AURANIA, the third ship of the trio, was not completed until early in 1916. She differed from the other two ships in that her twin screws were driven by single-reduction-geared turbines. AURANIA never

entered commercial service and never wore *Cunard* colours. She was completed as a troopship, but in February 1918, while off the north coast of Ireland, she was torpedoed by a German U-boat. She did not sink and was taken in tow. However, the tow ropes parted in the winter gales and the ship was driven ashore near Tobermory, where she broke up.

Above: SS ANDANIA fitting out in Scots yard at Greenock
in 1913. The battleship alongside is probably HMS
AJAX /*Cunard*

Below: SS AURANIA as a troopship, painted grey /*Cunard*

1913-1920

In the years immediately preceding World War I the German *Hamburg-Amerika Line (HAPAG)* decided to build three very large passenger liners for the transatlantic service. Their policy was to provide a very high standard of accommodation, cuisine and service in comfortable ships of moderate speed. The expensive competition to build the fastest liner in the world was abandoned, and in this *HAPAG* followed the policy of the British *White Star Line*.

The first of the great *HAPAG* trio was completed in 1913 by the Hamburg yard of Vulkan Werke and made a successful maiden voyage from Hamburg to New York in that year. Named IMPERATOR, she was of 52022tG, her overall length was 919ft and she had a beam of 98·5ft. She had four screws directly driven by two sets of Curtis–AEG–Vulkan steam tubines, developing a total of 62000shp at a speed of 22·5 knots. The high- and intermediate-pressure stages of each turbine drove the inboard shafts and the low-pressure stages drove the two outer shafts. She had 46 coal-fired boilers delivering superheated steam at 227psi (16kg/cm²) and her bunker capacity was 8500 tonnes of coal. Her after funnel was a dummy and the top was plated over about 5ft below the rim. Uptakes from the galley and from boiler safety valves were taken up inside the casing and through the top plating as also was a stairway, which emerged through a man-hole. Smoke and steam could thus be seen at times issuing from the foreward and after parts of the 'dummy' respectively. The lower part of the dummy funnel was occupied by storerooms and a large HSW gravity tank. Cowl ventilators were few and inconspicuous, being replaced by a number of rectangular intakes along the boat deck.

After making several voyages, it became obvious that the ship was 'tender' to the point of instability, and in order to correct the trouble her three funnels were reduced in height by 3m and much of the heavy panelling and decoration of her public rooms was replaced by a décor of much ligher material. She also had 2000tons of concrete poured into her bottom.

IMPERATOR should have left Hamburg on August 1st, 1914 on a scheduled voyage for New York, but this was cancelled and war was declared on August 4th. For the next four years the great ship remained in Hamburg until, after making some voyages as a US Navy transport, she was in 1919 ceded to Great Britain under the terms of the peace treaty. She went to the *Cunard Line* as BERENGARIA, but was in fact owned equally by *Cunard* and *White Star*. This

SS IMPERATOR leaving Hamburg before World War I / *Hapag*

arrangement was found to be impracticable and her ownership passed entirely to *Cunard Line*.

Her passenger capacity was enormous, with room for 700 first class, 600 second, 1000 third and 1800 fourth class passengers. The high proportion of third and fourth class accommodation was of course, intended for the emigrant traffic, but after the passing of the United States immigration laws in 1924 it was altered so that the ship carried 970 first class, 830 second class and 1000 third class passengers. Her officers and crew numbered 1100.

Her first voyage for her new owners was in April

1921 but later that year she was completely refitted and converted to oil burning. From 1922 until 1938 BERENGARIA worked the Southampton–New York service with AQUITANIA and MAURETANIA and, after the

Above: SS BERENGARIA (ex IMPERATOR) leaving Southampton. Note small column of smoke issuing from the third (dummy) funnel /NMM

Below: SS BERENGARIA in the Ocean Dock, Southampton. Photograph taken from LEVIATHAN, with OLYMPIC on right of picture and AQUITANIA on the far left in the Trafalgar dry dock /NMM

Cunard-White Star amalgamation of 1934, with the White Star liners MAJESTIC (originally BISMARCK of HAPAG) and OLYMPIC.

However, in October 1936 she suffered a serious fire in some of her cabins, and this was followed by another fire on board in March 1938. Neither of these events endeared her to the very fire-conscious Americans, and as she was also no longer profitable she was withdrawn from service and sold for scrapping late in 1938.

The second great ship of the HAPAG trio was completed at the Hamburg yard of Blöhm and Voss in 1914. Named VATERLAND, her length was 951·75ft oa and her beam was 100·28ft, the latter measurement being about 2ft more than that of IMPERATOR. With a gross tonnage of 54282 she was the largest liner in the world. Her four screws were driven by direct-drive turbines, the arrangement being similar to that installed in IMPERATOR (qv). As with IMPERATOR, her after funnel was a dummy. VATERLAND was the faster of the two ships, and developed 91000shp for 25·8 knots on trial.

She carried 1150 officers and crew and had accommodation for 978 first class, 548 second and 2117 third class passengers.

VATERLAND went into service in 1914 and she was in New York at the outbreak of World War I. Here she remained until 1917, when the Americans entered the war against Germany. Her crew then tried to sabotage the ship, but the Americans repaired the damage and she was commissioned as a heavily **1913** armoured troop transport in August 1917. She was renamed LEVIATHAN and could carry up to 11000 servicemen.

At the end of hostilities she was laid up until 1922, when after much argument and prevarication *United States Lines*, with help from the US Government, became owners of the ship and her complete refitting was commenced. She was almost completely reconstructed internally and was also fitted for burning oil fuel in her forty-six boilers.

She left New York on her first voyage under the American flag in July 1923, and for the next eleven years shared the transatlantic services with GEORGE WASHINGTON, REPUBLIC and other ships of *United States Lines*. Despite her luxurious accommodation and her speed (she frequently crossed at an average of more than 24 knots), LEVIATHAN was a financial failure and she was laid up in New York in 1934, her place to be taken much later by AMERICA (qv). In 1938 she made an eventful and difficult crossing to Inverkeithing in the Firth of Forth, there to be broken up by the British firm of Thomas W. Ward.

SS LEVIATHAN leaving Southampton /PR-W.

BISMARCK was the last of the three great *HAPAG* liners. She was launched from the Hamburg yard of Blöhm and Voss in June 1914 and was in the early stages of fitting out when war was declared on August 4th of that year. No work was carried out on her during the war and she was not completed until March 1922, by which date she had been handed over to the British under the terms of the peace treaty. She was purchased jointly by *Cunard* and *White Star Lines* (cf BERENGARIA), but carried the colours of the latter company and was renamed MAJESTIC. She was ultimately owned entirely by *White Star*. Her accommodation was for 700 first class passengers, 545 second class and 850 third class but these figures varied during her lifetime. She carried 1093 officers and crew.

MAJESTIC was 956ft overall (915ft pp) and her beam was 100·1ft. With a gross tonnage of 56551, she was not only the largest of the *HAPAG* trio but also the largest ship in the world until the advent of NORMANDIE in 1935. Her four screws were driven directly by eight Parsons turbines, built in Germany under licence, which developed 80000shp for her service speed of 23·5 knots, but she was capable of much better performances and often made crossings between New York and Southampton at over 24 knots average, her fastest recorded voyage being at 25·1 knots in 1925. She had forty-six single-ended

Above: SS MAJESTIC leaving Southampton. Note smoke issuing from third (dummy) funnel /PR-W

boilers which covered an area of five acres and supplied steam at 240psi. As in the previous two ships, her after funnel was a dummy.

Soon after her acquisition by *White Star*, she was refitted and her forty-six boilers altered to burn oil fuel.

With BERENGARIA she came under *Cunard-White Star* ownership in 1934 and two years later was laid up to be sold for scrapping. However, at this point the Admiralty stepped in and purchased her, to be converted by Thornycroft into a training ship for naval artificer cadets. In 1937 she arrived at Rosyth and was commissioned as HMS CALEDONIA. Soon after the outbreak of World War II the great ship was burned out and sank. She was raised a few months later, towed to Inverkeithing and there scrapped by Thomas W. Ward.

Thus ended the career of the last of three of the finest ships ever to serve on the North Atlantic.

Above: SS MAJESTIC in the floating dock at
Southampton /PR-W

1914

Recognising the need for a third ship to run with
LUSITANIA and MAURETANIA, *Cunard* in 1910 ordered
from John Brown a larger vessel than either of the
two record-breakers. AQUITANIA, 45647tG, was
launched in 1913 and sailed on her maiden voyage
from Liverpool to New York on May 30th, 1914.

AQUITANIA cost £2m and was paid for entirely out
of *Cunard*'s own resources, without any government
aid. She was not intended to equal the speeds of her
'running mates' and her contract 23·5 knots was
obtained from steam turbines of 62000ihp directly
driving four screws. She was built with twenty-one
coal-burning boilers supplying steam at 195psi. Her
passenger capacity was enormous, with accommodation for 750 first class, 600 second class and 2052 third
class. During her long life AQUITANIA carried more
passengers than any other ship in the world, even
though her passenger complement was later altered
and reduced to meet the changing patterns of transatlantic travel.

No expense was spared to make AQUITANIA the
most beautifully fitted ship in the world and her

first class public rooms and staterooms were regal in
their furnishings. The first class dining saloon was in
the style of Louis XVI and the smoking room was a
replica of part of Greenwich Hospital. Cuisine and
service were of the highest standard. Certainly she
deserved the many compliments bestowed upon her
by travellers of all nations, who referred to her as the
'Ship Beautiful'.

AQUITANIA was, however, able to make only three
round trips before the outbreak of World War I on
August 4th, 1914. She was then at Liverpool and was
promptly requisitioned and hurriedly converted to an
armed merchant cruiser. By extraordinary good luck,
before her conversion was completed she suffered a
collision while leaving the Mersey, and the Admiralty
came to the wise conclusion that she was not a
suitable ship for the purpose. Accordingly she was
laid up, joined later by MAURETANIA, until May 1915,
when both ships were fitted out as troopships to take
men out to the Dardanelles. Her career followed
closely that of MAURETANIA, and after trooping she
was converted to a hospital ship, serving as such with

distinction from August 1915 until February 1917, when she was again laid up until early 1918. Once again she went trooping, bringing American soldiers to Europe and, after the Armistice, taking them home again.

AQUITANIA resumed her commercial career in June 1919, but six months later was given a complete overhaul, with considerable alteration to her accommodation, and was converted to burn oil fuel. This reduced her engine and boiler room personnel by 198 men and, with the fitting of new screw propellers, made her a consistent 24-knot ship.

From 1920 to 1939 she worked regularly between Southampton, Cherbourg and New York, becoming the best loved of all the great liners of her time and often referred to as 'The Grand Old Lady of the Atlantic'.

In September 1939, at the outbreak of World War II, she was again requisitioned as an armed merchant cruiser. Again good sense prevailed and she was instead, for the next eight years engaged in trooping, carrying no fewer than 300000 men to and from Australia and South Africa, and across the Atlantic. She returned to commercial service in March 1948 and for the next 1½ years maintained an 'austerity'

Top: SS AQUITANIA showing her beautiful lines /PR-W

Above: SS AQUITANIA as a troop transport in World War II /PR-W

service between Southampton and Halifax, NS.

After thirty-five years of service, during which she had safely steamed more than 3 million miles, the great ship was broken up at Faslane in 1950.

The twin-screw steamship TRANSYLVANIA, 14315tG, was built by Scotts and delivered to *Cunard Line* in 1914. She was powered by single-reduction-geared steam turbines and was the first transatlantic liner to have geared turbines. Her service speed was 16 knots. She had accommodation for 263 first class passengers, 260 second class and 1860 in the third class.

TRANSYLVANIA was intended for the joint *Cunard-Anchor Line* service between New York and Mediterranean ports, *Anchor Line* having been a *Cunard* subsidiary since 1912. The outbreak of World War I brought the Mediterranean service to an end before the new ship could take up her duties. She was therefore used at the beginning of the war for the

Liverpool or Glasgow–New York service, and in 1915 she was purchased by *Anchor Line*, soon afterward becoming a troopship. The brief career of TRANSYLVANIA ended when she was torpedoed and sunk by a German submarine in the Mediterranean in 1917, with the loss of over 400 men.

Canadian Pacific Ocean Services SS EMPRESS OF FRANCE, 18481tG, was built by Beardmore in 1913-1914 for the *Allan Line* as their SS ALSATIAN. Her sister ship CALGARIAN was built by Fairfield and both ships entered the Liverpool–Canada service in 1914. They were the largest, fastest and most luxurious ships on the Canadian service, their quadruple screws driven by four sets of turbines giving them each a speed of 18 knots. The first transatlantic ships to have cruiser sterns, they were also the first to carry motor-propelled lifeboats. With the older turbine steamers VICTORIAN and VIRGINIAN (qv) they provided

Above: SS TRANSYLVANIA /NNM

Below: Canadian Pacific Ocean Services SS EMPRESS OF FRANCE, ex ALSATIAN /*Canadian Pacific*

a frequent and regular service for the *Allan Line*, one of the oldest companies trading on the North Atlantic.

ALSATIAN could carry 287 first class passengers, 504 second and 484 in the third class.

On the outbreak of World War I ALSATIAN and CALGARIAN were both taken over by the Admiralty as armed merchant cruisers. ALSATIAN had a very distinguished career, becoming flagship of the 10th Cruiser Squadron, but CALGARIAN was torpedoed and sunk by a German U-boat in March 1918.

In 1915 it was finally announced that the *Allan Line* had in 1909 been bought by *Canadian Pacific Ocean Services* (later *Canadian Pacific Steamships*)

and so, on being released from war service and refitted for passenger service in 1919, ALSATIAN was renamed EMPRESS OF FRANCE and went back on her prewar duties. In 1922, however, she started a new service between Hamburg, Southampton, Cherbourg and Quebec. She also made a number of cruises, being painted white for these occasions. She was the first Atlantic liner ever to be used for 'round-the-world' cruising. In 1924 she was converted to burn oil fuel.

In 1928 the ship was transferred to the Pacific services of the company, but was not very successful and was brought home to be scrapped in 1934.

1917

SS JUSTICIA, 32120tG, was laid down at Harland and Wolff's yard at Belfast in 1912 for *Holland-America Line*, as STATENDAM. By far the largest ship ever to have been ordered by Dutch shipowners, she was indicative of the prosperity of the company. She was designed to take her rightful place among the great luxury passenger liners of the North Atlantic. JUSTICIA was a triple-screw ship, with two four-cylinder triple-expansion engines driving the wing shafts and exhausting into a low-pressure turbine which drove the centre shaft. Her speed was 18 knots in service.

She was launched as STATENDAM in July 1914, just before the outbreak of World War I, and for the next three years no work was carried out on her. In 1917 she was requisitioned by the British Government and completed as a troopship, to carry 4700 officers and men. She was manned and managed by *White Star Line* and renamed JUSTICIA.

JUSTICIA began her valuable wartime service in late 1917, carrying Canadian and American troops to Great Britain. She was at first a uniform grey, but

was later 'dazzle painted'. On July 19th, 1918, while westward-bound, she was attacked by German submarines off the north coast of Ireland and, despite the efforts of her escort ship, she was hit by six torpedoes fired at intervals by at least two U-boats. The great ship sank seventeen hours after the first torpedo struck, with the loss of only seven lives.

The *Red Star* liner SS BELGENLAND, 27132tG was launched at Harland and Wolff's Belfast yard in December 1914. She was a triple-screw ship, having two four-cylinder triple-expansion engines driving the two wing shafts and a low-pressure exhaust-steam turbine the centre shaft. She developed a total of 21230shp for a speed of 17 knots.

SS JUSTICA /NMM

BELGENLAND was intended for the Antwerp–New York service of the *Red Star Line*, which was owned by the American company *International Mercantile Marine (IMM)*. World War I delayed her completion, but in 1917 she was completed as a cargo ship for *White Star Line*, also an *IMM* company, and with two funnels and three masts she sailed as BELGIC until 1921. She then returned to Belfast and was fitted out as a passenger liner, with accommodation for 500 first class, 700 second class and 1500 third class passengers. With a total of only 530 officers and crew she should have been a very economical ship to operate.

During her fitting-out at Belfast the opportunity was taken to convert her boilers from coal to oil burning, to remove one mast and add an after 'dummy' funnel. Her name was changed back to BELGENLAND, but her port of registry remained Liverpool and she sailed under the British flag. She worked with LAPLAND (qv) and other *Red Star* ships between Antwerp or London and New York until 1932, when the Depression closed the service. BELGENLAND then made a number of cruises, interspersed with long periods of inactivity at Tilbury.

In 1934 BELGENLAND was transferred to another *IMM* company, the *Atlantic Transport Company of West Virginia*. She now flew the American flag, was renamed COLUMBIA and painted white. However, after making a few voyages between New York and California via the Panama Canal, she was sold for scrap, crossed the Atlantic flying the British flag and was broken up at Bo'ness in the Firth of Forth in 1936. Her sale for scrap ended the ship-owning activities of the *Atlantic Transport Company* and brought to an end the chequered career of a beautiful ship.

1918

The *Red Star Line* SS WESTERNLAND, 16314tG, was completed by Harland and Wolff in 1918 as the *Dominion Line* SS REGINA. She was a handsome ship with a cruiser stern and an island bridge. Her sister ship was the *White Star* SS PITTSBURGH, which became the *Red Star Line* PENNLAND, and she was very similar to the *White Star* DORIC (qv).

WESTERNLAND was a triple-screw ship with two four-cylinder triple-expansion engines driving the wing shafts and an exhaust-steam low-pressure turbine the centre shaft. Her service speed was 15 knots. Originally she could accommodate 600 cabin class passengers and 1700 in the third class, but during her eventful career her accommodation was altered and she ended up carrying 583 tourist class passengers only.

As REGINA, she was completed as a troopship, and not until 1922 did she sail as a passenger liner on the *Dominion Line* Liverpool–Halifax–Portland service, though she was then nominally owned by *Leyland Line*. Both *Dominion Line* and *Leyland Line* were constituent companies of the giant American *International Mercantile Marine Company (IMM)* (page 189), as also was *White Star Line*. The policy

was to maintain *White Star Line* as the prestige company and to keep it supplied with the best and most modern ships. So the new REGINA became virtually a *White Star* ship, sailing on the *White Star-Dominion Line* joint service until 1925, when the ownership became wholly *White Star* and she sailed on their Canadian service carrying their colours.

In 1929 REGINA was transferred to the *IMM Red Star Line*, her name was changed to WESTERNLAND and she ran between Antwerp and New York. She sailed under the British flag and her port of registry was Liverpool.

When the original *Red Star Line* ceased operating in 1935 WESTERNLAND and her sister ship PENNLAND were sold to Arnold Bernstein of Hamburg, who continued to operate them under the *Red Star* name, which he had also purchased.

Bernstein was a Jew and in 1937 he was imprisoned by the Nazis and soon after, his company was dissolved. WESTERNLAND and PENNLAND were purchased by *Holland-America Line*, who operated them on the Antwerp–Southampton–New York service until the outbreak of World War II. PENNLAND was sunk in 1941 while trooping, but WESTERNLAND, after being also used as a troopship, was purchased by the Admiralty in 1942 for conversion to a repair ship. This never materialised and the ship continued trooping until 1947, when she was sold for scrapping.

SS STAVANGERFJORD, 13156tG, was the third passenger liner of the *Norwegian America Line*. She was a twin-screw steamship with quadruple-expansion engines and a speed of 16 knots.

She was laid down at Cammell Laird's yard in 1915, but as a result of other more important wartime

Above: The Red Star Line SS WESTERNLAND /NMM

Below: Norwegian American Line SS STAVANGERFJORD / *Norwegian America*

construction her completion was greatly delayed. It was in fact only allowed by the British Government to proceed as a result of the sinking of the KRISTIANIAFJORD (qv).

STAVANGERFJORD became a most reliable and well-loved ship on the North Atlantic. She had a straight stem, a flat-fronted bridge structure and a cruiser stern. She was converted to burn oil fuel in 1924, and in 1931 was re-engined and given exhaust-steam turbines which augmented the power to her two screw shafts through hydraulic couplings and double-reduction-gearing.

As built she had accommodation for 88 first class, 318 second and 820 third class passengers, but in 1931 this was altered to 147 cabin class and 207 tourist class, with third class unaltered. Her passenger accommodation was progressively improved over the years and her passenger to crew ratio was ultimately 2 to 1, with 90 first class, 172 cabin class and 413 tourist passengers, to 330 officers and crew.

Caught by the Germans in Oslo in 1940, she became a German submarine accommodation ship until 1945. She was then completely refitted and put back again on the Oslo–Christiansand–Stavanger–Bergen–New York service. Once again she became known as a comfortable and happy ship, and after forty-five years of service was sold to far eastern shipbreakers in 1963.

The two *Canadian Pacific* ships MINNEDOSA, **1918** 13972tG, and MELITA, 13967tG, were laid down in 1914 for the *Hamburg-Amerika Line* at the Scotstoun yard of Barclay Curle. As a result of World War I the ships were not launched until 1917, and the hulls were then towed to Belfast for completion as troopships at the Harland and Wolff yard. Towards the end of 1918, however, the ships were put into *Canadian Pacific* service between Liverpool and Canada, and in 1925 both were extensively refitted, their gross tonnages being increased to 15186 and 15183 respectively. Their passenger accommodation was for 550 cabin class passengers and 1200 third class.

These ships had triple screws, the two wing shafts being driven by four-cylinder triple-expansion engines and the centre shaft by an exhaust-steam turbine. They had a service speed of 17 knots. During their 1925 refits their boilers were provided with superheaters. In each ship the after funnel was a dummy and was used as a boiler room air intake.

Canadian Pacific Steamships SS MINNEDOSA outward bound from the Clyde in 1927. /PR-W

In 1935 both ships were sold to Italy for scrapping but were bought from the scrap yard by *Italia Line* for use as troopships during the Abyssinia campaign, being renamed PIEMONTE and LIGURIA respectively. They both became casualties during World War II.

PIEMONTE was torpedoed and later bombed and sunk in the harbour at Messina. She was scrapped in 1948.

Her sister ship was badly damaged at Tobruk and scuttled in the harbour. She was not raised and scrapped until 1950.

1920-1923

HOMERIC and COLUMBUS

Shortly before the outbreak of World War I the *Norddeutscher Lloyd* (*NDL*) ordered from the Danzig yard of F. Schichau two large steamships for transatlantic service. These ships were to be the reply of *NDL*, not only to such foreign competition as the large medium-speed *White Star* liners OLYMPIC and BRITANNIC, but also to the *Hamburg-Amerika Line* ships, of which VATERLAND (54348tG) was in service and IMPERATOR and BISMARCK, of similar size, were building.

Construction of the two *NDL* sister ships was held up by the war and not until 1920 was the first of them, COLUMBUS (34351tG), completed. This ship went to Great Britain under the terms of the peace treaty and became the *White Star* liner HOMERIC. She was the largest ship ever to be completely powered by reciprocating steam engines, her twin screws being driven by two four-cylinder quadruple-expansion

engines, each of which developed 16000shp for a speed in service of 19 knots. Her twelve boilers burned coal to provide steam at 210psi.

In 1924, soon after joining the *White Star* fleet, HOMERIC was given a complete overhaul; many of her public rooms and passenger cabins were altered and improved, while 'down below' her boilers were converted to burn oil fuel. HOMERIC was an excellent sea-boat and was very popular with transatlantic passengers. When she first went into service her accommodation was for 529 first class, 487 second and 1750 third class passengers. These figures were altered from time to time, and when cruising she carried a total of only 1550 passengers. Her officers and crew numbered 625, so from the aspect of

SS HOMERIC /PR-W

SS COLUMBUS /Real Photographs

passenger to crew ratio she was an economical ship.

Unfortunately her career was a short one, for as a result of the Depression of 1930-1931 she was taken off the North Atlantic and after 1932 was only used for cruising. In 1936 she was found no longer economic and was scrapped.

The second of the *NDL* sister ships was completed in 1923 by Schichau and was retained by *NDL* to enable that company to re-enter the transatlantic express service. This ship was also named COLUMBUS, 32354tG, and although slightly smaller than her sister ship, her machinery was identical, as was her speed in service. Before she was completed, her boilers were altered to enable her to burn oil fuel.

Her passenger accommodation was on a lavish scale, and she was perhaps the most comfortable and luxuriously appointed ship in the world at that time. She carried 480 first class passengers, 610 tourist class and 596 third class. Her appearance was different from that of HOMERIC, mainly because her funnels were very much shorter and of greater diameter.

In 1927 one of her main engines broke down and for two years she sailed at reduced speed, with a smaller engine replacing the one which had failed. In 1929 she was withdrawn from service to undergo extensive reconstruction. Her reciprocating engines were replaced by single-reduction-geared turbines and she was given new boilers with increased output, making her service speed now a useful 23 knots. She was given even larger diameter funnels. Thus altered, she became a slower but still adequate running mate for the two new *NDL* liners, BREMEN and EUROPA, and in appearance she was almost a smaller edition of these great ships.

Soon after the outbreak of World War II, in December 1939, COLUMBUS tried to run the British blockade and return to Germany from New York. She was intercepted by British naval forces and was scuttled by her crew to avoid capture. A sad end to a fine ship.

1906/1921

Canadian Pacific Steamships SS MONTREAL, 9720tG, was completed for *Hamburg-Amerika Line* Far East service by Blöhm and Voss in 1906 as KÖNIG FRIEDRICH AUGUST. She was ceded to the Allies as reparation after World War I and was purchased by *Canadian Pacific* in 1920. She was a twin-screw ship driven by two quadruple-expansion engines and her service speed was 15 knots.

After refitting at Antwerp, during which time her gross tonnage was raised from 8776 to the figure given above, she was put to work on the new

Trieste–Naples–Montreal service of *Canadian Pacific* in 1921. She had accommodation for 229 first class and 240 third class passengers. The service was not viable, so MONTREAL was converted to a 'cabin class' ship and put on the Liverpool–Quebec–Montreal service, but after two years she was again laid up.

In 1928 she was sold to the French *Fabre Line*, renamed ALESIA and for three years ran between Marseilles and New York, but was yet again laid up in 1931. Two years later she was sold to Italy for scrap.

1915/1921

Canadian Pacific Steamships SS MONTREAL /*Canadian Pacific*

Royal Mail Steam Packet Company (*RMSP*) SS ORBITA, 15486tG, was completed for the *Pacific Steam Navigation Company* (*PSN*) by Harland and Wolff in 1915. She was a 14-knot triple-screw ship with two four-cylinder triple-expansion engines driving the wing shafts and a low-pressure exhaust-steam turbine the centre shaft. She had accommodation for 880 passengers.

As a result of their defeat in World War I, the Germans in 1920 had not yet re-entered the transatlantic passenger trade. Under the circumstances, the British *Royal Mail Steam Packet Company* decided that it would be profitable for them to start services from Hamburg via Southampton and Cherbourg to

New York. The service was introduced by ORBITA in 1921 and she was joined by ORDUNA and OROPESA, all from the associated *Pacific Steam Navigation Company*'s South American service. Later SS ORCA from *PSN* and OHIO, which was to have been *Norddeutscher Lloyd* MÜNCHEN, joined the service.

By 1926 the German North Atlantic companies were operating again, and in 1927 *Royal Mail* bought out the *White Star Line*, entrusted the North Atlantic services to that company's ships, and sent the first three 'O' class ships back to *PSN*, while ORCA and OHIO went to *White Star Line* as CALGARIC and ALBERTIC respectively.

1904/1921

SS PRINZ EITEL FRIEDRICH, 8865tG, was built by the Vulkan yard at Stettin for the Hamburg–Australia–Far East services of *Norddeutscher Lloyd* (*NDL*) and went into service in 1904. She was a twin-screw ship driven by two quadruple-expansion engines and with a speed of 15 knots in service.

Although many of *NDL*'s far east ships served at times on the North Atlantic, there is no record of PRINZ EITEL FRIEDRICH ever having done so. Like many other German ships she was interned in New

York at the outbreak of World War I and, along with most of the interned vessels, seized by the United States Government when that country entered the war in 1917. PRINZ EITEL FRIEDRICH was renamed DE KALB and went to war as an armed troop transport.

After the war the *United American Lines* and *Hamburg-Amerika Line* joined in partnership to resume the service between Hamburg and New York, with Dover or Southampton as the British port of call. DE KALB was purchased from the United States

Above: Royal Mail Steam Packet Company (RMSP)
SS ORBITA /PR-W

Below: SS PRINZ EITEL FRIEDRICH /NMM

Shipping Board by *United American Lines* and was refitted to carry 99 cabin class and 1000 third class passengers. She plied between Hamburg and New York from February 1921 until 1924, when she was sold out of the service and finished her days on the Pacific coast of America.

1921

The Italian hospital ship CALIFORNIA was completed by Scotts in 1921 as the *Cunard* liner SS ALBANIA, 12768tG. The second ship to carry that name, she was one of the first to be built for *Cunard* after the end of World War I. She had steam turbines single-reduction-geared to two shafts which gave her a speed of 13 knots. She carried 500 cabin class passengers only and was used first on the Liverpool–New York service, but later mostly between Liverpool, Quebec and Montreal.

ALBANIA was originally intended to be one of the 'A' class ships of the *Cunard* Canadian service. She was, however, unlike any of the other *Cunard* vessels and was regarded as a misfit. Her career with the company was brief, for after being laid up for several years she was sold in 1930 to the Italians, who renamed her and converted her to a hospital ship during their aggression in Abyssinia. The photograph was taken in the Bitter Lakes of the Suez Canal in 1940.

SS PARIS, 34569tG, was built at Penhoët for *Cie Générale Transatlantique (CGT)* and was launched in 1916. As a result of World War I, work on her was stopped and the incompleted hull was laid up in Quiberon Bay until after the cessation of hostilities. Ultimately, she went into service between le Havre and New York in 1921. A call at Plymouth was included in her schedule from 1922.

PARIS was a quadruple-screw ship with direct-acting Parsons turbines supplied with steam from fifteen oil-fired water tube boilers, and developing 45000shp for a speed of 22 knots.

She was the second of the three projected express liners of *CGT* but her entry into service to join FRANCE (qv) was badly delayed by World War I. PARIS was laid down in 1913, launched in 1916 and not completed until 1921.

She was a luxuriously-appointed ship with accommodation for 340 first class, 163 tourist and 409 third class passengers. Her first class dining saloon was widely acclaimed as being the most beautiful room ever built into a ship.

PARIS was dogged by ill luck. In 1926 she collided with a pier at le Havre and made a hole 20m long in her hull. She was repaired very smartly at the Wilton-Fijenoord yard at Rotterdam, the work being finished 2½ days ahead of schedule. At that time she was the largest ship ever to enter Rotterdam.

In 1928 she was severely damaged by fire while in harbour at le Havre, but was repaired and put back into service. Her ill luck however recurred in April 1939, when she again caught fire while alongside at le Havre. This time she was completely gutted and capsized at her berth, becoming a total loss.

The *Dollar Steamship Line* SS PRESIDENT GARFIELD, 10533tG, was built as BLUE HEN STATE by the New York Shipbuilding Company and completed in 1921 for the United States Shipping Board. She was one of five identical 14-knot twin-screw ships, each powered by two four-cylinder triple-expansion engines. She

The Italian hospital ship CALIFORNIA ex *Cunard Line* SS ALBANIA /PR-W

Above: SS PARIS /NMM

Below: The *Dollar Steamship Line* SS PRESIDENT GARFIELD /Real Photographs

1921 carried 78 first class passengers and 690 third class, and went on charter to the *United States Steamship Company* to run between New York, Cobh and London in 1921.

On the failure of that company later the same year, BLUE HEN STATE was renamed PRESIDENT GARFIELD and chartered to *United States Lines* to operate between New York, Southampton and Hamburg or Bremen.

In 1924 this ship, with six other similar ones, was sold to the *Dollar Steamship Line* by the United States Shipping Board. All were named after United States presidents. In 1938 the *Dollar Steamship Company* got into serious financial difficulty and was taken over by the United States Government, who changed its name to *American President Line*. The ships were operated on a round-the-world service, crossing the Atlantic from east to west.

In 1940 the company obtained six new ships and the old PRESIDENT GARFIELD was renamed PRESIDENT MADISON. However, when the Japanese attacked Pearl Harbour in 1941, the United States Government took over all the *American President Line* ships and PRESIDENT MADISON, ex PRESIDENT GARFIELD, ex BLUE HEN STATE, finally became the United States hospital ship RESCUE.

The *United States Mail Steamship Company* was founded in 1920 to operate between United States and European ports. All its twelve ships were chartered from the United States Shipping Board. The company soon got into financial difficulty and was wound up by the Shipping Board in 1921. The ships were disposed of to other lines. BLUE HEN STATE is the nickname for the State of Delaware.

1921/1925

Anchor Line North Atlantic passenger services were mainly centred on a weekly sailing between Glasgow and New York. The company, whose origins date back to 1856, was taken over by *Cunard Line* in 1911 but retained its separate identity. In 1916 *Anchor Line* took over the *Donaldson Line*, which therefore also became a *Cunard* associate. In 1935, as a result of the Depression, financial difficulties caused a reconstitution of the company as *Anchor Line (1935) Ltd* (the date was soon dropped from the title) and *Cunard* had no interest in this new company.

Anchor Line had suffered severe shipping losses in World War I and between 1921 and 1925 five new liners were put into service. They all carried previous *Anchor Line* names and were, in order of introduction, CAMERONIA, TUSCANIA, CALIFORNIA, TRANSYLVANIA and CALEDONIA. All were twin-screw steamers driven by double-reduction-geared turbines and with a speed of 16 knots. They had cruiser sterns and the length of each ship was 552ft pp, with a beam of 70ft. These comfortable and well liked ships were very similar in dimensions and appearance to the *Cunard* vessels SCYTHIA, SAMARIA and LACONIA, though these had counter sterns.

SS CAMERONIA, 16365tG, was built by Beardmore and entered service in May 1921. She was a sister ship of TYRRHENIA (qv), which was taken over by *Cunard* and later became LANCASTRIA. CAMERONIA was always distinguishable from her four companion ships by having one deck less than they had. She could carry 265 first class, 370 second class and 1150 third class passengers. Later, when immigration to the United States was curtailed, she carried cabin and tourist class passengers only.

After her completion had been badly delayed by strikes, CAMERONIA's maiden voyage in May 1921 was from Liverpool to New York for *Cunard Line* and she did not sail in the *Anchor Line* Glasgow–New York service until later the same year. During the 1930s, she was laid up for a year and then made several voyages as a troopship to the Far East. After this she was employed on the Glasgow–New York service until 1940, when she became a Ministry of Transport troopship, remaining however under the management of her owners.

CAMERONIA was badly damaged by a torpedo from a German aircraft while off the North African coast in December 1942 but managed to reach the Clyde, where she was repaired and enabled to return to service. She survived the war and became an emigrant ship to Australia. In 1953 she was bought by the Ministry of Transport for a troopship, being renamed EMPIRE CLYDE (the second ship to carry the name), and was sold for scrap in 1955.

SS CALIFORNIA, 16792tG, was built by Alexander Stephen and entered the *Anchor Line* Glasgow–New York service in 1923. She was the third of the five new *Anchor Line* ships and was a sister ship of TUSCANIA.

During the difficult years of the 1930s CALIFORNIA was frequently used on the *Anchor Line* Bombay service. When on the North Atlantic her passenger accommodation was the same as that of CAMERONIA.

CALIFORNIA became an armed merchant cruiser at the outbreak of World War II and was allocated to

Above: SS CAMERONIA, *Anchor Line* /PR-W

Below: SS CALIFORNIA, the third of five new *Anchor Line* ships /PR-W

the Northern Patrol. In 1942 she became a troopship and the next year was sunk by aircraft off the Portuguese coast while in company with DUCHESS OF YORK, which was also lost.

SS TUSCANIA, 16991tG, was completed for *Anchor Line* in 1922 by Fairfield and ran on the Glasgow–New York service until 1926, when she was transferred to the *Cunard* London–New York service and carried their colours. After 1931 she was used for cruising and also on the company's Bombay service, but TUSCANIA was regarded as a surplus ship and in 1939 was sold to the newly formed *Greek Line* as their first vessel. She was renamed NEA HELLAS and operated between Piraeus and New York until the outbreak of World War II, during which she became a British troopship and was managed by *Anchor Line*. After the war she resumed her sailings between Piraeus, Mediterranean ports and New York, but in 1954 was completely refitted and afterwards carried

Top: SS TUSCANIA /NMM

Above: SS TRANSYLVANIA, the fourth of the new *Anchor Line* ships /Real Photographs

70 first class and 1300 tourist class passengers on a service between Bremen and New York which began in 1955. Her name was changed again, this time to NEW YORK.

The arrival of *Greek Line*'s new ship OLYMPIA (qv) displaced NEW YORK from many of her regular sailings and she was scrapped in 1961.

SS TRANSYLVANIA, 16923tG, was the fourth of the new *Anchor Line* ships, and was built by Fairfield, entering the Glasgow–New York service of the company in 1925. She was a sister ship of CALEDONIA, 17046tG, which went into service the same year and ended her career by being torpedoed by a German submarine while serving as HMS SCOTSTOUN, an armed merchant cruiser, in 1940.

TRANSYLVANIA and CALEDONIA were almost identical with their immediately preceding sisters, TUSCANIA and CALIFORNIA, but had three funnels instead of one. The first and third funnels were dummies, for appearance only.

TRANSYLVANIA carried 264 first class, 457 second class and 620 third class passengers, but her accommodation was later improved, the numbers reduced, and she carried cabin and tourist class only. She became quite popular as a cruising liner in the 1930s. At the outbreak of war she became an armed merchant cruiser and was torpedoed and sunk by the German submarine U-56 off Inistrahull on August 10th, 1940.

1920-1922

At the outbreak of World War I three passenger liners were building for the South American service of the *Hamburg-Amerika Line*. These were WILLIAM O'SWALD at the Weser yard, Bremen, JOHANN HEINRICH BURCHARD at Tecklenborg and TIRPITZ at the Vulkan yard, Stettin. All were very similar ships and the first two were sisters. Construction of TIRPITZ, which is described on page 94, was the furthest advanced of the three. Work on the first two, which had ceased at the commencement of hostilities, was resumed after the war, but in the meantime both had been ceded to the Netherlands to replace their (neutral) ships sunk by German submarines. Thus they were completed in 1920, as BRABANTIA and LIMBURGIA respectively, of the *Royal Holland Lloyd*.

The Allies objected to the transfer of these ships to the Dutch and litigation went on for two years, during which time both ships were trading to South America for their Dutch owners. In 1922 however, both ships were sold to the *United American Lines*, an

Below: Hapag triple screw SS RESOLUTE in cruising colours /*Hapag*

Bottom: Hapag triple screw SS RELIANCE leaving Hamburg on a cruise /*Hapag*

American-German company formed with United States Government backing to revivify the war devastated *Hamburg-Amerika Line*. The ships again changed names, becoming RESOLUTE 19653tG, and RELIANCE 19582tG respectively, and they began trading between New York, Southampton and Hamburg in 1922.

They were not well patronised, probably because being under the American flag and with prohibition in force at that time, they were 'dry' ships. They were therefore re-registered in Panama and ran profitably under this flag of convenience until 1926, when they were both sold back to *HAPAG*, their original owners.

For the next nine years the two ships worked on the North Atlantic, but they also had long spells as cruise liners and eventually did nothing else.

RESOLUTE was sold to the Italians as a troop transport in 1935, being renamed LOMBARDIA, and was finally sunk by Allied bombing in 1943.

RELIANCE remained with *HAPAG* until she was destroyed by fire in 1938 at Hamburg.

Both were very handsome steamships with only slight differences between them. They each had triple screws, the outboard shafts being driven by four-cylinder triple-expansion engines and the centre shaft by a low-pressure turbine. The after funnel was a dummy and was used as a boiler room intake. They were oil-burners with 17 knots speed.

They had very comfortable though not luxurious accommodation and each ship could carry 290 first class, 320 second and 400 third class passengers. For ships of nearly 20000tG, 1010 passengers was a very moderate total.

1922

Cunard Line SS LANCASTRIA, 16243tG, was completed by Beardmore in 1922 as SS TYRRHENIA. She was originally ordered for *Anchor Line*, at that time a *Cunard* subsidiary, and was a sister ship of the *Anchor Line* CAMERONIA (qv). The fleets of both companies had suffered grievous losses during World War I, and consequently in the immediate postwar years many new ships were built for them, TYRRHENIA being one of six on order for *Anchor Line* (see page 66).

TYRRHENIA was the first *Cunard* liner to have a cruiser stern. She was a twin-screw ship with Curtis-Brown turbines double-reduction-geared to each screw shaft and developing 12500shp for a speed of 16 knots. Six oil-fired boilers provided superheated steam at 220psi. She could accommodate 280 first class passengers, 364 second class and 1200 in the third class. She went into service on the *Cunard* Canadian service from Liverpool, but in 1924 her accommodation was altered and she became a cabin class ship carrying 580 in the cabin and 975 in the third class. At this time her name was changed to LANCASTRIA.

SS LANCASTRIA and other ships in the St Laurence River off Quebec /*Cunard*

Soon after this she began sailing from London to New York on a weekly service with CARMANIA, CARONIA and the *Anchor Line* TUSCANIA as her running mates. However, after 1932 the economic situation caused her withdrawal from this service and until the outbreak of World War II, she was engaged in cruising, often with a white hull.

In 1939 she became a troopship and while acting in this capacity she was sent to evacuate British troops from St Nazaire in June 1940. With probably more than 8000 men on board, she was awaiting sailing orders when she was heavily bombed by German aircraft and sank within twenty-five minutes. The loss of life was appalling and it is estimated that more than 4000 men were killed, either as the immediate result of the bombing or in the sea which, heavily polluted with fuel oil, was set alight and burned fiercely.

The sinking of LANCASTRIA remains the greatest sea tragedy of all time.

The *Cunard Line* SS SAMARIA, 19602tG, was completed by Cammell Laird in 1922. She was a 16-knot twin-screw ship powered by double-reduction-geared turbines using superheated steam at 220psi. She had accommodation for 350 passengers in the first class, 350 in the second class and 1500 in the third class. From 1924 the second class became known as 'tourist third cabin class'.

SAMARIA was the second of three ships built for the Liverpool–Boston–New York and other intermediate services of the *Cunard Line*. She was preceded by SCYTHIA, 19730tG, which went into service in 1921, and followed by LACONIA, 19680tG, which sailed on her maiden voyage on schedule, only a month later. LACONIA's construction had been badly

delayed by strikes so she was towed to the Wilton-Fijenoord yard for completion, which was achieved in ten days less than contract time. *Cunard* were delighted.

These three were in each case the second of the company's ships to carry the name. They were almost identical sister ships and excellent and steady seaboats, though they would probably have benefited from an extra two knots speed. Each ship had an island bridge, which made them similar in appearance to the smaller 'A' class but from which they could be distinguished by having an extra deck.

On the outbreak of World War II LACONIA became first an armed merchant cruiser and then a troopship. She was torpedoed and sunk in the South Atlantic in 1942. SAMARIA and SCYTHIA survived as troopships throughout the war, and after refitting went back into *Cunard* service, carrying first and tourist class passengers between United Kingdom ports, and occasionally Rotterdam, and Canada. SAMARIA was scrapped in 1956 and SCYTHIA two years later.

The *Holland-America Line* SS VOLENDAM, 15434tG, was purchased on the stocks from Harland and Wolff's Glasgow yard in 1921. She sailed on her maiden voyage from Rotterdam to New York in November 1922.

VOLENDAM was a handsome and comfortable ship with twin screws driven by single-reduction-geared steam turbines, giving her a speed of 15 knots. With her sister ship VEENDAM she maintained the intermediate service between Rotterdam and New York, with calls at Boulogne and Plymouth. During the

The *Cunard Line* SS SAMARIA /PR-W

winter seasons both ships became increasingly popular as cruise liners to the Caribbean and elsewhere.

As originally fitted out VOLENDAM carried 263 passengers in the first class, 436 in the second and 1200 in the third class. As a result of the United States laws limiting immigration, the third class accommodation was soon altered to tourist class for 480 passengers.

During the early months of World War II VOLENDAM was busy transporting tourists, emigrants and British children from Europe to the United States. In August 1940, while carrying several hundred children, the ship was torpedoed off the coast of Ireland. However, all but one of her passengers and crew escaped safely from the ship which, although badly damaged, did not sink and was ultimately taken in tow and beached on the island of Bute. She finally reached the Birkenhead yard of Cammell Laird where she was repaired and converted to a troopship. For the rest of the war she sailed safely to many parts of the world, carrying more than 100000 troops before she returned to commercial service as a one class ship in 1947, sailing between Rotterdam and New York.

VOLENDAM was withdrawn from service and scrapped in 1951 after a successful and adventurous career.

Above: The *Holland-America Line* SS VOLENDAM /*Holland-America*

Below: SS MONTCLARE as she appeared in 1932 /PR-W

1922

Canadian Pacific Steamships Ltd in 1922 put into service three sister ships for the Liverpool–Quebec–Montreal service. These were the steamships MONTROSE, 16401tG, built by Fairfield, MONTCLARE, 16314tG, and MONTCALM, 16418tG, both built by John Brown. They were twin-screw ships with double-reduction-geared turbines and a service speed of 16 knots. Between 1929 and 1931, all three ships were re-engined with single-reduction-geared turbines and their speed was raised to 17 knots. They maintained a regular and consistent service for seventeen years, and while never being spectacular, were reliable, comfortable and well-liked cabin class ships, carrying 542 cabin passengers and 1268 third class.

At the outbreak of World War II all three were taken over by the Admiralty. MONTCLARE retained her name, first as an armed merchant cruiser and then as a submarine depot ship. MONTCALM became first HMS MONTCALM, an armed merchant cruiser, and then in 1941 a submarine depot ship, being renamed HMS WOLFE. Both these ships were purchased by the Admiralty and were in service until sold for scrapping in 1958 and 1952 respectively.

MONTROSE became HMS FORFAR, an armed merchant cruiser. She was torpedoed and sunk in the Atlantic by the German Submarine U-99 in December 1940.

Below: HMS WOLFE, ex SS MONTCALM, a submarine depot ship, in the Holy Loch in 1943 /PR-W

1922-1923

The first Italian ship to have a gross tonnage in excess of 20000 was the twin-screw GIULIO CESARE of 21657tG. Driven by geared turbines and with a speed of 19·5 knots, this fine ship was completed by Swan Hunter in 1922 for the *Navigazione Generale Italiana*'s New York service.

A similar, but larger and slower, ship was completed for the same company by Ansaldo at Sestri Ponente in 1923 and joined GIULIO CESARE on the Genoa–Naples–New York service. This was SS DUILIO, a twin-screw two-funnelled ship of beautiful proportions and with a cruiser stern. Her gross tonnage was 24281 and her geared turbines gave her a speed of 18·5 knots when developing 22000shp. Her life on the North Atlantic was however short, for in 1928 she went to the South American service and, five years later, ran between Genoa and South Africa. She was then transferred to *Lloyd Triestino* and her end came in 1945 when she was bombed and sunk at Trieste.

1922-1923

Before World War I six Italian shipping companies were engaged in the North Atlantic trade, but they were largely concerned with emigrant traffic to the United States. The ships were comparatively small, most being of about 5000tG or less, and none was of more than 8000tG. However, some of the six companies were members of the International Atlantic Pool, which endeavoured to parcel out a fair share of the trade offering to each of its signatories.

The three most important companies concerned were *Navigazione Generale Italiana*, (*NGI*), *Lloyd Sabaudo* and *Lloyd Italiana*, and there was some competition between such ships as ITALIA (5372tG), of *NGI* and three ships of *Lloyd Sabaudo*, each of which was about 7950tG.

In 1915 the Italians entered World War I on the Allied side and promptly seized the *Hamburg-Amerika Line* MOLTKE, 12307tG, which after the war

Above: SS DUILIO in *Italia Line* colours at Capetown in 1933 /NMM

Bottom: HMS ARGUS, which was to have been the *Lloyd Sabaudo* CONTE ROSSO of 1915 /PR-W

became the *Lloyd Sabaudo* PESARO on the North Atlantic run. The company had before the war placed a contract with Beardmore to build a 15000-ton liner, to be named CONTE ROSSO. She was however taken over by the Admiralty and completed in 1917 as the aircraft carrier HMS ARGUS.

After the war a new CONTE ROSSO, a twin-screw turbine-driven liner of 18017tG was built by Beardmore and completed in 1922. This ship, and her sister CONTE VERDE of 1923, were the most important Italian liners up to that time and with a speed in service of 19 knots they were for a short time very successful on the North Atlantic. Each carried 208 passengers in the first class accommodation, 268 in the second class and 1800 in the third class. The

SS CONTE ROSSO of 1922 at speed /NMM

United States immigration laws had a very adverse effect upon their profitability and by 1928 both ships had been transferred to the South American run.

CONTE ROSSO was sunk by a British submarine in 1941 while acting as a troopship in the Mediterranean.

CONTE VERDE was in Shanghai in 1943 when she was scuttled to avoid capture by the Japanese, who however successfully raised her and used her as a troopship. Later she was again sunk by bombing from US aircraft. Once again she was salvaged, in 1949, and before being scrapped six years later saw service with the Japanese *Mitsui Line*.

1918/1923

The *White Star* liner SS CALGARIC, 16063tG, was completed by Harland and Wolff in 1918 as the cargo steamer ORCA for the *Pacific Steam Navigation Company*. She was rebuilt as a passenger liner in 1922 and she commenced sailing for the *Royal Mail Steam Packet Company* on their Hamburg–Southampton–Cherbourg–New York service in 1923 (page 62).

In 1927 she became CALGARIC of the *White Star Line* and was used, with ALBERTIC, on that company's Canadian service. During her service with both companies she was frequently used for cruising.

CALGARIC had a cruiser stern. She was a triple-screw ship with two quadruple-expansion engines driving the wing shafts and an exhaust-steam low-pressure turbine the centre shaft. Her speed was 16 knots. Like ALBERTIC, she carried only cabin class and third class passengers. She was withdrawn in 1933 and sold for scrapping at Rosyth in 1934.

1923

The *White Star* liner SS ALBERTIC, 18940tG, was laid down at the Weser yard, Bremen, as the *Norddeutscher Lloyd* SS MÜNCHEN in 1913. The outbreak of World War I delayed her construction and she was not completed until 1923 when, as reparation, she was handed over to the *Royal Mail Steam Packet Company (RMSP)* as their OHIO.

RMSP had started a passenger service on the North Atlantic in 1921 between Hamburg, Southampton, Cherbourg and New York, and OHIO went on to this run with ORCA, ORDUNA and ORBITA (qv) as running mates.

In 1927 *RMSP* bought *White Star Line* from the *International Mercantile Marine* and subsequently retired from the North Atlantic trade, handing its services and two of its ships, ORCA and OHIO, over to *White Star*, who renamed them CALGARIC and ALBERTIC respectively. They remained on the North Atlantic but were used on the Canadian service running between London, Southampton or Liverpool to Quebec and Montreal. They also made some cruises, ALBERTIC for a time to New York.

ALBERTIC was a twin-screw ship powered by two quadruple-expansion engines using steam at 220psi from six coal-fired boilers. Her engines developed 16000shp for a service speed of 16 knots. She carried 580 passengers in cabin class accommodation and 1700 in third class. She was a comfortable ship and carried many thousands of emigrants to Canada during the 1920s. She was laid up in 1933 and the following year was sold to Japan for scrapping.

Below: The *White Star Line* SS CALGARIC /NMM
Bottom: The *White Star Line* SS ALBERTIC /Cunard

1923

The *White Star Line* SS DORIC /NMM

The *White Star Line* SS DORIC, 16484tG, was completed in 1923 by Harland and Wolff and went into the company's Canadian service, running between Liverpool, Quebec and Montreal. She was a handsome, comfortable cabin class ship with good accommodation for 600 cabin and 1700 third class passengers.

DORIC was very similar to REGINA (later WESTERNLAND) (qv) which was built in 1918 for *Dominion Line* and which had been on the *White Star-Dominion Line* Liverpool–Canada service since 1922. But whereas REGINA was a triple-screw ship driven by two triple-expansion engines and a low-pressure turbine, DORIC had twin-screws driven by single-reduction-geared turbines. Her service speed was 15 knots, rather slow even for an 'intermediate' liner.

As a result of the world trade depression of the early 1930s DORIC was taken off the Canadian service in late 1932 and, after refitting, was used exclusively as a cruise ship.

In September 1935, while returning from a Mediterranean cruise, she collided off the Atlantic coast of Portugal with the French cargo ship FORMIGNY, 2166tG, and was seriously damaged below the waterline. Her passengers were taken off by the *Orient* line ORION and by the *P & O* liner VICEROY OF INDIA. DORIC then managed to reach Vigo, where temporary repairs were effected. She later sailed for Tilbury, where it was considered uneconomic to repair her and she was sold for scrap.

Cunard Line SS FRANCONIA, 20341tG, was the second *Cunard* ship to carry the name and she was completed by John Brown in 1923. She had six steam turbines double-reduction-geared to two screw shafts and her speed in service was 16 knots.

FRANCONIA and her sister ship CARINTHIA, 20277tG, which was completed in 1925, were almost identical with SAMARIA, SCYTHIA and LACONIA, but in each of the new ships the bridge formed part of the superstructure and was not of the island type. The passenger accommodation of FRANCONIA and CARINTHIA was also different and catered for 240 first class, 460 second class and 950 third class. In 1930-1931 this was altered to accommodate first and tourist classes only.

Both ships were used on the London–Southampton–New York and on the Liverpool–New York services, but they were also extensively used for cruising and their hulls were then painted white.

In 1939 CARINTHIA became an armed merchant cruiser and was torpedoed and sunk in 1940. FRANCONIA served throughout World War II as a troopship. She was used as a headquarters ship for Winston Churchill at the Yalta Conference in 1945. FRANCONIA returned to the *Cunard Line* Liverpool–Quebec service in 1949. She made her last voyage in 1956 and was then scrapped at Inverkeithing.

After World War I *Norddeutscher Lloyd (NDL)* was left with very few ships and had to employ several small and unsuitable ones to start their Hamburg–New York service on the North Atlantic.

The first of the new ships specifically designed for this service was the SS MÜNCHEN, which was built by the Vulkan yard, Stettin, and went into service in 1923. She was the third *NDL* ship to carry the name and was a twin-screw vessel of 13325tG, powered by two four-cylinder triple-expansion engines supplied with steam by coal-burning boilers and with a service speed of 15·5 knots. She carried 1078 passengers in three classes.

In 1930 MÜNCHEN caught fire while in New York harbour and was gutted, but did not sink. She was towed home to the Weser yard at Bremen, completely rebuilt and re-engined as an oil-burning ship of

1923 14690tG with a speed of 16·5 knots, and named GENERAL VON STEUBEN. Her passenger complement was reduced to 548. It is in this form she is seen here.

In 1938 she became one of Hitler's 'Strength through Joy' ships, being again renamed STEUBEN. Her end came in 1945 when she was sunk by a Russian submarine in the Baltic Sea.

Atlantic Transport Line SS MINNEWASKA, 21716tG, was built by Harland and Wolff and went into the company's London–New York service in 1923. She was a twin-screw oil-burning ship powered by two sets of Brown-Curtis turbines single-reduction-geared to the screw shafts. She had a service speed of 16 knots but was capable of 19 knots and made 20 knots on trial. She carried 368 first class passengers only, but had the largest cargo capacity of any passenger ship built up to that time, some 20500 tons dw.

MINNEWASKA and her sister ship MINNETONKA, 21998tG, which went into service in 1924, were the

Above: Cunard Line SS FRANCONIA /PR-W

Below: NDL GENERAL VAN STEUBEN ex MUNCHEN /NMM

largest ships ever built for *ATL* and many considered them too big for the work they had to do. They were built as replacements for ships of the same names which had been lost during World War I.

By the end of the 1920s *Atlantic Transport Line*, a constituent company of *International Mercantile Marine* (*IMM*) (qv), was in considerable financial difficulty and, after being laid up for a year, MINNEWASKA and MINNETONKA were transferred in 1932 to *Red Star Line*, another *IMM* company.

Carrying tourist class passengers, the two ships ran for a year between Antwerp and New York until being again laid up in 1933. Both ships were sold, very cheaply, for scrap in 1934.

The *Atlantic Transport Company* was wound up in 1934 and the *Red Star Line* was sold in the same year.

Atlantic Transport Line SS MINNEWASKA /NMM

1923-1924

SS ALBERT BALLIN, 20815tG, was the first of two sister ships built after World War I for the newly reconstituted *Hamburg-Amerika Line* (*HAPAG*) by Blöhm and Voss, Hamburg. She went into service in July 1923, being followed on the Hamburg–Southampton–New York service by her sister ship DEUTSCHLAND in March 1924. They were large, well-appointed, comfortable ships and were equipped with bulge-type Frahm anti-rolling tanks. They were driven by single-reduction-geared steam turbines

driving twin screws and developing 12500shp for a speed of 15·5 knots. Both ships had four masts and two funnels.

They were designed specifically to deal with the profitable emigration traffic from Europe to the United States and each ship carried 250 first class, 340 second class and 950 third class passengers.

During 1929-1930 both ships were re-engined and provided with new high-pressure water tube boilers by Blöhm and Voss. In consequence, their speed was

raised to 19·5 knots. In 1934 each ship was reconstructed, the forward part being lengthened by 39·3ft to give an overall length of 646ft, and a bulbous bow was fitted. This raised the gross tonnage of ALBERT BALLIN to 21131tG and of DEUTSCHLAND to 21046tG, and resulted in a saving of oil fuel of nearly 30 per cent at full speed.

In 1935 ALBERT BALLIN was renamed HANSA. This was in pursuance of the Hitler anti-Semitic policy; Albert Ballin, a Jew, had spent thirty years of his life bringing the *Hamburg-Amerika Line* to a position of eminence in world shipping, and consequently bringing much trade and prosperity to Germany.

Top: SS DEUTSCHLAND as built /NMM

Above: SS ALBERT BALLIN as reconstructed and lengthened /Real Photographs

Both ships were in Germany during World War II. HANSA was sunk by a mine in the Baltic in 1945 but was later salvaged. She was taken over by Russia, renamed SOVETSKY SOJUS and, in 1976, SOVIETSKY SOJUS. She is still in service, her home port being Vladivostock and her gross tonnage 23009.

DEUTSCHLAND was sunk by Allied bombing in 1945.

1924

SS PRESIDENT HARRISON, 10594tG, was built in 1920 by the New York Shipbuilding Company as WOLVERINE STATE of the United States *Pacific Mail Line*. It was, however, taken over when new by the United States Shipping Board *United States Lines* and was one of five ships which operated on their London–New York service carrying cargo and 78 first class passengers.

At the end of 1923 this ship and six others were sold by *United States Lines* to the *Dollar Steamship Company*, who used them on an east to west round the world service, making the Atlantic crossing from Marseilles to Boston.

In 1938, owing to financial difficulties, *Dollar Steamship Company* was bought by the US Government, who continued operating the company as *American President Line*.

PRESIDENT HARRISON was a twin-screw ship driven by two four-cylinder triple-expansion engines. She had a speed of 14 knots. In December 1941 she was deliberately wrecked by her crew in the China Sea to prevent her capture by the Japanese. The photograph shows her leaving Singapore in 1940.

SS PRESIDENT HARRISON /PR-W

1923-1925

The *Donaldson Line* began operating steamships between Glasgow and Montreal in 1879. The *Anchor Line* had operated steamships between Glasgow and New York since 1856 and later their ships were also sailing on a service to Canada. In 1916 a joint company, *Anchor-Donaldson Line*, was formed to operate a combined Glasgow–Canada service, but, as *Anchor Line* had been a *Cunard Line* subsidiary since 1912, the new company was brought under the *Cunard* 'umbrella'.

In 1935 *Anchor Line* was liquidated (page 66) and at the same time the company's interest in *Anchor-Donaldson* was sold to a *Donaldson Line* subsidiary, *Donaldson Atlantic Line*, which operated the two ships ATHENIA and LETITIA on the Glasgow–Quebec–Montreal service until the outbreak of World War II in 1939.

ATHENIA 13465tG, was completed by Fairfield in 1923 and she was obviously a 'Cunard type' ship, but had a cruiser stern. Apart from this, with her island

bridge her silhouette was nearly identical with the first three *Cunard* 'A'-class (page 47). She carried 516 cabin class passengers and 1000 third class, but later had accommodation for 314 cabin class, 310 tourist and 920 third class passengers. She was a twin-screw ship, her engines being two sets of steam turbines double-reduction-geared to the screw shafts. She developed 8700shp for a service speed of 15 knots, but could exceed this by at least two knots when required.

She was the second ship to carry the name. Her predecessor of 1904 had been torpedoed and sunk during World War I and, history repeated itself as the second ATHENIA had the unhappy distinction of being the first merchant ship casualty of World War II. She was torpedoed and sunk without warning by the submarine U-30 in the North Atlantic only three hours after the declaration of war on September 3rd, 1939. This early example of German ruthlessness caused the loss of 112 men, women and children.

SS LETITIA, 13475tG, was a sister ship of ATHENIA and was completed by Fairfield in 1925. Her career followed closely that of her sister until 1939, when she was commissioned by the Admiralty as an armed merchant cruiser with eight 6in guns in single mountings. At the end of 1941 she was taken out of service and converted to a troopship. During her service in this capacity she was badly damaged by bombing off the North African coast in 1943 and was sent to America for repair. The Canadian

Above: SS ATHENIA, the second ship to carry the name / NMM

Below: SS LETITIA /NMM

Government then took her over and converted her in 1944 to a hospital ship. Thus she followed the career of the first LETITIA, 8991tG, of 1912, which was wrecked while serving as a hospital ship in World War I.

In 1946, while repatriating Canadian sick and wounded from Europe, she was sold to the Ministry of Transport, who renamed her EMPIRE BRENT, and she continued on repatriation work until 1947. After a refit on the Clyde she first became an Australian emigration ship and then a New Zealand one, even-

The first LETITIA of 1912 which was wrecked while serving as a hospital ship in World War I /NMM

tually passing into the ownership of the New Zealand Government. They renamed her CAPTAIN COOK but she was still managed by the *Donaldson Line.*

After a further period of work as troopship, emigrant ship and briefly under charter to *Donaldson Line* as a transatlantic liner in 1955, she was broken up in 1961.

1920/1924

United States Lines (USL) SS AMERICAN BANKER, 7430tG, was built in 1920 by American International Shipbuilding Corporation for the United States Shipping Board as a transport for troops and military supplies. She was then named CANTIGNY and was one of seven ships built as US transports in 1920-1921. They were single-screw ships with double-reduction-geared turbines and a speed of 15 knots.

In 1924 five of the ships, including AMERICAN BANKER, were sold to *American Merchant Lines,* who used them as cargo-passenger ships carrying 12 tourist class passengers between London and New York. Their accommodation was improved and extended in 1928-1929 and they subsequently each carried 80 passengers.

As the result of a series of sales and mergers the five ships came under the flag of *United States Lines Company* in 1931, and the remaining two of the original seven also became *USL* ships in 1934, working between Liverpool and New York.

AMERICAN BANKER was sold to the *Société Maritime*

of Antwerp in 1940 and renamed VILLE D'ANVERS. In 1946 she was sold to Honduras as CITY OF ATHENS and, a year later, to the Panamanian *Incres Line,* being named PROTEA and sailing between Antwerp, Plymouth and Montreal. In 1952 the ship was purchased by the newly formed *Arosa Line,* a Swiss-owned company which registered its three ships in Panama.

PROTEA now changed her name for the fifth time and became AROSA KULM. Her accommodation was completely rebuilt and the general appearance of the ship was altered. She now carried 46 tourist cabin class passengers and 920 third class in dormitory accommodation and worked, very profitably, on the Canadian immigrant and tourist trade between Bremen and other European ports and Halifax, Montreal, and occasionally New York.

In 1959, however, *Arosa Line* went bankrupt and AROSA KULM was scrapped in Belgium, after thirty-nine years of more than usual variety and change of ownership.

1924-1953

As part of the rebuilding and expansion of their fleet after World War I the *Compagnie Générale Transatlantique (CGT)* ordered a new ship from Cammell Laird of Birkenhead, and the keel of SUFFREN was laid down in March 1919. As a result of labour and other troubles the ship was not launched until four years later and her name had by then been changed to DE GRASSE. She was completed in 1924 and made her maiden voyage to New York from le Havre in August of that year.

DE GRASSE was a twin-screw single-reduction-geared turbine-driven ship of 17707tG, with a speed of 16 knots. She had two funnels and a counter stern.

She was seized by the Germans on the invasion of France in 1940 and was used by them as an accommodation ship in the river Gironde. When the Germans withdrew from the area in 1944 they sank DE GRASSE, probably by gunfire, though some accounts say she was scuttled. She was salvaged in 1945

Top: CGT DE GRASSE *as built /NMM*
Above: Canadian Pacific EMPRESS OF AUSTRALIA, *ex* DE
GRASSE, *passing under Jacques Cartier Bridge, Montreal /*
Canadian Pacific

and completely refitted at St Nazaire, emerging in
July 1947 with one funnel only and with new and
excellent passenger accommodation. Her gross tonnage had now increased to 18435.

She returned to her former duties on the le
Havre–New York service, but by 1952, as a result of
the transference of FLANDRE from the West Indies run
to the North Atlantic, DE GRASSE was laid up.

In January 1953 the *Canadian Pacific* liner EMPRESS OF CANADA (ex DUCHESS OF RICHMOND) caught fire while in dock at Liverpool and sank at her berth. In order to cope with the very heavy traffic of that Coronation Year the company bought DE GRASSE, renamed her EMPRESS OF AUSTRALIA, and hurriedly put her into service between Liverpool and Quebec. She carried 220 first class and 444 tourist class passengers. She lasted only until the end of 1955 and then, after working briefly as a troopship, she was laid up and sold to an Italian company who refitted her, renamed her VENEZUELA and operated her between Mediterranean ports and Central America. After running aground at Cannes in 1962 she was sold for scrapping at Spezia. So ended the long and adventurous career of a famous British-built French liner.

1925

Cunard Line SS ALAUNIA, 14030tG, was completed by John Brown in 1925. She was a twin-screw ship driven by double-reduction-geared turbines and she had a speed of 15 knots.

ALAUNIA, the second *Cunard* ship to carry the name, was the last of six sister ships built after World War I for service between United Kingdom and Canadian ports, and generally known as the 'A' class ships. They were built in two batches: ANDANIA, 13950tG, (Hawthorn Leslie), ANTONIA, 13867tG, (Vickers) and AUSONIA, 13912tG, (Armstrong Whitworth) entering service in 1922, while AURANIA, 13984tG, (Swan Hunter) and ASCANIA 14013tG, (Armstrong Whitworth) followed in 1924 and ALAUNIA in 1925. In each of the first three ships the bridge was of the island type, whereas in the second three it was part of the superstructure. In other respects the ships were practically identical and each carried 500 cabin class passengers and 1200 in the third class. They were popular and economical ships.

At the outbreak of World War II five of the six became armed merchant cruisers, but ANTONIA became a troopship and later a repair ship, as HMS WAYLAND. ANDANIA was torpedoed and sunk in 1940. Of the remainder, AUSONIA, ALAUNIA and AURANIA were converted to fleet repair ships, the first two retaining their own names and AURANIA becoming HMS ARTIFAX. Only ASCANIA was returned to commercial service after the war and she sailed for

Cunard Line SS ALAUNIA /PR-W

Cunard, mostly on the Liverpool–Montreal service, until 1956 when she was scrapped.

Encouraged by the success of their ships CONTE ROSSO and CONTE VERDE and by the North Atlantic boom years of the middle twenties, *Lloyd Sabaudo* ordered from Beardmore a new and much larger ship. This was CONTE BIANCAMANO, 24416tG, which went into service between Genoa, Naples and New York in 1925. She had four steam turbines, double-reduction-geared to two screw shafts and developing 24000shp

Above: This photograph shows ALAUNIA as the repair ship HMS ALAUNIA /PR-W
Below: Lloyd Sabaudo Line SS CONTE BIANCAMANO of 1925. She later carried *Italia Line* colours /NMM

for a speed of 20 knots. Her seven boilers provided steam at 220psi.

She was a fine looking ship, elegantly fitted out with all the facilities of a modern express liner. Her accommodation was for 215 first class, 333 cabin class and 1030 third class passengers.

With her Italian-built sister, CONTE GRANDE, she became an *Italia Line* ship in 1932 and was then transferred to the South American service. In 1937 she went to *Lloyd Triestino*, running between Genoa and Buenos Aires.

The *Norddeutscher Lloyd* (*NDL*) SS BERLIN, 15286tG, the third ship to carry the name, was built by Bremer Vulkan and went into service between Bremen, Southampton and New York in 1925. She

was a 16-knot twin-screw ship powered by two four-cylinder triple-expansion engines and was the last transatlantic liner to be built with reciprocating engines. She was not a fast ship but was renowned for her comfortable accommodation.

BERLIN was one of six North Atlantic ships to be built for *NDL* in the immediate postwar years and which the company was allowed to keep. Others were handed over to the Allies as reparations.

In 1939 she became one of Hitler's 'Strength through Joy' ships, and in 1945 she struck a mine in the Baltic and sank. In 1949 the Russians salvaged the ship which was then repaired at Warnemunde. She was renamed ADMIRAL NAKHIMOV and since 1957 has been in service in the Black Sea, usually working between Odessa and Batum.

MV GRIPSHOLM, 18815tG, was built by Armstrong

Above The Norddeutscher Lloyd (NDL) SS BERLIN /Real Photographs
Below: Swedish Lloyd MV GRIPSHOLM 1925 /Swedish America
Right: SS LUSITANIA at sea /Painting by George F. Heiron
Next page: SS LEVIATHAN at Southampton. OLYMPIC ahead /Painting by George F. Heiron

Whitworth for *Swedish-American Line* and went into service between Gothenburg and New York in 1925. She had two Burmeister and Wain diesel engines driving twin screws and her service speed was 17 knots.

GRIPSHOLM was the first North Atlantic motor ship. She was named after Sweden's famed royal castle and

NDL MV BERLIN of 1945, ex GRIPSHOLM /Skyfotos
Left: NDL SS BREMEN /Painting by George F. Heiron

it was said that 'her spacious and lovely rooms made one realise what it was to live like a king'. Part of her decoration was in the form of panel paintings of Viking ships by well-known artists.

In 1924, shortly before the ship went into service, the United States Government introduced an act greatly restricting immigration and, as a result, there was much surplus transatlantic tonnage. *Swedish-American* promptly began organising cruises for their ships and GRIPSHOLM became one of the most success-ful cruise liners, as well as maintaining a reduced North Atlantic service.

During her nineteen years in Swedish ownership GRIPSHOLM was twice reconstructed and as a result her passenger accommodation was reduced from 1640 to 920, her crew was increased from 301 to 350 and her gross tonnage went up to 19049. In company with all *Swedish-American* passenger ships, her hull was painted white after 1930.

In 1954 GRIPSHOLM was sold to the *Bremen-American Line* and ran between Hamburg, Southampton and New York under charter to, and then owned by, *Norddeutscher Lloyd*, who renamed her BERLIN. She was withdrawn from service and scrapped in 1966 at Spezia.

1926-1927

SS HAMBURG, 21133tG, and SS NEW YORK, 21445tG, were built by Blöhm and Voss, Hamburg, and went into the Hamburg–Southampton–New York service of the *Hamburg-Amerika Line* in 1926 and 1927 respectively. They were regarded as ships of the 'ALBERT BALLIN Class' and, with ALBERT BALLIN and DEUTSCHLAND, formed a quartet which gave a regular and reliable weekly service across the North Atlantic.

The two new ships were, however, different in several respects from the earlier two. For example, they had two masts instead of four and their funnels were about 1m higher. As a result of the United States laws which drastically limited immigration, the accommodation for third class passengers was greatly reduced and each of the new ships was designed to carry 220 first class, 480 second class and 460 third class passengers.

Machinery, speed, anti-rolling tanks and hull dimensions were the same as for ALBERT BALLIN and DEUTSCHLAND, and HAMBURG and NEW YORK were re-engined and reconstructed in the same way and during the same periods as those two ships (page 79).

In 1945 HAMBURG was sunk by a mine off Sassnitz but was refloated and rebuilt in 1950 as the Russian JURY DOLGURUKY.

NEW YORK was bombed and sunk at Kiel by Allied air attack in April 1945.

The serious participation of Italian shipping companies in the North Atlantic express services may be said to have begun in 1922 with the completion of the *Lloyd Sabaudo* CONTE ROSSO and of the *Navigazione Generale Italiana* (*NGI*) GIULIO CESARE in the same year. These ships were followed by others of similar size and speed in rapid succession

Furthermore, the competition to be expected from the newly-formed *Cosulich Line*, as well as the current boom in transatlantic traffic, obviously influenced *NGI* in their building of the two largest passenger ships of the Italian merchant fleet.

In 1926 *NGI* put into service the larger of its two new ships, the ROMA, a two-funnel steamship of

32583tG which had been built by Ansaldo at Sestri Ponente. She had four screws driven by single-reduction-geared turbines and her service speed was 20 knots.

The second ship, AUGUSTUS, of 30418tG, went into service in 1927. Also built by Ansaldo, she was of great interest as being at that time the largest motor ship in the world. She also had four screws, and each was driven by an MAN six-cylinder, two-cycle, double-acting diesel engine built in Italy under licence. The total output of her four main engines was 28000shp for a service speed of 19 knots.

Both ships were designed with an eye to the booming emigrant traffic to the United States and ROMA could accommodate 1736 passengers in four classes, while AUGUSTUS carried no fewer than 2220. The passenger accommodation for the first and intermediate classes was of a very high standard but the majority of passengers in both ships were carried in large open-berth dormitories reminiscent of some of the pilgrim ships trading to the East.

The appearances of the two ships were very similar, both having straight stems and counter sterns, while the spacing and size of the funnels in both were almost identical.

In 1931 *NGI* became a constituent of the *Italia Line* and ROMA and AUGUSTUS were the new company's largest ships.

During World War II both ships were converted to aircraft carriers, ROMA being named AQUILA and AUGUSTUS becoming SPARVIERO. AQUILA was bombed and severely damaged by the RAF in 1944, finally being given the *coup de grâce* by Royal Navy frogmen in 1945. Her wreckage was disposed of in 1950. SPARVIERO ended her career as a block ship at Genoa, being scuttled there in 1944, raised in 1946 and scrapped the following year.

Below: NGI SS ROMA /NMM
Bottom: NGI MV AUGUSTUS /NMM

1927

SS LAURENTIC, 18724tG, was the second ship to carry the name and she entered the Liverpool–Quebec–Montreal service of the *White Star Line* in 1927. She was built by Harland and Wolff and was a 17-knot triple-screw ship powered by two four-cylinder triple-expansion engines and a low-pressure turbine. She was a coal-burning ship for the whole of her life. She was fitted with telescopic metal topmasts to enable her to pass under the Quebec Bridge to reach Montreal.

After the construction of the oil-burning twin-screw turbine steamship DORIC (qv) in 1923 it seems very strange that the next ship built for *White Star Line* by Harland and Wolff should have reciprocating engines and burn coal.

LAURENTIC was, however, a large and comfortable ship which could carry 594 cabin class, 406 tourist third cabin class and 500 third class passengers, and her public rooms were exceedingly well appointed for an 'intermediate' cabin class liner. Later in her career she sailed between Liverpool and Boston, and also called frequently at Greenock, lying off the Tail o' the Bank.

With the Depression she was used more and more for cruising and in 1932 she became an exhibition ship for British goods, visiting major Canadian Atlantic ports.

LAURENTIC was involved in two serious collisions, the first with the Belfast ship LURIGETHAN in fog in the Belle Isle Strait. Both ships were able to proceed without assistance. The second collision was much more serious and happened in August 1935, after the ship had been taken over by *Cunard-White Star Line*. She was four hours out from Liverpool when she collided, also in fog, with the *Blue Star Line* NAPIER

SS LAURENTIC /*Cunard*

CGT SS ILE DE FRANCE /NMM

STAR. Six of LAURENTIC's crew were killed and later both ships were held equally to blame. LAURENTIC had to return to Liverpool and her passengers were transferred to other ships.

After being repaired, LAURENTIC spent much of the next four years laid up. It was said she was kept in reserve as a coal-burning ship in case of a shortage of oil fuel.

On the outbreak of World War II she became, one would think, a most unsuitable armed merchant cruiser. She met her fate in November 1940 when she was torpedoed and sunk by the German submarine U-99 off Bloody Foreland.

SS ILE DE FRANCE, 42050tG, was built at Penhoët for the *Cie Générale Transatlantique (CGT)* and went into service between le Havre, Plymouth and New York in 1927. She had four screws directly driven by Parsons turbines, the high-pressure turbine driving the port outer shaft, the intermediate-pressure driving the starboard outer, and the two low-pressure turbines the two inner shafts. She developed 52000shp at 23·5 knots but was able considerably to exceed these figures. She had thirty-two fire- and water-tube boilers which were oil-fired and provided saturated steam at 231psi. The boiler uptakes were equally divided between the first two funnels, and the third funnel, following the fashion of the time, was a dummy, which acted as an engine-room air intake.

Before World War I *CGT* was preparing to build a fleet of three large and fast passenger ships to compete with the British and German express liners in what was at that time the very lucrative North Atlantic trade. Only one ship, FRANCE (qv), was in service before the outbreak of hostilities; the second ship, PARIS (qv), had been laid down at Penhoët in 1913, launched in 1916 but not completed until 1921. In order to try to accelerate this much delayed programme, ILE DE FRANCE was built in the extraordinary time of two years and seven months. She had accommodation for 1680 passengers in seven classes, varying from extreme luxury to dormitory-type third class. She carried a crew of 816.

She was fitted with an aircraft catapult and in 1928 a small biplane flying-boat was launched when the ship was about 400 miles from New York, to carry mails on a special delivery service. The reverse service was carried out with mails for le Havre on the west to east run. This never became a regular feature, high cost and the uncertainties of the weather making it uneconomical and irregular, and the flying-boat service was withdrawn, it is believed, after about three months (page 182).

During the years before World War II, ILE DE FRANCE had an extensive refit in 1931 involving the rebuilding of much of her accommodation, and smaller improvements were made during the next eight

years. FRANCE was withdrawn from service in 1932 and NORMANDIE joined ILE DE FRANCE and PARIS in 1935 to make a trio of some of the finest ships on the North Atlantic.

On the outbreak of World War II the ship was taken over by the French Government as a troopship and at the fall of France her officers and ship's company joined the Free French forces. Thus ILE DE FRANCE became an Allied troop transport and was one of the most valuable of our wartime assets, a large fast ship able to carry nearly 9000 men at a time. She saw service all over the world and, from 1942 until she returned to CGT in 1947, was managed by the *Cunard-White Star Company*.

During the period 1947 to 1949 the ship was completely rebuilt at the Penhoët yard, and when she again went into service she had two large but hand-

CGT ILE DE FRANCE as rebuilt with two funnels /Real Photographs

some funnels in place of her former three. The hull was externally unaltered but the whole of her accommodation and facilities had been renewed and she could now carry only 1350 passengers in three classes, first, cabin and tourist. Her gross tonnage was then 44356. She at once became one of the most popular North Atlantic liners and ran regularly until the end of 1958, when she was thirty-two years old.

With the reduction in passenger trade on the North Atlantic, ILE DE FRANCE became uneconomic and she was sold to Japanese shipbreakers in 1959. She was renamed FURANZO MARU for the voyage to Japan.

1919/1927

Of the three important passenger liners building at the outbreak of World War I for the South American service of the *Hamburg-Amerika Line*, TIRPITZ was the nearest to completion. (See also page 69). She had been launched from the Vulkan yard at Stettin in November 1913 and work stopped on her in August 1914. However, her fitting-out was resumed two

years later and, with many interruptions, was completed after the end of hostilities in 1919. She was then handed over to Great Britain as reparation and for the next two years worked as a troop transport under the management of the *P & O Line*.

TIRPITZ was an elegant ship of 21861tG with three funnels, the after one being used only as an engine-

Canadian Pacific SS EMPRESS OF AUSTRALIA, ex TIRPITZ /
PR-W

room air intake. In this she followed the German fashion of the time, and the uptakes to her other two funnels were divided. Technically the most interesting feature of the ship was her machinery. Two sets of impulse-reaction turbines each drove her twin screws through a form of hydraulic transmission known as a Fottinger. Hydraulic Transformer. This brilliantly conceived but experimental drive had the merit of being reversible, thus obviating the need for astern turbines. In service, however, it proved to be very inefficient and its inherent 'slip' reduced the ship's designed speed of 17·5 knots to little more than 15·5 while absorbing nearly 15000shp. At full speed the transmission reduced a turbine speed of 775rpm to a shaft speed of 144rpm.

Shortly before changing their name to *Canadian Pacific Steamships Ltd, Canadian Pacific Ocean Services Ltd* in July 1921 bought TIRPITZ and renamed her EMPRESS OF CHINA. For the next year the ship was refitted on the Clyde and converted from coal- to oil-burning. She then went into the company's trans-Pacific service as EMPRESS OF AUSTRALIA. During this period of her career she was instrumental in saving many lives during the Yokahama earthquake of 1923. But her machinery gave much trouble and caused repeated delays. As a result she was withdrawn in August 1926 and sent to the Clyde for extensive reconstruction and re-engining.

After very considerable constructional problems, but without upsetting her magnificent public rooms, her original fourteen boilers were cut up in the ship and removed piecemeal, to be replaced by six double-ended boilers and a small single-ended auxiliary. Her turbines and 'transformers' were replaced by Parsons turbines driving through single-reduction-gearing. As a result she could achieve 20 knots at a very economic rate of oil consumption.

EMPRESS OF AUSTRALIA now went into the trans-atlantic service of the Company and left Southampton on her first voyage in June 1927. She carried 400 first class passengers, 150 second class and 630 third class. She filled in her off-peak periods as a very successful cruise liner. She was by and large a very popular ship and was again extensively refitted in 1938.

At the outbreak of World War II, she was taken over as a troopship and after serving all over the world she was retained in this capacity until 1952, when she was sold out of service and scrapped at Inverkeithing.

95

1927-1928

The Italian *Cosulich Line* was founded in 1920 and began trading between Trieste and New York with three old ships, the most famous being the ex-*Hamburg-Amerika* liner FURST BISMARCK of 1890, which sailed for *Cosulich* for four years as SAN GIUSTA.

In 1925 *Cantieri Navale Triestino* laid down two large ships for *Cosulich*, and SATURNIA of 23940tG sailed on her maiden voyage to South America in 1927. She was followed in 1928 by VULCANIA, 23970tG, which sailed to New York and which was soon to be joined on the North Atlantic by her sister ship.

These two ships may be regarded as most successful experiments. They were the largest motor ships ever to have been built up to that time and the first important North Atlantic ships to adopt diesel propulsion. They had twin screws and each ship had two four-cycle double-acting Burmeister and Wain engines which developed 18000shp for a service speed of 19·5 knots.

In 1935 both ships were re-engined with diesel engines developing 26000shp, the most powerful marine diesels of their time. The new engines in VULCANIA were by Fiat, those in SATURNIA were by

Below: Italia Line MV SATURNIA at Palermo in 1962 / PR-W
Bottom: Italia Line MV VULCANIA at Naples in 1962 / PR-W

Sulzer. Both ships could now achieve a service speed of 21 knots and with their excellent accommodation, especially for the tourist class, they were popular and successful ships. Each ship could carry 240 first class, 270 second and 860 tourist class passengers.

In 1932 *Cosulich* had joined the other principal Italian shipping companies, *Navigazione Generale Italiana* and *Lloyd Sabaudo*, to become the *Italia Line*, and the two great motor ships continued their profitable service wearing the funnel colours of the new line, white with a narrow green band and a red top.

During World War II VULCANIA became a United States troopship, returning in 1947 to her North Atlantic duties, with Genoa as her home port, having been completely refitted and reconditioned and her

gross tonnage increased to 24496. She was laid up at Trieste in 1965 for disposal, but was bought the same year by *Siosa Line*, who renamed her CARIBIA and used her for cruising. In September 1972 she grounded on submerged rocks off Nice and was severely damaged, flooding part of her engine room. She managed to proceed on one engine to Genoa and then to Spezia, where she was laid up. In November 1973 the ship was towed to Barcelona for breaking up, but was re-sold to Taiwan and was broken up at Kaohsiung.

SATURNIA in 1944 became the United States Navy hospital ship FRANCIS Y. SLANGER. She also survived the war and returned to service with her sister ship in 1947, with her gross tonnage increased to 24346. She was withdrawn from service in 1965.

1928

MV KUNGSHOLM, 21256tG, the second ship to carry the name, was built for *Swedish-American Line* by Blöhm and Voss of Hamburg and entered the Gothenburg–New York service in 1928. Like MV GRIPSHOLM of 1925 (qv) she was also used for cruising. In appearance both ships were very similar and both were twin-screw vessels powered by Burmeister and Wain diesel engines. With a speed in service of 18 knots KUNGSHOLM was slightly the faster ship. She was luxuriously but tastefully appointed and was said at the time of her introduction, to justify her name

by being indeed a 'home for kings'. Her passenger accommodation was for 115 first class, 490 second and 970 third class passengers.

In 1942, during World War II, KUNGSHOLM was sold to the United States Government as a troopship and was renamed JOHN ERICSSON. She served in the Pacific, and later at the invasion of France in 1944.

MV KUNGSHOLM was built for *Swedish American Line* / PR-W

1928 After the war she was purchased in 1947 by Panamanian *Home Lines*, an associated company of *Swedish-American*, and after refitting following a fire she was renamed ITALIA and subsequently carried 120 first class passengers and 1320 in the tourist class. She ran first between Genoa and South America,

then between Genoa, Lisbon and New York and finally on the Hamburg–Southampton–le Havre–Halifax–New York service.

In 1964 she was sold to become a floating hotel at Freeport, Bahamas and renamed IMPERIAL BAHAMA. She was broken up the following year.

1928-1929

During 1928-1929 *Canadian Pacific Steamships Ltd* put into service four 20000-ton twin-screw passenger liners for their Liverpool (and Greenock)–Canada services. These sister ships were each designed to carry 580 cabin class, 480 tourist class and 510 third class passengers. They were twin-screw vessels driven by single-reduction-geared steam turbines developing about 18500shp for a speed of 18 knots. The ships were named after various duchesses: DUCHESS OF BEDFORD, 20123tG, built by John Brown; maiden voyage from Liverpool, June 1st, 1928. DUCHESS OF ATHOLL, 20119tG, built by Beardmore; maiden voyage from Liverpool, July 13th, 1928.

DUCHESS OF RICHMOND, 20022tG, built by John Brown; maiden voyage from Liverpool, March 15th, 1929. DUCHESS OF YORK, 20021tG, built by John Brown; maiden voyage from Liverpool, March 22nd, 1929.

There can be few instances of a single company putting into service four large new ships in such a short space of time.

Below: Canadian Pacific SS DUCHESS OF YORK /NMM
Bottom: Canadian Pacific SS EMPRESS OF FRANCE, ex DUCHESS OF BEDFORD /*Canadian Pacific*

They were very comfortable and reliable ships but were inclined to roll, becoming known on the North Atlantic as the 'Rolling Duchesses'. Their service before World War II was free from serious incident, though DUCHESS OF ATHOLL lost her rudder in mid-Atlantic in 1935 and was steered to Liverpool on her engines.

All four ships were requisitioned for service as troopships during 1939-1940 and while serving in this capacity DUCHESS OF ATHOLL was torpedoed and sunk by the German submarine U-178 while east of Ascension Island in October 1942.

DUCHESS OF YORK was bombed and sunk by German dive-bombers off the coast of Morocco in July 1943.

The two surviving ships were both de-requisitioned in 1947 and completely refitted by Fairfields. DUCHESS OF BEDFORD was renamed EMPRESS OF FRANCE, painted white, and returned to her prewar service. She was withdrawn and sold for scrap in 1960.

DUCHESS OF RICHMOND was renamed EMPRESS OF CANADA, painted white and sailed from Liverpool on her first postwar voyage in July 1947. In 1953 this ship unfortunately caught fire in Gladstone Dock, Liverpool, heeled over and sank, becoming a total loss. She was ultimately righted and towed away to Spezia for scrap. Her place was taken by the French liner DE GRASSE, renamed EMPRESS OF AUSTRALIA (qv).

1920/1929

Canadian Pacific SS EMPRESS OF CANADA, 21516tG, was a twin-screw turbine-driven ship, built by Fairfield in 1920 for the company's trans-Pacific service.

In 1924 she made the company's first 'round the world' cruise, which started from and ended at New York. Five years later she came home to Fairfield to be re-engined and then worked for a time on the Southampton–Quebec service, before returning to the Pacific.

EMPRESS OF CANADA was requisitioned by the Ministry of War Transport as a troopship in November 1939 and she was often seen in the Clyde in this capacity during the early months of World War II.

In March 1943 she was torpedoed and sunk in the South Atlantic by the Italian submarine LEONARDO DA VINCI.

Canadian Pacific SS EMPRESS OF CANADA. The photo shows her in wartime colours and with an old 6in gun on her poop, leaving the Clyde in 1941 /PR-W

1929

SS STATENDAM, 29511tG, the third *Holland-America* liner to carry the name, was laid down at Harland and Wolff's Belfast yard in 1921 and launched in 1924, the year in which the United States Government passed the first of its laws severely limiting immigration into their country. As a result, work on the ship was suspended and when in 1927 it became possible to resume, strikes by Belfast shipyard workers delayed the ship so much that she was towed to the Wilton-Fijenoord yard at Rotterdam for fitting out and completion. She was the second largest ship to be dealt with at the Wilton yard up to that time. She made her maiden voyage to New York in 1929.

STATENDAM was a twin-screw vessel having six steam turbines, single-reduction-geared to her two shafts. They developed 19500shp for a speed of 19 knots, and received superheated steam from six water-tube boilers at a pressure of 430psi. She was beautifully appointed, her public rooms being amongst the finest of any ship in the world, and she was often referred to as the 'Queen of the Spotless Fleet'. Her passenger accommodation was in four classes, and she carried 510 first class, 344 second class, 374 tourist class and 426 third class passengers.

Soon after the outbreak of World War II STATENDAM was laid up at Rotterdam, and when the Germans invaded Holland in 1940 she was set on fire and became a total loss.

Hamburg-Amerika MV MILWAUKEE, 16694tG, was built by Blöhm and Voss, Hamburg, and with her sister ship ST LOUIS, built by Bremer Vulkan at Vegesak, went into service between Hamburg, Southampton and New York in 1929. Her passenger

Below: SS STATENDAM /Robert S. Mathews
Bottom: Hamburg America MV MILWAUKEE **shown here as a cruise liner at Funchal, Madeira, in 1934 /PR-W**

capacity was for 270 cabin class, 287 tourist class and 416 third class. She carried a crew of 328. Her accommodation was comfortable and modern without being luxurious, and both MILWAUKEE and ST LOUIS became known as steady sea-boats.

With the general fall-off of transatlantic travel both ships were used more and more for cruising and their hulls were painted white.

These sister liners were of interest in that they were the first cabin class motor ships on the North Atlantic. They were twin-screw ships, MILWAUKEE having two MAN six-cylinder double acting two-cycle diesel engines, one driving each shaft through single-reduction-gearing; 14235shp was developed for a speed of 15 knots. ST LOUIS had four diesel engines of the same aggregate power, two geared to each shaft.

In 1939 ST LOUIS was involved in one of the most vile episodes of Nazi terrorism. As a piece of propaganda she was allowed to be chartered by over 950 Jewish refugees, each of whom had paid a large sum in passage money and for visas to be evacuated from Germany to Cuba. Unbeknown to the passengers, to the ship's officers and to most of the crew, the Government of Cuba was then corrupt and anti-

semitic: so, on arrival at Havana, none of the refugees was allowed to leave the ship. After delay and negotiations, many of which were thwarted by SS and Gestapo agents among the crew, attempts were made to persuade the United States to accept at least some of the Jews. These attempts failed and ST LOUIS headed back to Europe. After many further heart-rending delays the ship docked at Antwerp. From there, 224 of the refugees reached France, 214 remained in Belgium and 181 were accepted by Holland. Nearly 300 managed to reach Britain. The rest were returned to the concentration camps in Germany. It is estimated that only some 25 per cent of those who embarked in ST LOUIS survived, many being killed as a result of German invasions of Holland, Belgium and France.

ST LOUIS was heavily damaged by bombing at Hamburg in 1944 and became a hulk, used for a time as a restaurant. She was broken up in 1950.

MILWAUKEE survived World War II and, after being briefly used to repatriate American troops, was handed over to Britain and renamed EMPIRE WAVENEY. In 1946 she caught fire at Liverpool and was destroyed. The hulk was raised and scrapped at Troon.

Left: NDL SS BREMEN /NMM

1929-1930

Despite their losses in World War I, by the mid-1920s the two principal German passenger shipping companies were able to re-enter the profitable North Atlantic passenger trade. The *Hamburg-Amerika Line (HAPAG)*, having ceded its three large and fast passenger liners VATERLAND, IMPERATOR and BISMARCK to the United States and Britain, followed the policy of our own *White Star Line* in concentrating on comfortable ships of medium size and speed. It was left to *Norddeutscher Lloyd (NDL)* to develop the fast giant liners which were to compete so successfully not only with *Cunard*, but also with French and Italian ships of similar size and speed.

In May 1927 the first of two great ships, BREMEN, was laid down at the Weser yard at Bremen, and two months later her sister ship, EUROPA, was laid down at the Blöhm and Voss yard at Hamburg. Both ships were launched in August 1928, EUROPA on the 15th and BREMEN on the 16th of that month.

BREMEN sailed for New York via Southampton on July 16th, 1929, and on this her maiden voyage averaged 27·83 knots westward and 27·92 knots eastward, thus capturing the Atlantic Blue Riband

from *Cunard*'s MAURETANIA, which had held the distinction for twenty-two years.

BREMEN was a beautiful and well-proportioned ship of 51656tG, with a bow-fronted bridge structure and two large squat pear-shaped funnels. She had a rounded raked bow, leading to a bulbous fore-foot below the waterline, and a cruiser stern. Her twenty oil-fired water-tube boilers provided superheated steam at 23kg/cm² to four sets of single-reduction-geared turbines, which drove four screws and developed 140000shp at 28·5 knots on trials. Her one shortcoming was that her funnels were too squat, and boiler fumes and smuts descended in profusion upon the after parts of her promenade and boat decks. This trouble was largely eradicated by increasing the height of both funnels by 4·5m.

Her accommodation was of a very high standard, and amenities included an art gallery and a rifle range as well as the usual library, swimming pool and winter garden. She carried 600 first class passengers, 500 second class, 300 tourist class and 600 third class.

She was, for a time, fitted with a catapult between the funnels, from which an aircraft was launched to carry mails for the last 600 miles of their journey westward to New York and eastward to Bremerhaven.

EUROPA was a slightly smaller ship, with a gross tonnage of 49746. There were some differences between her and BREMEN, the most important being that she had twenty-four boilers instead of twenty,

NDL SS BREMEN at sea /Real Photographs

though her machinery was of identical output to that of her sister. Her funnels were oval in shape but of equal height, and were later extended by the same amount as those of BREMEN when it was found that she too suffered from the same troubles with fumes and smuts. Her accommodation and appointments were equally luxurious, though in a different style from those of her sister ship. The passenger capacity was about the same in both ships.

EUROPA was at first dogged by ill luck. She was badly damaged by fire while fitting out in the Blöhm and Voss yard, and on trials she had troubles with her high-pressure turbines, stripping some blading. As a result, instead of the two ships entering service together as planned, EUROPA was only able to make her maiden voyage in March 1930, eight months late. However, on that voyage she proved to be well up to BREMEN's standards and improved marginally on the latter's crossing times.

Both these great liners settled down to provide a fast reliable service for the next nine years, and they were always very popular. BREMEN proved slightly the faster, but both ships were soon eclipsed in speed by the arrival of the Italian liners REX and CONTE DI SAVOIA, and later the French NORMANDIE and the British QUEEN MARY.

On the outbreak of World War II BREMEN was in New York and, after her sailing had been twice delayed, she sailed for home, ultimately reaching Bremerhaven via Murmansk in December 1939. She was laid up and never sailed again. She was destroyed by fire in March 1941 while still at her berth, the blaze having been started by a crew member who was mentally unbalanced.

EUROPA was at her home port of Hamburg when war was declared and as far as is known her only sailing during the war was to return to Bremerhaven, where she was found undamaged by the Americans who occupied that port in May 1945. After being used by the Americans for a short time as a troopship, she was ceded to France and went to the *Compagnie Générale Transatlantique (CGT)* as a replacement for NORMANDIE, which was burnt out in New York during the war. She was renamed LIBERTÉ

Above: NDL SS EUROPA with original short funnels /Real Photographs
Below: NDL SS EUROPA, showing final appearance under the German flag /NMM

CGT SS LIBERTE ex EUROPA /*CGT*

and was sent to le Havre for reconstruction. On December 9th, 1946, during a severe storm, she broke adrift in the harbour and collided with the half-submerged wreck of the PARIS (qv), sustaining severe damage to her hull below the waterline. In order to prevent her capsizing she was scuttled. Later, she was successfully raised and urgent repairs were made to her hull before she was towed to St Nazaire; there her reconstruction was completed in 1950, but only after further delay had been caused by a fire in her passenger accommodation. Her gross tonnage was raised to 51839, her draught was increased and her

speed reduced to 23·5 knots. Her funnels were further increased in height and altered in shape. In no way did the profile of LIBERTÉ resemble that of BREMEN. Her passenger accommodation was altered to carry 569 first class, 562 second class and 382 tourist class passengers.

She made her last voyage to le Havre in November 1961 and was broken up the next year.

1930

Canadian Pacific SS EMPRESS OF SCOTLAND, 26032tG, the second ship to carry the name, was built by Fairfield as EMPRESS OF JAPAN and completed in 1930. Intended for the trans-Pacific service, her maiden and several subsequent voyages were in fact made between Southampton and Quebec. She sailed for the Pacific late in 1930. Perhaps the most beautifully-proportioned of all *Canadian Pacific* ships, she had three funnels, the last of which was a dummy serving as an air-intake for the engine room. She had twin-screws driven by six single-reduction-geared turbines which gave her a service speed of 22 knots. Her original accommodation was for 400 first class passengers, 164 second class, 100 third class and 548 in a fourth class used mostly by Asiatics.

Soon after the outbreak of World War II she came home and was requisitioned as a troopship. Her name was changed to EMPRESS OF SCOTLAND in October 1942. Her trooping activities continued safely until May 1948, when she was extensively refitted and her gross tonnage increased to 26313. She then carried 458 first class and 205 tourist class passengers only. In 1950 she entered the Liverpool–Greenock–Quebec service and in 1952 her masts were shortened to enable her to pass under the Quebec Bridge to reach Montreal.

As a result of the falling off of seaborne Canadian passenger trade, EMPRESS OF SCOTLAND was laid up in 1957, but was immediately sold to the *Hamburg Atlantic Line* and renamed SCOTLAND. She was largely

reconstructed at Hamburg, her dummy funnel was removed and she was given two new funnels of more modern appearance. Her gross tonnage was again increased, to 30030, and her name was changed to HANSEATIC. She was completely air-conditioned and carried 85 first class passengers and 1165 in tourist class accommodation.

Her service with her new owners was mainly between Cuxhaven, Southampton, Cobh and New York, but also she was used for cruising. In September 1966 she caught fire while in New York harbour and was so badly damaged that she was towed to Hamburg and scrapped.

MV LAFAYETTE, 25178tG, was built at Penhoët and went into service for *Compagnie Générale Transatlantique (CGT)* in 1930. She was a quadruple-screw ship powered by four MAN two-cycle double-acting diesel motors with a total of 22000bhp, which gave her a service speed of 18 knots.

LAFAYETTE was one of the few large transatlantic motor passenger liners, and was of the same generation as the only two British transatlantic motor ships, BRITANNIC and GEORGIC. She was also a 'cabin class' ship and provided accommodation for 623 cabin class

Above: SS EMPRESS OF SCOTLAND /*Canadian Pacific*
Below: SS HANSEATIC, ex EMPRESS OF SCOTLAND /Skyfotos

and 308 tourist class passengers, with a mere 122 third class. In the British ships however, fewer first and more tourist class passengers were carried. The standard of comfort was very high in all these ships and they were by far the most luxurious 'intermediate' liners on the North Atlantic at that time.

LAFAYETTE was on the le Havre–Plymouth–New York service of *CGT*. In 1938, while in dry dock at le Havre, she caught fire and was completely gutted, her

hull being scrapped at Rotterdam later the same year. She was the first of three great *CGT* ships to be destroyed by fire in four years, followed by PARIS at le Havre in 1939 and NORMANDIE at New York in 1942.

CGT MV LAFAYETTE. (note *White Star* liner, probably ADRIATIC, on horizon) /Real Photographs

1930-1932

The *White Star Line* Motor Ships

The success of the *White Star Line*'s 'Big Four' as 'cabin class' liners decided the company to order from Harland and Wolff two modern and luxurious 'cabin class' ships to replace the older ships on the 'intermediate' services. A complete break with tradition was made when it was decided, for reasons of economy of operation, that the new liners should have oil engines.

BRITANNIC and GEORGIC were the first and only British passenger motor ships ever to be built for the North Atlantic and remain so to this day. They were fine looking ships, with straight stems and cruiser sterns, and each had two squat funnels, the forward one being a dummy and used as an engineer's lounge.

It was difficult to distinguish between them, but BRITANNIC had a flat-fronted bridge structure whereas that of GEORGIC was bow-fronted.

They were twin-screw ships, each powered by two Burmeister and Wain ten-cylinder four-cycle double-acting diesel motors with a total of 18500bhp for a speed in service of 18 knots. They were very well-equipped ships, each carrying 479 cabin class, 557 tourist class and 506 third class passengers, all in excellent accommodation, which in some instances was a great deal better than that provided in some of the luxury express liners of the day.

BRITANNIC entered service in 1930 and GEORGIC two years later. Both ships originally ran on the

Liverpool–New York service, with calls at Belfast and the Clyde according to the traffic offering. They occasionally sailed from Southampton, and during the winter months they were used for cruises to the West Indies. After the *Cunard-White Star* merger both ships were transferred to the London (Tilbury)–New York service and they were at that time the largest passenger ships to use the port of London. They retained their *White Star* colours.

It was unfortunate that the advent of these two fine ships could do nothing to save the *White Star Line* from the financial disaster which finally overcame it in 1934.

MV BRITANNIC, 26943tG, was the first of the *White Star* motor ships. She served throughout World War II as a troopship and was not returned to her owners until 1947. She was refitted, her gross tonnage was increased to 27650, and her accommodation was altered to carry 429 first class and 564 tourist class passengers.

Cunard-White Star put her on to the Liverpool–New York service, again with winter cruising. She was withdrawn from service in 1960 and scrapped at Inverkeithing.

MV GEORGIC, 27759tG, was the last ship to be built

Above: MV BRITANNIC served during World War II as a troopship /PR-W
Below: White Star MV GEORGIC, second of the *White Star* motorships /Cunard

for *White Star Line* and a sister ship to BRITANNIC. She was requisitioned as a troopship in 1940, but in 1941 was bombed and badly damaged by fire at Port Tewfik. After being temporarily repaired at Port Sudan and then at Karachi, she eventually reached Belfast, where she was reconstructed as a permanent troopship. Her appearance was altered by giving her only one funnel and one mast. Her owners were then the Ministry of War Transport, though she was managed by *Cunard-White Star*.

GEORGIC survived the war and her further service for the Government was as an emigrant ship to Australia and a troopship. She was scrapped in 1956 at Faslane.

1931

The largest and most luxurious passenger liner to be built for *Canadian Pacific* was completed by John Brown in 1931. This was EMPRESS OF BRITAIN, 42348tG, the second *Canadian Pacific* ship to carry the name, a quadruple-screw steamship driven by single-reduction-geared turbines using superheated steam at 425psi from nine oil-fired boilers. Her normal speed was 24 knots but soon after entering service she made several crossings at over 25 knots. She was the fastest ship on the Canadian run and was capable of making the return journey inside twelve days, enabling her comfortably to maintain a fortnightly service between Southampton and Canada.

EMPRESS OF BRITAIN made an annual world cruise and in this capacity she was the largest ship ever to pass through the Suez and the Panama canals. When cruising she used only her two inboard screws and her speed did not then exceed 18 knots.

She was in every way a successful luxury liner, carrying 1095 passengers and a crew of 700, but in no way was she a beautiful ship. Her length, 733ft oa, had been kept to a minimum to enable her to pass through the Panama Canal, and she had a generally 'top-heavy' appearance with a high free board and with three very large funnels, the after one a dummy and used as an engine-room ventilating air intake.

In November 1939 she was requisitioned as a troopship and eleven months later, while homeward bound from Egypt, she was bombed and severely damaged by German aircraft off the west coast of Ireland. She was taken in tow by the Polish destroyer BURZA but was torpedoed and sunk by the German submarine U-32 three days later.

Canadian Pacific SS EMPRESS OF BRITAIN leaving Southampton in 1934 /PR-W

1931-1948

American Export Lines were mainly cargo ship owners and operators until 1931, when they put into service four new cargo-passenger liners to provide a 46-day scheduled 'round-trip' service between New York and Mediterranean ports. These four ships, which became known as the 'four aces', were sisters of 9360tG named EXOCHORDA, EXCALIBUR, EXETER and EXCAMBION. They were single-screw ships with single-reduction-geared turbines giving a speed of 16 knots. They carried a substantial amount of cargo but were not refrigerated. They had excellent accommodation for 125 first-class passengers (this was later extended to 147). Various political and economic factors caused changes in their Mediterranean itinerary, but all four continued trading until 1940, when EXOCHORDA was requisitioned by the US Government

Below: SS EXCALIBUR of 1930 /NMM
Bottom: SS EXCAMBION of 1948 /Duncan

as a transport and renamed HARRY LEE. She survived the war and was sold to Turkish interests in 1946 as their TARSUS, later being destroyed by fire in 1960.

The remaining three ships were requisitioned as troopships in 1941, becoming JOSEPH HUGHES, EDWARD RUTLEDGE (both torpedoed and sunk off North Africa in 1942) and JOHN PENN (bombed and sunk in the Pacific in 1943) respectively.

After World War II the Company began a similar service to Mediterranean ports in 1948 with four ships purchased from US Navy. These four had been built in 1944-5 as troopships and they revived the names of the original 'four aces'—EXOCHORDA (ex-DAUPHIN), EXCALIBUR (ex-DUTCHESS), EXETER (ex-SHELBY) and EXCAMBION (ex-QUEENS). All were single-screw steamships of 9644tG with double-reduction-geared turbines providing a speed of 17 knots. Each carried 124 first-class passengers and all accommodation was air-conditioned. With the reintroduction of transatlantic services by the principal Mediterranean countries, *American Export Lines* found their ships becoming uneconomic and they were sold, two in 1959 and the last two EXCALIBUR and EXETER, in 1965.

1932

SS CHAMPLAIN, 28124tG, was a twin-screw 'intermediate' cabin class passenger liner, which was completed in 1932 at Penhoët for *Compagnie Générale Transatlantique (CGT)*. She was powered by single-reduction-geared steam turbines and had a service speed of 19 knots.

Her passenger accommodation, 623 first, 308 tourist and 122 third class, was about the same as that of the *CGT* 'intermediate' motor-driven liner LAFAYETTE, and CHAMPLAIN was regarded as a larger steam-driven version of that ship. Certainly the two could be regarded as the French equivalent of the contemporary British cabin class ships BRITANNIC and GEORGIC.

CHAMPLAIN had a short life for, while evacuating refugees from St Nazaire in June 1940, she exploded a magnetic mine off La Pallice and sank very rapidly, with the loss of about 350 lives.

Having in 1922 entered the 'big ship clique' in the North Atlantic trade, the Italians soon considered building ships which could compete in size and speed with the giant express liners of Britain, France and Germany. The first Italian company to react to such competition was *Navigazione Generale Italiana (NGI)* who at the end of 1929, with encouragement from the Italian Government, ordered from Ansaldo of Sestri Ponente a high-speed 50000-ton liner to be named GUGLIELMO MARCONI, later altered to REX.

This challenge was immediately taken up by *Lloyd Sabaudo* who ordered, also with Government support, a similar ship from Cantieri Riuniti dell' Adriatico, to carry the name CONTE DI SAVOIA. Before either ship was completed, *NGI*, *Lloyd Sabaudo* and *Cosulich* had been grouped together to form the *Italia Line* and so neither ship ever sailed for her original

CGT SS CHAMPLAIN /Real Photographs

Top: Italia Line SS REX, ex GUGLIELMO MARCONI */Italia*
Above: Italia Line SS CONTE DI SAVOIA */Italia*

owners. The considerable financial aid the Italian Government had granted to both the original companies to build these ships was continued. Furthermore, Mussolini was very impatient to show that his Italy could achieve supremacy on the North Atlantic, so both ships were completed in record time.

On September 27th, 1932, REX sailed on her maiden voyage. She was a truly magnificent ship, with a beautiful counter stern. Her gross tonnage was 51062 and she had four screws driven by single-reduction-geared turbines, there being three turbines to each shaft. Her total shaft horsepower was 120000 for 28 knots, though she handsomely exceeded these figures on trials. She had fourteen boilers supplying superheated steam at 385psi. Her passenger accommodation was the most lavish and beautiful of any ship in the world at that time, though she could carry 2032 passengers in four classes.

Her maiden voyage was disastrous. After leaving Genoa amid scenes of great rejoicing she developed severe trouble in her high-pressure turbines and had to put into Gibraltar for urgent repairs which lasted for four days, during which time many of her first class passengers left her. Even then her troubles were not ended, as further turbine faults developed in

mid-Atlantic, and she limped into New York nearly a week behind schedule. Her troubles were generally ascribed to the rush to get her into service.

While in New York comprehensive repairs and replacements were carried out and thereafter REX became a much loved and very reliable ship. In August 1933 she made the east to west crossing at an average speed of 28·92 knots, thus taking the honour of making the fastest voyage away from BREMEN of *NDL*.

CONTE DI SAVOIA, a slightly smaller quadruple-screw ship of 48502tG, had similar machinery to REX but only ten boilers. These were built by Yarrow and supplied superheated steam at 425psi. She exceeded 30 knots on trials. She was one of the first transatlantic liners to be equipped with stabilisers.

Her appointments were different from those of REX but equally lavish and beautiful. She carried 2060 passengers.

She left Genoa on her maiden voyage on

November 30th, 1932, and her troubles started when, 800 miles east of the Ambrose light vessel, a turbo-generator exhaust valve fractured and blew a considerable hole in the ship's side below the waterline. One turbo-generator room immediately flooded and the ship was hove-to while the hole was filled with concrete. Again the trouble was said to have been the result of too-hasty construction.

CONTE DI SAVOIA was never so fast a ship as REX, though she was just as popular and her appearance was equally magnificent. She was easy to distinguish from REX because she had a cruiser stern.

Both these great ships were laid up when Italy entered World War II. After the fall of Italy both were taken by the Germans and were ultimately bombed and sunk by the RAF, REX at Capodistria in 1944 and CONTE DI SAVOIA off Venice in 1943. They were later raised but each was considered to be a constructive total loss and was scrapped. A sad end for two of the finest ships in the world.

1932-1933

The *United States Line* sister ships SS MANHATTAN and SS WASHINGTON, each of 24289tG, went into service between New York, Plymouth and Hamburg in 1932 and 1933 respectively. They were built by the New York Shipbuilding Corporation and were the largest merchant ships to have been constructed in the United States up to that time. They were twin-screw ships, each having six steam turbines, single-reduction-geared to the two screw shafts and developing 36000shp for a speed of 20 knots; six water tube boilers in each ship provided superheated steam at 400psi. As built, both ships had short and rather small diameter funnels; larger funnels were later fitted.

They were 'cabin class' ships, each carrying 500 cabin, 500 tourist and 200 third class passengers, in accommodation which was far superior to that provided for first and second class passengers in many transatlantic liners. All cabin class passengers had private baths and toilet facilities.

At the outbreak of World War II the two ships ceased sailing to Britain and Germany and made Genoa their European terminal port until Italy came into the war in 1940.

United States Lines SS MANHATTAN, showing original short funnels /*United States Lines*

In 1941 the ships became United States Army transports and ferried many thousands of American troops across the North Atlantic. Their names were changed, MANHATTAN becoming WAKEFIELD and WASHINGTON becoming MOUNT VERNON. In 1942 WAKEFIELD was badly damaged by fire while at sea but was towed to Halifax, NS, and subsequently rebuilt as a transport. In 1946 she was placed in reserve and was broken up in 1965. MOUNT VERNON survived the war, was renamed WASHINGTON in 1945 and refitted for commercial service, but now with accommodation for 1100 passengers in one class. Her gross tonnage became 23626.

United States Lines SS WASHINGTON with larger funnels which greatly enhanced the appearance of both ships /NMM

She was now owned by the United States Department of Commerce and from 1948 ran between New York, Cobh, Southampton and le Havre. Late in 1951 she was withdrawn from service and laid up. She was broken up in 1965 at Kearny NJ.

1921/1934

SS LEERDAM, 8854tG, of the *Holland-America Line* was built by Nieuwe Waterweg in 1921 and rebuilt in 1934, after which she was used on the North Atlantic service.

After the end of World War I the *Holland-America Line* purchased four sister ships for their Mexico and Cuba services. These ships, MAASDAM, EDAM, LEERDAM and SPAARNDAM, were all built by Dutch yards and went into service in 1921-1922. They were single-screw ships driven by double-reduction-geared turbines with a speed of 13 knots. They each had two funnels, the after one being a dummy.

The four ships were each of about 8850tG, with counter sterns and straight stems. Much of the 60600 tons of shipbuilding material ceded to Holland after World War I, in part compensation for her war

losses, was used in the construction of these vessels.

In 1934 the four were reconstructed, the dummy funnels removed and their accommodation modernised and made suitable for North Atlantic travel. They each carried 30 cabin class passengers and 60 third class, as well as a large quantity of cargo. They provided a slow but comfortable and regular service between Rotterdam, New York and Baltimore.

MAASDAM and SPAARNDAM were sunk during World War II. LEERDAM and EDAM were scrapped in 1954.

Top: Holland-America SS LEERDAM rebuilt with one funnel /*Holland-America*

Above: SS EDAM as rebuilt /*Holland-America*

1935

MV PILSUDSKI, 14294tG, was completed in 1935 by Cantieri Riuniti dell' Adriatico for the Polish *Gdynia-America Line*. She had twin screws driven by two nine-cylinder two-cycle single-acting Sulzer diesel motors, which gave her a service speed of 17·5 knots. She carried 370 tourist class passengers and 400 third class.

She was employed on the Gdynia–New York service of the company until the outbreak of World War II, when she became an armed merchant cruiser. She was torpedoed and sunk off the mouth of the Humber in late November 1939.

Her sister ship BATORY went into service between Gdynia and New York in 1936, then, during the war served as an infantry landing ship and later as a troopship. After the war she sailed for a time on the North Atlantic and then ran between Poland and India. She was scrapped in 1971.

In the ten years before the outbreak of World War II the transatlantic express luxury liner was developed in size, speed and magnificence to an extent never seen before and which certainly will never be seen again.

In those years the principal competitors were *Cunard* for Britain, *Norddeutscher Lloyd* for Germany, *Italia* for Italy and *Compagnie Générale Transatlantique* for France. It was the French company which provided by far the most interesting of the great liners and the one which undoubtedly embodied the most advanced, if controversial, design.

The quadruple-screw SS NORMANDIE, 79283tG, was built at a cost of £8¼m at Penhoët for *Compagnie Générale Transatlantique (CGT)*, though the French Government provided about eighty per cent of the

Top: MV PILSUDSKI in the Thames in 1936 /PR-W
Above: SS NORMANDIE—the launch /NMM

money. She went into service in 1935, a year before *Cunard Line*'s QUEEN MARY. She had a beautiful but rather unusual hull, with a clipper bow and a bulbous forefoot. Forward she had a pronounced flare, but on the waterline, fore and aft, her hull was very fine

while being extremely full amidships. The forecastle deck was clear of all obstruction and was in the form of a turtle-back, which emphasised her marked sheer forward.

Her machinery was a particularly bold experiment. Up to that time turbo-electric propulsion had been used only in much smaller and slower ships, such as the *P & O* 22300-ton twin-screw ships STRATHAIRD and STRATHNAVER, with 23 knots speed and 28000shp. So the decision to use this form of propulsion in a quadruple-screw vessel of nearly 80000 tons gross, with more than 30 knots speed and requiring 170000shp, was to say the least courageous.

Four main turbo-generators were provided, with a total output of 133600kW, while auxiliary generators provided a further 13200kW. Current from the main generators supplied power to the four 30100kW three-phase ac synchronised propulsion motors, one of which drove each of the four screw shafts. Super-heated steam for the turbines was generated at 400psi in twenty-nine water-tube boilers and the uptakes from these and from four auxiliary boilers were led into the first two funnels. Still, it seems, clinging to a twenty-year-old tradition, a third, dummy funnel was provided, in NORMANDIE used for dog kennels.

Top: SS NORMANDIE in service /Beken
Centre: SS NORMANDIE—the bridge /NMM
Above: SS NORMANDIE—the dog run in the dummy funnel /NMM

Passenger accommodation was superb and provided the 848 first and 'grand luxe' passengers with the most magnificent public rooms and the most luxurious cabins ever to be built into a ship. The 470 tourist class passengers and the 454 third class were also very well cared for, and of her 1345 officers and crew no fewer than 975 were stewards, waiters, cooks and others directly concerned with passenger comfort.

NORMANDIE had few teething troubles, despite her many innovations. She had some trouble with condenser tubes on her maiden voyage, but although it was necessary to shut down one turbo-generator she kept all four screws turning and lost very little speed. Her big drawback was, however, vibration which was very serious at high speeds. Her four three-bladed screw propellers were changed to ones with four blades, but this made only a partial improvement. Much of her hull was strengthened, some 'open spaces' were enclosed and this brought the vibration down to a tolerable level, though the trouble was never completely eliminated. These alterations to her hull increased her gross tonnage to 82799.

On her maiden voyage from le Havre to New York she averaged 29·68 knots and on the return voyage 30·34 knots, thus easily beating the speeds set up by both BREMEN and REX and gaining for France the Atlantic Blue Riband. She finally lost the record to QUEEN MARY but she was always a challenger.

At the outbreak of World War II NORMANDIE was laid up in New York, but in December 1941 she was taken over by the United States Government, renamed LAFAYETTE and her conversion to a troopship was begun. During the work of conversion welders were using their torches in the main saloon, in close proximity to a large quantity of highly inflammable mattresses which had been stacked there. These caught fire, the men on fire-watching duty were grossly inadequate, and by the time the fire was brought under control by the New York Fire Brigade, the ship was so full of water, much of which had frozen in the extreme cold, that she capsized at her berth. She was later raised but was considered to be a constructive total loss after consideration had been given to convert her to an aircraft carrier. Her hull was not scrapped until 1946.

Thus, by nothing less than gross carelessness and ineptitude, the world's most beautiful ship ended her short career.

1936

QUEEN MARY

The 1920s were the most prosperous years in the history of North Atlantic shipping. For *Cunard*, AQUITANIA, BERENGARIA and MAURETANIA were operating the express service between Southampton and New York, but all were by the end of the twenties relatively old ships. Notwithstanding their continued popularity, by 1928 the company was preparing for their replacement by two new liners of greatly increased size and speed.

In 1930 John Brown received the contract for the first of these great ships and by the end of that year the keel of 'No 534' was laid at Clydebank. By this time, however, the great slump in world trade had started. So great was the recession that by the end of 1931 it was found impossible for *Cunard* to guarantee

SS QUEEN MARY on her first visit to Southampton, March 1936 /PR-W

payment to the builders and all further work on the ship ceased.

For more than two years 'No 534' remained uncompleted on the stocks and not until April 1934 was her construction resumed. This was made possible by a Treasury loan to the company of £4½m and the promise of a further £5m towards the construction of a second ship of comparable size and speed. But in return for these loans it was agreed that the North Atlantic interests of *Cunard* and of the bankrupt *White Star Line* should be merged, and *Cunard-White Star Ltd* came into being in 1934, with *Cunard* being a majority shareholder. To anticipate, *Cunard* purchased the remainder of the *White Star* holding in 1947 and from 1949 completely took over *Cunard-White Star Ltd*, thus rendering obsolete the famous *White Star* name.

Above: SS QUEEN MARY on her first visit to Southampton, March 1936 /PR-W
Below: SS QUEEN MARY at sea /Skyfotos

SS QUEEN MARY as a troopship, leaving the Clyde /PR-W

On September 26th, 1934 'No 534' was launched by HM Queen Mary and was named by her QUEEN MARY. The ship was fitted out in eighteen months, her public rooms, cabins and all her passenger appointments being on a magnificent scale but always in good taste. Her accommodation was for 776 cabin class passengers, 784 tourist class and 579 third class.

She was of 80744tG, and had four four-bladed screw propellers driven by sixteen single-reduction-geared turbines developing 160000shp. Superheated steam at 425psi was provided by twenty-four water-tube boilers and there were three boilers for auxiliaries. Her fuel consumption in service was almost identical with that of the smaller and slower BERENGARIA.

On March 24th, 1936, QUEEN MARY left the Clyde for Southampton, where she was dry-docked in the King George V Graving Dock for hull inspection, cleaning and painting and for her propellers to be changed. She then returned to the Clyde for her very successful trials, during which she attained a speed only fractionally less than 33 knots. Her maiden voyage from Southampton to New York began on schedule on May 27th, 1936. In 1938 she regained for Britain the Atlantic Blue Riband, then held by the French liner NORMANDIE, by achieving average speeds of 30·99 knots westbound and 31·69 knots eastbound.

The outbreak of World War II found QUEEN MARY in New York and there she remained until March 1940, when she left for Hong Kong and Sydney to be converted for trooping service, duties which she carried out with conspicuous success until the end of the war. With her running mate QUEEN ELIZABETH (qv) she worked mostly across the North Atlantic, her chief protection from submarine attack being the great speed which she could maintain, even in the roughest weather.

The two ships were unescorted, except in the Western Approaches. On October 2nd, 1942, her escort there was the old anti-aircraft cruiser CURACAO, and soon after the two ships had joined company

QUEEN MARY, which was on a zig-zag course, rammed and sank CURACAO with a loss of 338 of the cruiser's company. This was the only major mishap to occur to either of the 'Queens' during their war service, in which together they carried over 1½ million servicemen and steamed well over one million miles. QUEEN MARY made thirty-two Atlantic crossings during 1942 and 1943 alone and carried up to 15000 troops on each occasion. For most of the war both ships worked to and from the Clyde but from August 1945 they both used Southampton as their home port.

QUEEN MARY was released from war service in September 1946 and ten months later, after being completely refitted, she sailed for New York in commercial service, joining the previously released QUEEN ELIZABETH in a two ship transatlantic express service. Her passenger accommodation was now for 711 first class passengers, 707 cabin class and 577 tourist class. Her gross tonnage was increased to 81237.

In July 1952 QUEEN MARY yielded the Blue Riband to the new *United States Lines'* ship UNITED STATES (qv), which covered the 2938 nautical miles between Ambrose Channel Light Vessel and Bishop Rock at an average speed of 35·59 knots.

QUEEN MARY was consistently kept up-to-date and her accommodation was improved from time to time, with much air conditioning being introduced for her eventual cruising in hot climates. As a result of the successful introduction of Denny-Brown stabilisers in MEDIA (qv), two sets of this anti-rolling device were fitted to QUEEN MARY in 1954.

However, the postwar prosperity of transatlantic shipping was comparatively short-lived, as more and more passengers travelled by air, and in winter particularly, the transatlantic traffic fell off badly. Both 'Queens' therefore engaged in cruising, but even this was not economic.

QUEEN MARY made her last Atlantic crossing in September 1967, from New York to Southampton. Then, after making two cruises, she was withdrawn from *Cunard* service and sold to the city of Long Beach, California, where she has become a floating hotel and conference centre, and also houses a permanent marine exhibition.

So has ended the distinguished career of what His Majesty King George V once described as 'The Stateliest Ship in Being'.

HMS CURACOA, which was sunk after a collision with with QUEEN MARY in October 1942 /PR-W

1938

One of the most beautiful ships ever built, NIEUW AMSTERDAM, 36287tG, entered service between Rotterdam and New York in 1938. She was built for the *Holland-America Line* by the Rotterdam Drydock Company and was by far the largest ship ever to be constructed in Holland up to that time. She was the second ship to carry the name, which commemorates the original name of the city of New York.

NIEUW AMSTERDAM's passenger accommodation reflected the usual Dutch passenger ship policy—the greatest possible comfort and luxury without ostentation—and she was 'as beautiful inside as outside'. From the time of her introduction until the outbreak of World War II she made seventeen round trips across the Atlantic and was fully booked for each one. At that time she carried 556 first class passengers, 455 tourist class and 209 third class. Her officers and crew numbered 768.

NIEUW AMSTERDAM had eight steam turbines,

single-reduction-geared to two screw shafts giving her a speed in service of 21 knots.

After the outbreak of World War II she was first laid up in New York but later made a few short Caribbean cruises before the invasion of Holland in 1940. She was then taken to Halifax, NS, and provided with about thirty-six guns of various calibres, before sailing to Singapore, where her accommodation was stripped of all luxury and altered to enable her to carry up to 8000 troops. From then until the end of the war she was one of those great and valuable ships which performed such yeoman service transporting men and material, first between Cape Town and Suez but later between North America and the Clyde. She steamed more than 525000 miles and carried 378361 men and women on war service.

She returned to Rotterdam in 1946 to be extensively refitted and rebuilt into nearly her original

condition, but with altered passenger accommodation. She sailed for New York in October 1947 and thereafter maintained a regular transatlantic schedule, calling at Southampton and le Havre, but with an extensive programme of cruises in the winter off-season periods.

NIEUW AMSTERDAM was again refitted and modernised during the winter of 1956-1957 and went back into service with her hull painted light grey instead of black. A further extensive alteration and refit was

carried out five years later, when her accommodation was largely rebuilt to make her an air conditioned 'two class only' ship, carrying a total of 1274 first and tourist class passengers, with many 'interchangeable' cabins. At this time her turbine rotors were

Above: SS NIEUW AMSTERDAM in service as a troopship during World War II /PR-W
Below: SS NIEUW AMSTERDAM at Southampton in 1971 / PR-W

renewed and all her machinery refitted and replaced where necessary. She also was provided with stabilisers.

NIEUW AMSTERDAM remained as popular as ever and, with ROTTERDAM, STATENDAM and the two *German-Atlantic Line* ships HANSEATIC and HAMBURG, she maintained a complicated and intensive transatlantic and cruising schedule until late 1973.

She was then withdrawn from service and sold to Taiwan shipbreakers, arriving at Kaohsiung early in 1974.

MV NOORDAM, 10726tG, was built by P. Smit Jr, Rotterdam, for the *Holland-America Line* and she entered service between Rotterdam, New York and Philadelphia in 1938. Her sister ship ZAANDAM, 10909tG, was built by Wilton-Fijenoord and entered service six months later. These were large and hand-

some twin-screw cargo liners each with two twelve-cylinder two-cycle single-acting MAN diesel motors providing a useful 18 knots service speed.

Each ship carried 148 tourist class passengers in excellent accommodation.

After the invasion of Holland in 1940 the two ships saw service in many parts of the world and ZAANDAM was torpedoed and sunk 400 miles off the Brazilian coast in November 1942. NOORDAM survived the war, during which she had been intensively employed as a troopship and in 1946 she resumed her sailings

Above: Holland-America Line MV NOORDAM /Real Photographs
Below: Norwegian America Line MV OSLOFJORD /
Norwegian-America

between Rotterdam and New York. In 1963 she was sold to Panamanian owners as OCEANIEN and then was on time charter to *Cie des Messageries Maritimes*.

Her gross tonnage (Panamanian measurement) was then given as 9673. She was broken up at Spezia in 1967.

MV OSLOFJORD, 18673tG, was the fourth trans-atlantic passenger liner owned by the *Norwegian America Line*. A twin-screw diesel-engined ship with a speed of 18 knots, she was of fine appearance, with a raking stem and a cruiser stern. She was built at the Weser yard in Bremen, being completed in 1938.

OSLOFJORD was on the Oslo–Bergen–New York service until 1940, when the German invasion of Norway found her in New York and she was laid up. Later the same year she was put into service between Halifax and UK ports but exploded a magnetic mine off Tynemouth on December 13th, at the end of her first voyage, and became a total loss.

1930/1939

MV JOHAN VAN OLDENBARNEVELT, 19787tG, was built for the *Nederland Line* by the Netherland Shipbuilding Company, Amsterdam, and entered service in 1930. With her sister ship MARNIX VAN ST ALDEGONDE, which was sunk during the war, she became very popular on the service between Amsterdam and the Dutch East Indies. She was a twin-screw ship powered by two ten-cylinder Sulzer diesel motors and with a speed of 18 knots.

The *Holland-America Line* chartered her in 1939 for their Rotterdam–New York service, on which she was engaged for several months. She made only two voyages on her original Far East run before the invasion of Holland, after which she was in service as a troopship until 1946. Her next appearance on the North Atlantic was in 1954, this time under charter for the Netherlands Government-owned *Trans-Ocean*

Steamship Company, for whom she sailed between Rotterdam and New York and between Rotterdam and Canadian ports, first carrying emigrants and later students on educational tours.

In 1958 JOHAN VAN OLDENBARNEVELT was largely rebuilt for her original owners and was engaged in round-the-world cruising until 1963, when she was sold to the *Greek Line* and renamed LAKONIA. She was again reconstructed, somewhat hurriedly, before she sailed on her first cruise under the Greek flag. Four days out from Southampton she caught fire and was burned out with heavy loss of life among passengers.

Nederland Line MV JOHAN VAN OLDENBARNEVELT /PR-W

1939

The second *Cunard* liner to be named MAURETANIA was a twin-screw steamship of 35738tG, driven by single-reduction-geared turbines developing 40000shp and with a speed of 23 knots. She carried a crew of 604 and could accommodate 1165 passengers—475 first class, 390 second and 300 tourist class. MAURETANIA was completed by Cammell Laird in 1939 and went into service sailing between Liverpool and New York. Soon afterwards, she sailed briefly from London and Southampton, before the outbreak of World War II temporarily stopped her commercial service, and for a time she was laid up at New York.

From 1940-1946 she served with the fleet of large ocean liners engaged in trooping. Surviving the war, she returned to *Cunard* and then worked between

Above: SS MAURETANIA: maiden voyage from Liverpool, 1939 /PR-W
Below: SS MAURETANIA: last voyage from Southampton, 1965 /PR-W

Southampton and New York. Her best crossing was made eastbound in 1947, at 24·35 knots. As the passenger trade on the North Atlantic diminished MAURETANIA was increasingly used for cruising, and towards the end of her life she made some voyages between Naples and New York.

The second MAURETANIA was a very different ship from her predecessor. Viewed from ahead, she had none of the fine lines of the earlier ship and her two large and closely spaced funnels, while giving a well-balanced appearance, provided none of the rakish urgency of the record holder. Nonetheless, she was a very comfortable and well-loved ship. She was broken up at Inverkeithing in 1965.

1928/1941

In 1928 *Canadian Pacific Steamships* put into service five 10000-ton twin-screw cargo ships with names commencing with 'Beaver'. They were easily distinguished by their four sets of twin king-posts and were 14-knot turbine-driven coal-burning ships with specially ventilated holds for the carriage of perishable cargo. All were destroyed during World War II, four by enemy action in 1940-1941 and one by stranding on Hillyards Reefs, New Brunswick, in 1944.

This, the last of the 'Beavers', was named BEAVERHILL, 10041tG, and she is included in this book by virtue of the fact that in 1941 she was provided with accommodation for 138 passengers and made a number of war-time transatlantic crossings as a passenger–cargo liner.

Canadian Pacific SS BEAVERHILL in convoy HXM 292 in mid-Atlantic, 1943 /PR-W

1934/1946

MV JUTLANDIA, 8532tG, was completed in 1934 by Nakskov for the Danish *East Asiatic Company*. She was a 15-knot twin-screw ship powered by two Burmeister and Wain eight-cylinder four-cycle single-acting diesel motors, and was one of the first motor ships to dispense with conventional funnels. She operated between Copenhagen and the Far East but in 1946 was transferred to the North Atlantic and

established a new service between Copenhagen and New York, to share in the profitable postwar cargo and passenger trade between Europe and the United States. She carried 60 first class passengers.

In 1950 she became a hospital ship in the Korean War, and in 1953 resumed her sailings to the Far East, the company by then having abandoned its North Atlantic service.

1939/1946

The *Gdynia-America Line* MV SOBIESKI, 11030tG, was a twin-screw ship with two double-acting two-cycle diesel motors and a speed of 17 knots. She was completed by Swan Hunter in 1939 for the Poland–South America service. The outbreak of World War II, however, prevented her sailing and she was taken over by the British Admiralty as an infantry landing ship. Later she served as a troopship. She survived the war and sailed between Italian ports and New York for three years before being sold to Soviet Russia in 1950. She was named GRUZIA and was in service in the Black Sea. In April 1975 she arrived under tow at Spezia for demolition.

Above: MV JUTLANDIA /PR-W
Below: MV SOBIESKI as landing ship infantry /PR-W

1940/1946

The *United States Lines* SS AMERICA was built by Newport News Shipbuilding Company and completed in 1940. She was a replacement for LEVIATHAN (qv), but owing to the outbreak of World War II, she initially made no Atlantic crossing but was used for cruising from New York.

In July 1941 she was requisitioned by the United States Government and converted to an armed troopship, being renamed WEST POINT. She carried over half a million men during the war. She was returned to her owners as AMERICA and entered transatlantic commercial service in 1946, running between New York and Southampton with calls at le Havre and Cobh.

AMERICA is a twin-screw ship powered by six steam turbines double-reduction- and single-reduction-geared to the two screw shafts. She develops a total of 34000shp for a service speed of 25 knots. By British measurement her gross tonnage is 33532 and on the North Atlantic she carried 516 first class, 371 cabin class and 159 tourist class passengers, with 692 officers and crew.

By 1964 it was no longer considered economic to run her on the Western Ocean and she was sold to *Chandris Lines*, who renamed her AUSTRALIS, and after an extensive refit in Greece she now operates to Australia and New Zealand as well as cruising.

Above: United States Transport SS WEST POINT, ex AMERICA /PR-W
Below: United States Lines SS AMERICA /PR-W

1940/1946

QUEEN ELIZABETH

John Brown were successful in their bid to build the second giant Cunarder and, backed by a £5m treasury loan, the *Cunard* company gave the go-ahead for work to start on 'No 552'. The keel was laid in December 1936 on the same slipway as that on which QUEEN MARY had been built. The ship was launched by HM Queen Elizabeth on September 27th, 1938, and was named QUEEN ELIZABETH.

The new ship was slightly larger than her predecessor, having a gross tonnage of 83673. She was also different in that the design of her bridge and superstructure conformed with the ideas of a later era. More important, as a result of greatly improved boiler design she had need of only half the number of boilers, though her machinery was the same as that of QUEEN MARY and she developed the same shaft horsepower. This also meant that she required only two funnels, instead of the three as in the older ship.

While QUEEN ELIZABETH was still fitting out at Clydebank, war was declared, so installation of her planned luxury accommodation was stopped. Under conditions of strict secrecy the great ship, still uncompleted, slipped quietly down the Clyde on February 26th, 1940, and arrived safely in New York nine days later. After eight months she left for Hong Kong and Sydney to join QUEEN MARY in the business of trooping. From then until the end of hostilities her career followed the same pattern as that already described for QUEEN MARY (pages 117 - 120).

SS QUEEN ELIZABETH in service as a troopship during World War II /PR-W

As with that ship, her safety from U-boat attack was largely due to her great speed. In fact, probably the worst hazard she met during the war occurred when, fully laden with troops and equipment, she was steaming eastwards in September 1943. Off the coast of Greenland she encountered an episodic wave and after plunging some 60ft into the trough was hit by the following mountainous wave estimated by eyewitnesses as at least 60ft in height. What damage she sustained has never been divulged, but a naval officer who was a passenger in the ship stated that most of the equipment on the forecastle was wrenched away and thrown against the bridge structure in which all glass was shattered. There was wreckage and debris in profusion on her upper decks and the great ship was thrown about as if she had been no more than a skiff.

She was returned to civilian service in March 1946 and was at once sent to the Clyde for fitting out as the most luxurious liner afloat. To the great credit of all at Clydebank, the work was completed in the remarkably short time of seven months and she left Southampton for New York on October 16th, 1946. Her passenger accommodation was for 823 first class, 662 cabin class and 798 tourist class passengers.

QUEEN ELIZABETH never held the Atlantic speed record. This was probably a reflection of the then current *Cunard* policy, which was to discourage wasteful high-speed competition, though it was always generally believed that the new ship was never as fast as QUEEN MARY. What was undoubtedly more important was her immediate postwar record of twenty-three round trips from Southampton to New York in 11 months 24 days, during which time she carried 102476 passengers.

Stabilisers were fitted to the ship in 1955 and during the next ten years her accommodation, like that of QUEEN MARY, was made more suitable for cruising in hot climates by installation of air-conditioning in many cabins and public rooms. Despite all this she became uneconomic to operate and in 1967 it was decided to dispose of her to a consortium of American business men in Florida, to be used as a hotel ship at Port Everglades. She left Southampton for the last time on November 29th, 1967, and on arrival at her new home quickly became both a tourist attraction and a financial failure, as well as being regarded as a fire hazard and a source of pollution.

SS QUEEN ELIZABETH at New York in 1954 /*Cunard*

1946 Her owners became bankrupt and the ship was sold for £1·3m at auction, her new owner being Mr C. Y. Tung, a Chinese shipping magnate who intended to use her as a seagoing university in Hong Kong. Renamed SEAWISE UNIVERSITY, she sailed from Port Everglades, Florida, on February 10th, 1971, under the command of her former *Cunard* captain.

Even now she had to suffer further indignity, for she set out on two shafts only and steam was supplied by six of her twelve boilers. Between Haiti and Cuba her boilers failed and, after being adrift for two days, she was towed to Curaçao for repairs. She ultimately reached her destination, but while in Hong Kong harbour undergoing conversion for her new role she was sabotaged and set on fire on January 9th, 1972. She became a total loss and capsized the next day.

SS SEAWISE UNIVERSITY, ex QUEEN ELIZABETH, leaving Port Everglades, February 1971 /AP

1946

At the time of the German invasion of Holland in 1940 two sister ships were being built by Wilton-Fijenoord for the *Holland-America Line*. These were the twin-screw motor ships ZUIDERDAM and WESTERDAM. To prevent their falling into German hands, they were scuttled. WESTERDAM was twice salvaged by the Germans, only to be scuttled again and again. ZUIDERDAM was raised, but then sunk again by the Germans as a block-ship. She was ultimately scrapped as being a constructional total loss.

WESTERDAM, 12149tG, was however finally completed and entered the Rotterdam–New York service in July 1946, making the first postwar transatlantic sailing for *Holland-America Line*. She was powered by two five-cylinder double-acting two-cycle Fijenoord-MAN diesel motors and her speed in service was 16 knots. She carried only 134 first class passengers but had considerable cargo space. After eighteen years of hard work WESTERDAM was scrapped in 1964.

1947

SS NOVA SCOTIA, a passenger-cargo liner of 7438tG, was built by Vickers Armstrong for *Johnston-Warren Line*'s Liverpool–St Johns–Halifax–Boston passenger and cargo services. She was a single-screw ship driven by double- and single-reduction steam turbines and went into service in 1947. She carried 105 cabin class and 80 third class passengers. Her sister ship NEWFOUNDLAND was identical and the pair replaced two ships of the same names which were destroyed during World War II.

Johnston-Warren Lines is a subsidiary of Furness, Withey & Co Ltd, who are also the managers.

The two ships maintained a regular service until 1962, when the decline of passenger services caused the company to replace them by two cargo-only ships. NOVA SCOTIA and NEWFOUNDLAND were sold to *Dominion Navigation* of Nassau, Bahamas, trading between Australia, Japan and Hong Kong. Their names were changed to FRANCIS DRAKE and GEORGE ANSON respectively. They were sold for breaking up in December 1970.

Above: Holland-America Line SS WESTERDAM */Holland-America*
Below: SS NOVA SCOTIA */NMM*

1947 The *Cunard Line* sister ships MEDIA, 13345tG, and PARTHIA, 13362tG, were the first ships built for the company after World War II. They were 17-knot twin-screw steamships driven by double-reduction-geared turbines, MEDIA being completed by John Brown in 1947 and PARTHIA, the first Cunarder ever to be Belfast-built by Harland and Wolff, in 1948. They were the first *Cunard* ships to be designed as 'cargo-passenger liners', each having a large amount of cargo space and excellent air-conditioned accommodation for 250 cabin class passengers. In 1953 MEDIA was fitted with Denny-Brown stabilisers, the first transatlantic liner to be so equipped.

They operated a regular service between Liverpool and New York until 1961, when the recession in the trade rendered them uneconomic and they were withdrawn. MEDIA was sold to Italian owners, extensively rebuilt as the cruising liner FLAVIA and is operated by the *Costa Line*. Her gross tonnage is now 15465.

PARTHIA was sold first to the *New Zealand Shipping Company* as their REMUERA, and later became ARAMAC of the *Eastern and Australian Steamship Company*. She was broken up in 1970.

Below: SS MEDIA entering New York Harbour on the conclusion of her maiden voyage, August 1947. /Cunard
Bottom: SS PARTHIA at sea. Note the absence of a mainmast in these two ships /Cunard

1938/1947

The *Canadian Pacific* MV BEAVERBRAE, 9034tG, was built as HUASCARAN by Blöhm and Voss and went into service in 1939 on the *Hamburg-Amerika Line*'s South American service. She was a single-screw ship with diesel-electric drive. Three MAN seven-cylinder two-cycle single-acting diesel engines were direct-coupled to generators to provide power for the electric motor which drove the screw shaft. Her speed was 16 knots.

She was used by the German Navy as a submarine depot ship during World War II, at the end of which she was ceded to Canada as war reparations. *Canadian Pacific Steamship Company* bought her in 1947 and, after completely refitting her and renaming her BEAVERBRAE, put her to work between Bremerhaven (and later Bremen) and Canadian ports carrying displaced persons. She had berths for 773 passengers and between 1948 and 1954 she carried more than 38000 emigrants to Canada in fifty-one westbound voyages. Her eastbound voyages were made carrying cargo only.

In 1954 she was sold to *Compagnia Genoviese d'Armamento* of Genoa and, after being completely reconstructed and her appearance greatly altered, she sailed between Hamburg and Australia for the *Cogedar Line* as AURELIA, 10480tG. She has now been scrapped.

Canadian Pacific MV BEAVERBRAE /Skyfotos

1948

Cunard SS CARONIA, 34183tG, was completed in 1948 by John Brown and was at that time the world's largest passenger ship to be built since the war. She was a twin-screw ship powered by two sets of steam turbines; in each set the high-pressure turbine was double-reduction-geared to the screw shaft while the intermediate and low-pressure turbines were single-reduction-geared to the shaft. Six boilers supplied superheated steam at 625psi. Her speed in service was 22 knots.

CARONIA, the second ship to carry the name, was built as a dual-purpose ship and carried 528 first and 332 second class passengers when on the Southampton–New York run and one class only when cruising. She was a massive but beautiful ship with a single tripod mast and a single large funnel, both of which were raked. She was painted in four shades of green, which contrasted well with the dignity of the *Cunard* red and black funnel. Her career however, was marred by frequent troubles in her

SS CARONIA /PR-W

turbines and gearing, and she was often a liability to her owners.

Nonetheless the luxury and grace of this ship, both inside and out, together with the often expensive and luxurious cruises which she undertook earned her many epithets, the 'Green Goddess', 'Cunard's luxury yacht' and 'the millionaires ship' being among the politest.

In 1968 she was sold to the Franchard Corporation of New York and renamed COLUMBIA. Almost immediately, however, she was resold to the *Universal Line SA* of Panama and again changed her name to CARIBIA. She made a few cruises but suffered more engine failures and a fire, and was laid up in New York in 1969.

In February 1974 she was sold to shipbreakers in Kaohsiung. After leaving New York in charge of the German tug HAMBURG, the old ship nearly foundered as a result of water leaking into her shaft tunnels. Then on August 15th, during a severe tropical storm off the island of Guam, HAMBURG suffered a partial engine failure, was unable to control CARIBIA and cast off the tow. As a result CARIBIA struck the breakwater at the entrance to Apra harbour, Guam, and tore a 40ft gash in her starboard side. She sank and then broke into three pieces, the 150ft bow section completely blocking the entrance to the harbour. The entrance was ultimately cleared by an American salvage firm.

MV STOCKHOLM, 12165tG, was completed in 1948 by Gotaverken for the *Swedish-American Line's* Göthenburg–New York service. She was a twin-screw cargo-liner with accommodation for 120 first class and 450 tourist class passengers. Her two diesel engines together developed 14600shp for a service speed of 17 knots.

STOCKHOLM of 1948 was the fourth *Swedish-American Line* ship to carry the name. The first has already been noted (page 15), the second was a liner of 28000tG laid down by Riuniti, Trieste, and launched in 1938. She was completely destroyed by fire while fitting out. The third STOCKHOLM was a duplicate of the second and was launched from the same yard in 1940. As a result of World War II she was never delivered to Sweden but became the Italian troopship SABAUDIA and was bombed and sunk at Trieste in 1944.

The fourth STOCKHOLM was also dogged by ill-luck, for on July 26th, 1956, off the American coast, she was badly damaged after colliding with the Italian ANDREA DORIA (qv). As a result of the collision the Italian ship sank with the loss of forty-three lives. Four lives were lost in STOCKHOLM.

STOCKHOLM was repaired and went back into North Atlantic service until January 1960, when she was sold to the German Democratic Republic and named VÖLKERFREUNDSCHAFT.

1913/1949

SS KATOOMBA, 9424tG, was built by Harland and Wolff in 1913 for the Australian ship-owners *McIlwraith, McEacharn*. She was a 15-knot triple-screw ship with two four-cylinder triple-expansion engines driving the wing shafts and a low-pressure exhaust steam turbine the centre shaft.

In 1949 she was purchased by the *Greek Line*, which had been founded in 1939 and whose first four ships, including KATOOMBA, were purchased second-hand. KATOOMBA was renamed COLUMBIA and registered with the Cia Maritima del Este of Panama, flying a 'flag of convenience'. She carried 52 first class and 754 tourist class passengers on the Piraeus–Genoa–New York service, but was transferred to the Bremen–Southampton–Montreal service in 1950. She was really too small a ship for the North Atlantic passenger service but most of her voyages were made in the summer months and in the winter she cruised in the Mediterranean.

She was sold to Japan in 1959 for scrapping.

Above: MV STOCKHOLM /*Swedish American*
Below: SS KATOOMBA /NMM

1949

MV OSLOFJORD, the second ship to carry the name, was built for the *Norwegian America Line* by the Netherlands Dock and Shipbuilding Company, Amsterdam, and went into North Atlantic service between Norwegian ports, Copenhagen and New York in 1949. She was designed as a dual-purpose ship and used for cruising as required. In North Atlantic service she carried 189 first class and 477 tourist class passengers. As a cruise liner she carried 350 passengers in one class.

She was a twin-screw diesel-engined ship with a speed of 20 knots, fitted with stabilisers and fully air-conditioned. Her gross tonnage was 16844.

With the general fall-off of North Atlantic trade, OSLOFJORD was used increasingly for cruising and in 1970 she went on charter to *Costa Line*, who renamed her FULVIA and increased her capacity to carry 450 tourists.

On July 20th, 1970, while on a cruise and about 150 miles north of Las Palmas, a fire broke out in her engine room and this beautiful ship became a total loss. All her passengers and crew were saved.

MV OSLOFJORD /PR-W

1950

SS INDEPENDENCE, 23754tG, was built by the Bethlehem Steel Corporation in 1950 for *American Export Lines'* service between New York, Gibraltar, Naples and Genoa. She was the first of two sister ships, CONSTITUTION being put into service a year later.

They were attractive-looking ships, each with a raking bow and a counter stern. Their speed was 22·5 knots, this being achieved by four steam turbines double-reduction-geared to two screw shafts. The ships were completely air-conditioned. As built, each carried 374 first class, 350 second class and 254

tourist class passengers. In 1959, however, the ships were partly reconstructed, their passenger accommodation being improved and cabins for an extra 110 first class passengers provided in each of them.

In 1960 Isbrandtsen Co Inc of New York obtained a controlling interest in *American Export Lines*, which now became *American Export Isbrandtsen Lines Inc.* Soon afterwards, as a result of the decline of the Mediterranean passenger trade, both ships were withdrawn from their original duties and fitted out as cruise ships, their gross tonnage being increased to

29496. They were not successful and in 1969 both were laid up.

In 1974 both ships were sold to the *Atlantic Far East Line Inc* of the C. Y. Tung Group of Hong Kong being renamed OCEANIC CONSTITUTION and OCEANIC INDEPENDENCE respectively. Both ships have been laid up in Hong Kong but, in 1977, this latter ship was sold to Atlantic Far East Lines of Panama and re-named SEA LUCK.

SS INDEPENDENCE /Curt Frick

1937/1950

P & O SS STRATHEDEN, a turbine-driven twin-screw ship of 23732tG whose usual itinerary was between the United Kingdom and Australia, was chartered by *Cunard* in 1950 and made a number of North Atlantic voyages between Southampton and New York.

STRATHEDEN was one of three beautiful sister ships, STRATHMORE and STRATHALLAN being the other two. All three ships were Ministry of Transport troopships during World War II, STRATHALLAN being sunk during the North African invasion. STRATHEDEN and STRATHMORE were sold to a Greek company in 1963 and are now used as hotel ships for pilgrims in the Mediterranean.

Right: P & O SS STRATHEDEN /PR-W

1951-1952

SS RYNDAM, 15015tG, was built for *Holland-America Line* by Wilton-Fijenoord and went into service in 1951. She was laid down as DINTELDYK, an 11000-ton cargo ship with accommodation for about 60 passengers, but was altered while on the stocks and completed as a passenger liner. She was designed mainly for the tourist class traveller, carrying only 39 first class passengers but 822 tourist class. Her accommodation is of a high standard and she is fully air conditioned.

RYNDAM is a single-screw ship with two steam turbines double-reduction-geared to the screw shaft. Her speed in service is 16·5 knots and she has two water-tube boilers supplying superheated steam at 525psi. She is fitted with Denny-Brown stabilisers.

RYNDAM sailed first on the Rotterdam–New York service, but was soon transferred to the Canadian service, running between Rotterdam and Montreal with calls at Southampton and le Havre. She was also extensively used for cruising. From 1966 she sailed under the German flag for the *Europe-Canada Line* on the Bremerhaven–Canada and Bremerhaven–New York services. In 1967 she was transferred to the Dutch Government-owned *Trans-Ocean Steamship Company* and renamed WATERMAN. After only a year,

however, she reverted to her old name and to the ownership of *Holland-America Line*. As a result of the decline of the North Atlantic passenger trade, RYNDAM was sold in May 1971 for £2·5m to Cosmos Tours Ltd, who operated her solely as a cruise ship. Late in 1972 she was again sold, this time to World Wide Cruises SA of Panama, and is now named ATLAS. Since early 1976 her owners have been the Greek *Epirotiki Line*.

SS MAASDAM, 15024tG, is an almost identical sister ship to RYNDAM and was built for *Holland-America Line* by Wilton-Fijenoord to the same design. She went into service in 1952 and was used mainly between Rotterdam and New York, but also made extensive cruises. She took over the Canadian service for a brief period after 1966, until she was sold late in 1968 to the *Polish Ocean Lines*. She now sails mainly between Gdynia and Canada via Southampton or Tilbury, and on cruises. Her name is STEFAN BATORY, and she is seen here as such.

SS RYNDAM /*Holland-America*

1944/1952

SS GROOTE BEER, 9140tG, was built in 1944 by Permanente Metals Corporation as COSTA RICA VICTORY, 7643tG, for the United States Government. She was one of three similar ships purchased by the Netherlands Government for their *Trans-Ocean Steamship Company*. These ships were needed to assist in the emigration of Dutch subjects from Holland to the United States in the postwar period.

GROOTE BEER was a single-screw ship having two steam turbines double-reduction-geared to the screw shaft. She had a speed of 16 knots.

The *Trans-Ocean Steamship Company* greatly improved and extended her passenger accommodation,

Above: Polish Ocean Lines SS STEFAN BATORY, EX MAASDAM /PR-W
Below: SS GROOTE BEER /PR-W

thereby increasing her gross tonnage. She could carry about 800 passengers. The ship saw service in many parts of the world but for much of her life she worked between Rotterdam and New York and Rotterdam and Canadian ports. She was managed by *Holland-America Line*.

In 1963 GROOTE BEER was sold to Greek owners, but for the next three years was on charter to the Netherlands Government to make four educational voyages each year between Rotterdam and New York.

In 1970 she was renamed MARIANNE IV but was broken up in 1971.

1952

The twin-screw SS FLANDRE, 20464tG, was completed in 1952 by Ateliers et Chantiers de France at Dunkirk for the *Compagnie Générale Transatlantique* (*CGT*). FLANDRE and her sister ship ANTILLES were the first large passenger ships to be built in France after the end of World War II and they were intended for the *CGT* West Indies service. While FLANDRE was still under construction it was decided to transfer her to the North Atlantic service to provide, with LIBERTÉ and ILE DE FRANCE, a weekly sailing between le Havre and New York.

The design of FLANDRE was unusual, embodying the Carlotti-ACF hull form, in which a markedly curved stem ends in a bulbous forefoot and the two screw shafts are so arranged to achieve maximum water flow round each screw, thus reducing cavitation to a minimum. Fifteen per cent economy in the power required for any given speed is claimed for this system. The hull was divided transversely into eleven watertight compartments and some of her superstructure was fabricated in aluminium alloy.

The machinery of FLANDRE consisted of two groups of Rateau-Bretagne steam turbines driving the two screw shafts through double-reduction-gearing. Her normal speed in service was 22 knots but with her turbines developing 44000shp she had a top speed of 25 knots. Steam at 900psi and with 896°F of superheat was supplied by four water-tube boilers.

Completely air-conditioned accommodation was provided for 303 first class, 385 cabin class and 53 tourist class passengers. A very high standard of comfort and luxury was enjoyed in all three classes. She could also carry 3000 tonnes dw of cargo, some of it refrigerated.

FLANDRE sailed on her maiden voyage in July 1952,

SS FLANDRE /*CGT*

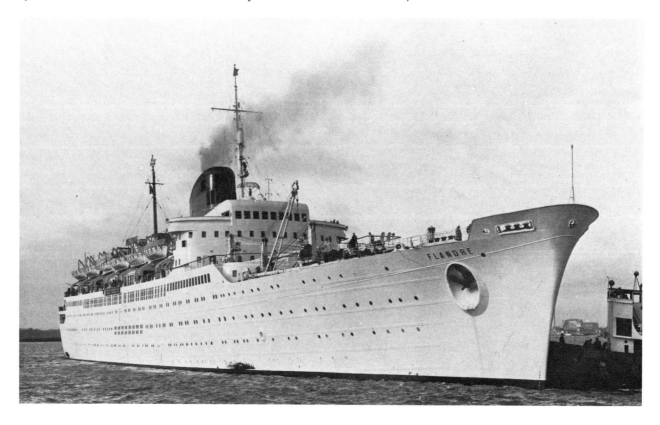

but serious faults developed in her electrical system and she broke down in mid-Atlantic, completing her voyage to New York under tow by two tugs. She returned to her builders for rectification and was not able to sail again until April 1953.

For the next ten years FLANDRE successfully maintained the service for which she was built, but in 1963 joined ANTILLES on the West Indies route and also went cruising.

In 1968 she was sold by *CGT* to the Italian *Costa Line* and renamed CARLA C. Now with a gross tonnage of 19975, she is still in service.

Below: SS UNITED STATES leaving Southampton Ocean Dock on her maiden voyage, July 1952 /PR-W
Bottom: SS UNITED STATES outward bound from Southampton /PR-W

The *United States Lines* SS UNITED STATES, 53329tG, was completed by Newport News Shipbuilding Company in 1952. She was constructed in a dry dock, being floated out when her hull and machinery were completed. Much of her superstructure was built up from riveted aluminium alloy.

UNITED STATES is the largest passenger ship ever built in the United States and also the fastest passenger ship in the world. She was constructed to perform a dual purpose, to be a luxury transatlantic liner in times of peace but to be easily convertible to a fast armed troopship in times of war. Her peacetime passenger capacity on the North Atlantic was 516 in first class, 508 in second class and 549 in tourist class accommodation. Her officers and crew numbered 1060 and she has 148000 cubic feet of cargo space, about a third of which is refrigerated. As a troopship in wartime she could carry 14380 troops.

1952

The United States Government paid $32m of the total $77m which the ship cost to build and they insisted on very high standards of safety and security. She is for example built and furnished throughout with non-inflammable materials, and her subdivision is the most complete of any merchant ship in the world. Her damage control system, operated from the bridge, is more comprehensive than that of many great warships.

As a result of the ship's intended military function, the deckheads in her cabins and public rooms are much lower than in the luxury liners of the past and completely lack the grace and elegance to which previous eras were accustomed. The décor of her public rooms has been thought by many travellers to be dull and depressing. Apart from this her passengers have enjoyed a high standard of luxury and amenities, though the metal furnishings in her cabins were not always appreciated. This ship is, of course, completely air-conditioned, but is not fitted with stabilisers. However, her bilge keels are exceptionally long and wide.

She is a quadruple-screw ship: the two forward, or outboard, screws are four-bladed, while the two after, or inboard, screws each has five blades. In service, each pair of screws turns at a different speed. For example, at 29·5 knots, her usual cruising speed in transatlantic service, the forward screws turn at 139rpm, while the rotational speed of the after pair is 141rpm, all screws turning outboard. These factors help to reduce vibration.

Her main engines consist of four sets of cross-compound turbines, one set driving each of the four screw shafts through double-reduction gearing. Each set of turbines develops 55000shp to give a total of 220000shp. The ship has eight Babcock & Wilcox boilers, each with ten sprayers (burners) and capable of supplying 269000lb of steam per hour at a pressure of 970psi and with a superheat temperature in the region of 1000°F. The layout and design of the machinery of UNITED STATES are generally similar to those of the USS MIDWAY class aircraft carriers, but without cruising turbines. The machinery and boiler spaces are subdivided into seven watertight compartments, but there is a complete system of cross piping to enable any boiler to supply steam to any of the four turbines independently.

On special trials UNITED STATES attained a reported speed in excess of 42 knots and on her maiden voyage from New York to Southampton in July 1952 she averaged 35·59 knots. Westbound, her average was 34·19 knots. These performances comfortably gave her the Blue Riband and it is unlikely that they will ever be surpassed by a passenger ship on the North Atlantic. Furthermore, these records were achieved with only six of her eight boilers in steam—indeed, during her transatlantic service she never used more than six boilers at a time and even those usually were steamed at only 60 per cent capacity. But she is a costly ship to run and requires a staff of 47 engineers: at sea, three officers are on duty in each engine room and two in each boiler room.

UNITED STATES was used for cruising in the winter seasons, but in the face of the huge operating costs of the present time she became completely uneconomic and was laid up at Hampton Roads late in 1969, after making more than 400 Atlantic crossings. This ship still has considerable military potential and she was purchased by the US Federal Maritime Administration in 1973. In March 1974 the Mallard Investment Corporation made a bid of $30·7 million for her, but a month later all bids were rejected and at the present time the ship is in Norfolk, Va. New bids for the ownership of UNITED STATES were to be received on March 1st, 1977. Transpacific Cruise Corpn. of Washington were proposing to turn her into a floating hotel. The US Government had insisted that her sale be only to a US company and it is understood that the reserve price was to be in excess of $5·0 million.

1953

SS OLYMPIA, 17269tG, was completed in 1953 by Alexander Stephen for the transatlantic service of the *Greek Line*. She is a twin-screw ship with four water-tube boilers supplying superheated steam at 600psi to four steam turbines double-reduction-geared to two screw shafts. Her speed in service is 21 knots and she is stabilised on the Flume system.

Originally she was completely air conditioned and carried 50 to 196 first class passengers and 1160 to 1306 tourist class. In 1971 she was extensively refitted as a one-class ship to carry 1030 passengers in exceptionally good accommodation.

The *Greek Line* was founded in 1938 and purchased second-hand ships to operate a service between Piraeus, Mediterranean ports and New York. The first ship so purchased was the *Anchor* liner TUSCANIA (qv), which was renamed NEA HELLAS and later NEW YORK. To date, the last ship so acquired was the *Canadian Pacific* EMPRESS OF BRITAIN (qv) which since 1964 has sailed as QUEEN ANNA MARIA.

OLYMPIA is the only important ship to be built new for the *Greek Line* but, as it is the policy of the owners to operate each ship as a separate company, she is registered in Monrovia, flies the Liberian flag and her owners are the *Transatlantic Shipping Corporation*. At first she sailed between Bremerhaven and New York but her itinerary was soon changed and she worked between Haifa and New York with calls at several Mediterranean ports. After being engaged in cruising for several years OLYMPIA was

found no longer to be economically viable and in 1974 she was laid up at Piraeus, where she still remained in 1977.

SS OLYMPIA /Skyfotos

1940/1953

The *Europe-Canada Line* MV SEVEN SEAS, 12375tG, was laid down by the Sun Shipbuilding Company in 1940 as the *Moore, McCormack Line* MORMACMAIL. Before completion she was taken over by the United States Navy and converted by Newport News Company to an escort aircraft carrier, serving until 1949 as USS LONG ISLAND. She was a single-screw ship powered by four Sulzer seven-cylinder two-cycle single-acting diesel motors with electro-magnetic slip couplings and single-reduction-gearing. Her service speed was 16 knots.

She was then reconverted for merchant service, carrying about 1000 passengers in dormitory accommodation. She made a number of transatlantic voy-

ages under charter, flying the Panamanian flag and named NELLY, 11086tG. In 1955 she was purchased by the newly formed *Europe-Canada Line*, a company owned jointly by *Rotterdam Lloyd* and *Holland-America Line* but registered in Germany.

SEVEN SEAS, carrying 25 first class and 1066 third tourist class passengers, sailed profitably between Bremen, Halifax and New York, mainly carrying emigrants. Later she carried students on transatlantic tours to New York.

In 1966 she was sold to the University of Rotterdam as an accommodation ship for students. Later she was moored alongside at Parkhaven, Rotterdam as a hotel ship and was scrapped in Belgium in 1977.

1953

The third *Swedish-American Line* ship to carry the name KUNGSHOLM was built by De Schelde, Flushing, and went into service in October 1953. She carried 132 first class and 637 tourist class passengers and her crew numbered 355. She was employed on the company's Gothenburg–New York service and on cruising.

A fine looking ship of 21164tG, she is a motor vessel with twin screws driven by two eight-cylinder two-cycle single-acting Burmeister and Wain diesel engines, which give her a speed of 19 knots.

In 1965 KUNGSHOLM was sold to *Norddeutscher Lloyd*, who renamed her EUROPA. With BREMEN (ex

Above: MV SEVEN SEAS /Real Photographs
Below: Swedish American MV KUNGSHOLM of 1953 /
Swedish American

Top: Hapag-Lloyd MV EUROPA, ex KUNGSHOLM /Skyfotos

Above: Italia Line SS ANDREA DORIA. She was never painted white /Italia

PASTEUR), she maintained for a time their Bremerhaven–Southampton–Cherbourg–New York service. In 1970, however, *Hapag-Lloyd* (the amalgamated company of *Hamburg-Amerika* and *Norddeutscher Lloyd*) withdrew both ships from transatlantic service. BREMEN was retained by the company and is used solely as a cruise liner; her hull is now painted white. PASTEUR (qv) was sold to *Chandris Lines*, who renamed her REGINA MAGNA and also used her only for cruising.

The *Italia Line* SS ANDREA DORIA, 29083tG, was built by Ansaldo, Genoa, and went into service in January 1953. She was the first of the beautiful and elegant steamships built in Italy for the North Atlantic passenger trade after the end of World War II.

She had a bulbous bow and a very fine hull with a cruiser stern. Her twin screws were driven by two sets of turbines, each set comprising a high-pressure turbine double-reduction-geared to the screw shaft

and intermediate- and low-pressure turbines, both of which were single-reduction-geared. She had four water-tube boilers providing superheated steam at 633psi. She developed 35000shp for a speed of 23 knots in service.

ANDREA DORIA had excellent accommodation for 202 first class passengers, 244 cabin class and 703 tourist class. All the first and cabin class cabins had private facilities, as did more than half of those in the tourist class. The décor of her public rooms was beautiful and bore no trace of vulgarity. She boasted three swimming pools and four cinemas, and was fully air-conditioned.

She ran between Genoa, Naples, Cannes, Gibraltar and New York, and was joined in 1954 by her sister ship CRISTOFORO COLOMBO (qv).

In the early hours of the morning of July 26th, 1956, ANDREA DORIA, nearing the end of an eight-day voyage from Genoa, was in patchy fog about a mile to the south of the Nantucket lightship. Largely as the result of an amazing confusion of radar signals, she

1953 was suddenly in violent collision with the outward-bound Swedish Lloyd MV STOCKHOLM, 12644tG, whose ice-strengthened bow struck deeply into the starboard side of the Italian ship. Both ships were travelling at nearly full speed at the time of impact and ANDREA DORIA went ahead, listing badly, for nearly two miles after the collision. After about eleven hours she sank, but not before all survivors had been got away to the many rescue ships, which included the *CGT* liner ILE DE FRANCE. Out of her 1706 passengers and crew 1663 were saved, the casualties having probably all been killed at the time of the collision or shortly afterwards.

In the badly crushed bow of STOCKHOLM three crew members were killed and four were injured. None of her passengers was hurt.

In the subsequent legal action to apportion blame, things seemed to be going in favour of the Swedish ship when the two companies reached a compromise out of court, thus avoiding further expensive litigation. The terms of this compromise were never made public.

1931/1954

The *Matson Line* SS MARIPOSA, 18563tG, was completed in 1931 by the Bethlehem Shipbuilding Corporation of America. In 1954 she was bought by *Home Lines* of Panama, who renamed her HOMERIC, had her re-engined by her builders and then completely refitted at Trieste.

She was a twin-screw ship with single-reduction-geared turbines which gave her a service speed of 20 knots. She had accommodation for 147 first class and 1096 tourist class passengers.

For *Home Lines* she worked first between New York and Italian ports and then between Quebec and Southampton. She was afterwards engaged entirely on cruising.

Late in 1973 she was sold to Nan Feng Steel Enterprises Corporation and arrived at Kaohsiung for scrapping in January 1974.

Matson Line SS MARIPOSA which became *Home Lines* HOMERIC /NMM

146

1954

Italia Line SS CRISTOFORO COLOMBO, 29249tG, was completed by Ansaldo, Genoa, in 1954 and went on to the Genoa–Naples–Cannes–Gibraltar–New York service in 1954 as running mate to ANDREA DORIA (qv), her sister ship. She had identical hull and machinery but her accommodation was differently laid out and she carried rather fewer first and cabin class passengers than did her sister. Her beautiful public rooms are elegantly decorated and depict the life and times of Christopher Colombus. She is completely air conditioned but did not have stabilisers until 1963, when four of the Denny-Brown type were fitted.

After the sinking of the ANDREA DOREA the two motor ships GIULIO CESARE and AUGUSTUS from the South American service maintained the Genoa–New York service with CRISTOFORO COLOMBO until LEONARDO DA VINCI was completed in 1960. These two ships then ran on a slower service, calling at several additional Mediterranean ports and at Boston, Mass., on their Genoa–New York run. In January 1973 CRISTOFORO COLOMBO replaced GUILIO CESARE on the South American service and GUILIO CESARE has since been scrapped.

From 1965 MICHELANGELO and RAFFAELLO maintained the North Atlantic express service, which has however been greatly reduced in recent years and the ships were diverted to cruising. Both these ships have now been withdrawn from service and CRISTOFORO COLOMBO has been sold to Venezuela as a floating hotel at Puerto Ordaz.

Italia Line SS CRISTOFORO COLOMBO /*Italia*

1930/1955

The *Arosa Line* MV AROSA SUN, 17080tG, was completed by Ateliers et Chantiers de la Loire in 1930 for the *Messageries Maritimes* as FELIX ROUSSEL (16744tG). She had two square funnels and her rather ugly hull had a straight stem and counter stern. She was a twin-screw ship with two Sulzer ten-cylinder two-cycle single-acting diesel motors giving her a speed of 17 knots. She never worked on the North Atlantic under French ownership, but in 1949 her appearance was improved by her being lengthened and given a single elliptical funnel. Her gross tonnage was increased.

In 1955 she was bought by *Arosa Line* and her name changed. She had an extensive refit and sailed first between Trieste and Mediterranean ports and New York and then between Bremen, Southampton and Quebec. She carried 100 first class passengers and nearly 1000 tourist class.

When *Arosa Line* became bankrupt in 1959 she was bought by a company in Holland and moored near Ijmuiden as an accommodation ship for workmen.

She was withdrawn and scrapped at Bilbao in 1974.

Arosa Line was a Swiss-owned company, registered in Panama. During the seven years of its existence it operated two other ships on the North Atlantic. The first, AROSA KULM, 8929tG, went into service in 1952. She was built as CATIGNY in 1920, and had several owners and three other names between 1920 and 1952.

The second ship, AROSA STAR, 9070tG, was built as BORINQUEN in 1931 and entered North Atlantic service in 1954.

Both ships have now been broken up.

Arosa Line MV AROSA SUN /Real Photographs

1955

SS MANCHESTER MARINER, 7850tG, was a single-screw ship with two turbines geared to one shaft. She was built in 1955 for *Manchester Liners Ltd* and was a good example of a medium-sized cargo liner, carrying about a dozen passengers to Canada and American inland ports through the St. Lawrence Seaway and the Great Lakes.

Manchester Liners Ltd was formed by Furness Withey in 1898, soon after the completion of the Manchester Ship Canal, to connect the city with north American ports. The company no longer carries passengers and owns a fleet of container ships, all with MANCHESTER in their names.

SS MANCHESTER MARINER /*Manchester Liners Ltd*

1955-1956

SS ISRAEL, 9853tG, was built by Deutsche Werft, Hamburg, for the Israeli *Zim Lines'* transatlantic service between Haifa, Naples and New York. She was completed in 1955 and, with her sister ship ZION, 9855tG, which came from the same builders in 1956, she was used for cruising as well as on the North Atlantic. These ships replaced JERUSALEM, which was *Zim Lines'* first transatlantic ship, purchased in 1953. JERUSALEM was built in 1913 as the *Norwegian American* Bergensfjord (qv). In 1956 she was renamed ALIYA and was scrapped in 1959.

ISRAEL and ZION were handsome and very well-appointed ships being fully air conditioned. They each had accommodation for 25 first class passengers and 300 in the tourist class. Each ship was driven by two Parsons turbines double-reduction-geared to a single-screw shaft with a speed of 18 knots. They had anti-roll stabilisers but nonetheless were small for the North Atlantic luxury service.

In 1964 the new *Zim* liner SHALOM entered service and in 1966 the two smaller ships were sold, ISRAEL becoming ANGRO DO HEROISMO of the *Empresa Insulana de Navejacao* of Portugal. She was broken up in 1974.

ZION also went to Portugal, as AMELIA DE MELLO of the *Sociedade Jeral de Comercio Industria e Transportes*. In 1972 she was sold to Greece and renamed ITHACA. She was refitted, her gross tonnage increased to 12500 and has since been engaged entirely in cruising, being operated by Strand Cruises.

Above: SS ISRAEL /*Zim Lines*   *Below:* SS ZION /*Zim Lines*

1955-1957

Between the years 1955 and 1957 *Cunard* took delivery of four fine modern steamships to replace ASCANIA, FRANCONIA, SAMARIA and SCYTHIA, which had been the mainstay of the Canadian services since the end of World War II. These new ships were all built by John Brown and were named SAXONIA, 21637tG, IVERNIA, 21717tG, CARINTHIA, 21946tG, and SYLVANIA, 21989tG, in chronological order of their completion. They were nearly identical sister ships and the first two operated from London to Quebec and Montreal via le Havre and Cobh and the last two from Liverpool via Greenock to the same destination.

All were twin-screw vessels driven by double-reduction-geared steam turbines and with a speed of 21 knots. They were handsome ships, each with a massive but shapely single funnel and no mainmast.

They carried first and tourist class passengers only, about 150 and 800 of them respectively, although numbers varied slightly in each ship.

In 1962 SAXONIA and IVERNIA were extensively refitted and made suitable for cruising, primarily from the USA. They were renamed CARMANIA and FRANCONIA, being the second and third ships respectively to carry those names. CARINTHIA and SYLVANIA maintained North Atlantic services to Canada and to New York until 1967 and 1968 respectively, when *Cunard* withdrew completely from the Canadian passenger trade, and the two ships were ultimately sold to the Italian *Sitmar Line* becoming FAIRSEA and FAIRWIND respectively.

After lying in the River Fal for more than a year, CARMANIA and FRANCONIA were bought for cruising by Russia. CARMANIA became LEONID SOBINOV and FRANCONIA was renamed FEDOR SHALYAPIN. Both ships are on charter to *CTC Lines* and operate between Southampton and Australia and New Zealand.

Below: Cunard SS SAXONIA, 21637tG, leaving Tilbury for Quebec and Montreal in 1959. This ship was renamed CARMANIA in 1962 /PR-W

Bottom: Cunard SS CARMANIA, ex SAXONIA, when exclusively a cruising liner: /*Cunard*

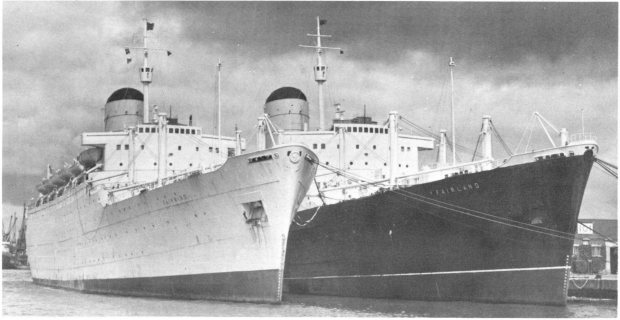

Top Cunard SS FRANCONIA, ex IVERNIA, 22637tG, in
light green cruising colours at sea in 1967 /*Cunard*

Above: Sitmar Line SS FAIRWIND and FAIRLAND at
Southampton in 1969. These ships were *Cunard* SS
CARINTHIA and SYLVANIA /PR-W

Below: USSR SS LEONID SOBINOV, ex CARMANIA, at
Southampton in 1974 /PR-W

1951/1956

The *Italia Line* MV GIULIO CESARE, 27078tG, was a twin-screw motor ship built by Cantieri Riuniti dell' Adriatico, Monfalcone. She had two twelve-cylinder two-cycle double-acting Fiat diesel motors which were built in 1941. They developed a total of 26000shp and gave her a speed of 21 knots.

She was fully air conditioned and had excellent cabin accommodation for 178 first class passengers, 288 cabin class and 714 tourist class. She later became a two-class ship carrying 181 first class and 1050 tourist class passengers.

She was the first large Italian liner to be constructed after the end of World War II and she went into service on the Genoa–South America service in 1951. She was joined the next year by her identical sister ship AUGUSTUS, 27090tG, completed by Cantieri Riuniti dell' Adriatico, Trieste, in 1952, and these two fine ships remained on the South American service until 1956, when they were both transferred to the North Atlantic. For the next four years they ran between Genoa and New York, making calls at Cannes, Naples and Gibraltar, as a replacement for ANDREA DORIA (qv) and as running mates to CRISTOFORO COLOMBO (qv).

With the arrival of the new LEONARDO DA VINCI in 1960, GIULIO CESARE and AUGUSTUS returned to the South American service.

GIULIO CESARE was sold for scrap in 1973 and AUGUSTUS was laid up at Naples in January 1976 and was sold in 1977 to a Hong Kong firm being re-named GREAT SEA.

Below: MV GUILIO CESARE /Italia
Bottom MV AUGUSTUS /Italia

1956

MV BERGENSFJORD, the second ship of the name, was built by Swan Hunter for the *Norwegian America Line* and her maiden voyage between Oslo, Bergen and New York was made in May 1956. She is a twin-screw motor vessel of 18739tG, with a speed of 20 knots.

BERGENSFJORD is a very similar but slightly larger ship than the older and ill-fated OSLOFJORD of 1949 (qv). She is fully air conditioned and has Denny-Brown stabilisers. She is a dual-purpose ship and carried 125 first class passengers and 748 tourist class on the North Atlantic, but when used as a cruise liner 450 passengers are carried in one class.

When on the transatlantic service, she had a high reputation for comfort and excellent cuisine and was one of the best looking liners on the Western ocean.

In March 1971 BERGENSFJORD was sold to the French *Compagnie Générale Transatlantique* (*CGT*) as a replacement for their cruising liner MV ANTILLES, which was wrecked on a reef in the Caribbean in January 1971. She was renamed DE GRASSE and engaged in cruising.

In December 1973 she was reported sold to Coral Riviera Ltd of Tel Aviv, but later was on charter to a Hong Kong company, carrying the name CORAL RIVIERA and operating under the Panamanian flag.

MV BERGENSFJORD /PR-W

1956-1961

During the five years 1956-1961 *Canadian Pacific Steamships* put into service three very beautiful 'Empress' ships, to work mainly between Liverpool, Quebec and Montreal but also to serve as cruise liners during the off-season of Atlantic travel.

The first two ships were sisters: EMPRESS OF BRITAIN, 25516tG, was built by Fairfield and went into service in April 1956; EMPRESS OF ENGLAND, 25585tG, was built by Vickers Armstrong and went into service in April 1957. On North Atlantic service these ships each carried 148 first class passengers and

896 tourist class. Their capacity when cruising was for 1050 passengers in one class.

In April 1961 EMPRESS OF CANADA, 27284tG, entered service. Built by Vickers Armstrong, this ship was a little longer and had more beam than the previous ships and her accommodation was for 192 first class and 856 tourist class passengers, with 1080 one-class berths available when cruising.

All three ships have twin screws and each screw shaft is driven by a set of three turbines (high, intermediate and low pressure) through double-reduction-gearing. Superheated steam at 690psi is supplied in each ship by three water-tube boilers. The published designed speed of these three ships is 20 knots, but all have made crossings between Liverpool and Rimouski (the landfall at the mouth of the St Lawrence) at over 21 knots in each direction. EMPRESS OF CANADA is said to be slightly slower than the other two ships.

All three ships are air conditioned and stabilised.

EMPRESS OF BRITAIN was sold to the *Greek Line* in 1964 and was registered in Monrovia, her owners being *Trans-Oceanic Navigation Corporation*. She carried the name QUEEN ANNA MARIA and after considerable reconstruction her gross tonnage was 21716. As well as cruising, she occasionally operated between the Piraeus and New York. In January, 1975, she was laid up at the Piraeus and next year was taken over by *Carnival Cruise Line Inc.* of Panama and renamed CARNIVALE. She cruises from Miami to the Caribbean with her sister ship MARDI GRAS (qv).

EMPRESS OF ENGLAND was sold to *Shaw Savill Line* in 1970, renamed OCEAN MONARCH and extensively refitted and modernised. She sailed between United Kingdom ports and Australia, but was mostly engaged in cruising. In June 1975 she left Southampton for Kaohsiung, where she was scrapped.

EMPRESS OF CANADA was the last large passenger liner in the *Canadian Pacific* fleet. She was painted in the garish modern style adopted by the company. The design included two different shades of green, which in certain conditions of light clashed horribly.

EXPRESS OF CANADA was withdrawn from service in 1971 and after lying at Tilbury for some months was sold in February 1972 to *Carnival Cruise Lines* of Miami. She was renamed MARDI GRAS and now cruises under the Panamanian flag with her sister ship CARNIVALE.

Below SS EMPRESS OF ENGLAND /*Canadian Pacific*
Bottom: SS EMPRESS OF BRITAIN at sea /*Canadian Pacific*

1957

The fourth STATENDAM, 24294tG, was built for the *Holland-America Line* by Wilton-Fijenoord and entered service in 1957. She was constructed in a dry-dock and floated out. Unconventionally, she was christened while on her trials by Princess Beatrix. She was built for the Rotterdam–Southampton–New York service and also for extensive luxury cruising.

STATENDAM is a twin-screw steamship with double-reduction-geared turbines developing 22000shp for a service speed of 19 knots. She has Denny-Brown stabilisers and is air conditioned throughout.

Her accommodation and public rooms are of the very high standard always associated with ships of the *Holland-America Line* and the tourist class cabins are exceptionally comfortable. Some interchange between

Above: SS EMPRESS OF CANADA leaving Southampton for New York /PR-W
Below: SS STATENDAM /Holland-America

MV GRIPSHOLM /PR-W

first and tourist class accommodation can therefore be made when required. Normally STATENDAM carries 84 first class and 867 tourist class passengers, but when cruising she becomes a one-class ship.

STATENDAM may be regarded as a development of the highly successful ships RYNDAM and MAASDAM (qv). She is at present engaged in cruising, mostly in tropical waters. Her hull is now painted midnight blue and her funnel carries the new insignia of the line on an orange background.

The *Swedish-American Line* MV GRIPSHOLM, 23215tG, was built by Ansaldo, Genoa, and went into service in 1957. She is a white-painted ship and the second to carry the name. Like most transatlantic liners she was mostly engaged in cruising but occasionally sailed between Gothenburg and New York. She carries 778 passengers, a crew of 355 and

has a garage for thirty motor cars. Her twin screws are driven by two nine-cylinder Götaverken diesel engines which develop 16200bhp to give the ship a service speed of 19 knots. She has Denny-Brown stabilisers and is completely air conditioned.

In November 1967, while crossing from Gothenburg to New York, GRIPSHOLM was south of Newfoundland when an explosion in the crank-case of her starboard engine completely disabled her, but she was ultimately able to reach New York without assistance.

In 1976 she was sold to *Nautilus Armadora S.A.*, Greece, and re-named NAVARINO. She is now entirely engaged in cruising.

1931/1958

The quadruple-screw turbo-electric steamship ARKADIA, 20648tG, was built by Vickers-Armstrong in 1931 as the *Furness-Withy* liner MONARCH OF BERMUDA for the New York–Bermuda service. She had two steam turbines connected to electric generators driving four screw shafts. Her service speed was 18·5 knots.

During World War II she was intensively used as a British troopship and in 1947 was sent to the Hawthorn Leslie yard on the Tyne to be refitted. While there she was severely damaged by fire but was later completely rebuilt by Thornycroft for the Ministry of Transport, who recommissioned her as the emigrant ship NEW AUSTRALIA in 1949. She was operated on the Australian service by *Shaw Savill Line*.

Her appearance was drastically changed by her rebuilding. Having had three funnels and two masts when MONARCH OF BERMUDA, she now emerged with a single large funnel and two other uptakes combined in a bipod funnel surmounted by a short mast.

In 1958 she was purchased by the *Greek Line* subsidiary *Arcadia Steamship Company*, and was again largely reconstructed at Hamburg by Blöhm and Voss. As ARKADIA she was used both for cruising and on the North Atlantic between Bremen and Canada, with intermediate calls at Amsterdam, le Havre and Cobh.

ARKADIA was withdrawn in 1966 and was sold to Spanish shipbreakers the next year.

Above: SS MONARCH OF BERMUDA in service as a troopship /PR-W

Left: SS NEW AUSTRALIA, ex MONARCH OF BERMUDA /PR-W

Below: SS ARKADIA, ex NEW AUSTRALIA, ex MONARCH OF BERMUDA /Real Photographs

1958

Before his purchase of PENNLAND and WESTERNLAND in 1935 (see page 58) Arnold Bernstein of Hamburg had, in 1933, initiated a comfortable, one-class trans-atlantic service with three refitted but elderly, twin-screw steamships, GEROLSTEIN (7772tG), ILSENSTEIN (8216tG) and KONIGSTEIN (9630tG). These were originally the *Shaw Savill* liners MAMARI (1904), MATATUA (1904) and ARAWA (1907) and each was capable of 13 knots speed.

Bernstein's company flourished and the purchase of the *Red Star* liners PENNLAND and WESTERNLAND in 1935 together with that company's name, brought even more prosperity. Then, in 1937, Bernstein was arrested by the Nazis and spent the next 2½ years in a concentration camp, all his ships and assets being disposed of. Through the good offices of influential American friends, he was released in 1940 and went to the USA.

After the end of the war, Arnold Bernstein tried to start a similar service but various circumstances delayed his ability to do this until 1958 when he founded the *American Banner Line* to carry tourist class passengers between New York, Zeebrugge and Amsterdam. To start the service, the fast freighter, SS BADGER MARINER, 9214tG, was purchased. This ship was built in 1953 at Chester, Pennsylvania. She

had two turbines geared to a single shaft and a speed of 21·5 knots.

The new company had the ship completely rebuilt on a lavish scale. She was air conditioned throughout and the cabins for her 900 passengers set a new standard of comfort for tourist accommodation in a ship of that size. Her conversion from a cargo to a passenger ship raised her gross tonnage to 14136 and lowered her speed to 20 knots. Her name was changed to ATLANTIC.

Bernstein was unable to raise the capital to purchase a second ship and ATLANTIC alone proved uneconomic. The company ceased trading in 1959 and the ship was sold to *American Export Isbrandtsen Lines* who used it for several years on cruises between New York and Mediterranean ports. However, the ship again proved unprofitable and she was laid up. In 1971 she was sold to *Seawise Foundation Incorporated* and renamed UNIVERSE CAMPUS. Her port of registry is Hong Kong.

SS ATLANTIC, 14136tG of the *American Banner Line* in in the Nordsee Canal, leaving Amsterdam for Zeebrugge and New York /PR-W

1939/1959

The *Norddeutscher Lloyd* (*NDL*) 'flagship', SS BREMEN, 32360tG, was built at Penhoët for the French *Compagnie de Navigation Sud-Atlantique* as PASTEUR, 30447tG, and completed in 1939. She was intended for the Bordeaux–River Plate service but the outbreak of World War II prevented her sailing, and in 1940 she sailed to Halifax, NS, where she was taken over by the Ministry of War Transport and converted to a troopship. Under *Cunard-White Star* management PASTEUR made many wartime Atlantic crossings. She was returned to the ownership of the French Government in 1945 and after refitting she was put on to the South American service under the management of her original owners.

In 1957 she was laid up and later the same year was purchased by *NDL* for their transatlantic service and renamed BREMEN.

After very extensive reconstruction at Bremerhaven, during which her gross tonnage was increased by 2000, BREMEN in 1959 went into service between Bremen and New York with calls at Southampton and Cherbourg. She maintained this service until the end of 1970, making some cruises in the winter. It was then announced that *Hapag-Lloyd* were withdrawing from the North Atlantic passenger trade and

that in future BREMEN and her running mate EUROPA (ex KUNGSHOLM) were to be exclusively cruise liners. The decision was short-lived, for in 1971 BREMEN was sold to the Greek *Chandris Lines* and renamed REGINA MAGNA. She was then used entirely for cruising.

She is a quadruple-screw ship, a set of Parsons turbines (high, intermediate and low pressure) driving each screw shaft through single-reduction-gearing. Her engines develop a total of 60000shp for a service speed of 23 knots. She has four water-tube boilers supplying superheated steam at 610psi. On the North Atlantic her passenger capacity was for 216 first class and 906 tourist class. She is completely air conditioned and she has two Denny-Brown stabilisers.

Late in 1974 she was laid up at the Piraeus. She was then sold to Middle East buyers for use as an accommodation ship in the Arabian Gulf.

In 1977, her name was changed to UNIVERSE.

Below: SS PASTEUR during her wartime service as a troopship /PR-W
Bottom: SS BREMEN, ex PASTEUR, in transatlantic service /PR-W

1959

SS ROTTERDAM, 38645tG, is Holland's largest passenger liner and she was completed in 1959 for the *Holland-America Line* by the Rotterdam Drydock Company at a cost of £13½m. It was always intended that another luxury liner should be provided for the Rotterdam–New York service as a running mate for NIEUW AMSTERDAM. World War II upset these plans and it was not until 1956 that the new ship was laid down.

ROTTERDAM is a twin-screw ship with six steam turbines developing 35000shp and driving the two screw shafts through double-reduction-gearing. Her speed in service is 20·5 knots. She has four water-tube boilers supplying superheated steam at 710psi.

Above: SS REGINA MAGNA, ex BREMEN, ex PASTEUR, as a *Chandris* cruise liner /PR-W
Below: SS ROTTERDAM.The photograph shows her beautiful hull /PR-W

SS ROTTERDAM, 38645tG, is Holland's largest passenger liner /PR-W

Boilers and machinery are all in the after part of the ship and in place of conventional funnels she has two slender uptakes joined at their tops by a cross beam. She is equipped with Denny-Brown stabilisers and she is fully air conditioned. ROTTERDAM has a beautiful hull and much of her superstructure, her 'funnels' and mast are made of corrosion-resisting aluminium alloy.

As a result of the disposition of her machinery much extra space can be provided for public rooms, swimming pools and passenger accommodation. She has for example a magnificent first class lounge and one of the largest theatres, seating 600 people, ever to be built into a ship. On the North Atlantic service she can carry a total of 1360 passengers in first and tourist classes. The exceptionally high standard of her tourist class accommodation makes it possible to interchange many cabins between the two classes according to current requirements. When engaged in luxury winter cruising she carries 730 passengers in one class.

ROTTERDAM, the fifth *Holland-America Line* ship to carry the name, is at present engaged entirely in cruising from United States ports. For some years she ran in conjunction with NIEUW AMSTERDAM, STATENDAM and with the *German-America Line* ships HANSEATIC and HAMBURG on a schedule which included some transatlantic voyages. Now however she has been transferred to *Holland-America Line* (*Netherlands Antilles*) for cruising mainly in tropical waters.

1960

Italia Line SS LEONARDO DA VINCI, 33340tG, was completed in 1960 by Ansaldo, Sestri, for the North Atlantic express service between Genoa and New York with calls at Naples and Cannes. She joined CRISTOFORO COLOMBO (qv) on this service as a replacement for the ill-fated ANDREA DORIA.

LEONARDO DA VINCI is a beautiful ship inside and out and is completely air conditioned. She has four Denny-Brown stabilisers. Her passenger capacity is for 413 first class, 342 cabin class and 571 tourist class. All cabins have private facilities and closed circuit television is provided in the first class cabins and in all public rooms. Her décor is dignified and in excellent taste.

LEONARDO DA VINCI is a twin-screw ship with one set of cross-compound impulse-reaction turbines double-reduction-geared to each screw shaft. Four water-tube boilers supply superheated steam at 626psi and 850°F. Her speed in service is 23 knots.

With the advent of MICHELANGELO and RAFFAELLO (qv) on the express service between Genoa, intermediate Mediterranean ports and New York, CRISTOFORO COLOMBO and LEONARDO DA VINCI changed their European terminals from Genoa to Trieste and

Naples respectively and they then returned to the South American service. MICHELANGELO and RAFFAELLO then became extensively engaged in cruising from North American ports, but usually made about six transatlantic voyages each way every year. Both these great ships have now been withdrawn and LEONARDO DA VINCI is mainly engaged in cruising, but makes

Italia Line SS LEONARDO DA VINCI. Two views of the great liner taken on a rare visit to Southampton in 1976 /PR-W

some voyages between Genoa and New York. She is due for retirement in 1977.

1961

MV PRINSES MARGRIET, 9336tG, was built by De Merwede, Hardinxveld for the Rotterdam–Great Lakes (Canada) service of the *Oranje Line*. She went into service in July 1961. She was a single-screw ship powered by one ten-cylinder single-acting two-cycle MAN diesel motor and had a service speed of 17 knots. She carried 111 first class passengers in fully air conditioned and extremely comfortable accommodation. She had Denny-Brown stabilisers.

The *Oranje Line* began trading between Rotterdam and Canada in 1937 but only started its passenger services in 1953. It owned three passenger ships, all

of them single-screw motor vessels: PRINS WILLEM VAN ORANJE, 7328tG (1953), PRINSES IRENE, 8526tG (1959) and PRINSES MARGRIET. The company has now been merged into the *Fjell Line* and the three passenger liners have been disposed of. PRINSES MARGRIET was chartered by *Holland-America Line* in 1965, who later purchased her and used her on the Rotterdam–New York service. Three years later, however, she left the transatlantic route for service between New York and the West Indies under charter to the *Royal Netherlands Steamship Company*.

1962

SS FRANCE, 66348tG, was built at Penhoët for *Compagnie Générale Transatlantique (CGT)* and went into service in February 1962. At that time she was not the largest passenger ship in the world: QUEEN MARY and QUEEN ELIZABETH both exceeded her in gross tonnage by a substantial margin. She was, however, the longest of the world's liners, her overall length of 1035ft 2in being greater by 4ft than that of QUEEN ELIZABETH, although the British ship had the greater beam, 119ft against the 110ft 11in of FRANCE.

Now the two great 'Queens' have gone, FRANCE can claim the distinction of being, not only the longest, but also the largest passenger liner in the world.

Despite her size, she is a beautiful and elegant ship and has well upheld the standards of ILE DE FRANCE and LIBERTÉ, which she replaced.

FRANCE has quadruple-screws driven by sixteen steam turbines, one high-pressure, two intermediate-pressure and one low-pressure turbine being single-reduction-geared to each screw shaft. There are two engine-rooms, each with four boilers immediately ahead and forming a compact machinery unit. The

Above: MV PRINSES MARGRIET /Skyfotos
Below: SS FRANCE /CGT

spacing of these units in the ship can be established by the fact that each group of four boilers is immediately below a funnel and the two funnels are widely separated. The turbines in the forward engine-room drive the outboard shafts while those in the after engine-room drive the two inboard shafts. A total of 160000shp gives a speed of 30 knots, but the ship can attain 34 knots as maximum, and during her first year in service she steamed 158000 nautical miles at an average speed of 30·3 knots. She has two pairs of Denny-Brown stabilisers. The forecastle, like that of NORMANDIE, has a 'breakwater deck', completely free of all obstruction. Winches and anchor gear are below this deck.

Much of her superstructure, her funnels and masts are made from welded aluminium alloy, more than 1600 tons of this metal having been used in her construction. Her funnels are fitted with lateral 'wings' which are in fact large ducts through which the boiler gases escape on either side of the funnel structure proper.

Above: SS FRANCE docking at Southampton /PR-W
Below: An evening departure of SS FRANCE /PR-W

Non-combustible materials are used almost entirely in her furnishings and in the modern décor of her magnificent public rooms. The ship is of course completely air conditioned.

She was designed essentially for the North Atlantic service between le Havre, Southampton and New York and her passenger accommodation is for 407 to 617 in the first class and 1247 to 1637 in the tourist class. As indicated by these figures, some of her cabins are interchangeable between the two classes according to requirement. When engaged in winter cruising she carries 1600 passengers in one class. Her officers and crew number 1144.

At the foreward end of the ship there is a garage for ninety-four cars and there are kennels, complete with 'lamp-posts' and 'fire hydrants', for twenty dogs on the sundeck.

FRANCE cost £30m to build, of which £7m was paid to Penhoët in the form of a government subsidy. Although she was frequently booked to eighty per cent of her full capacity, she became uneconomic and was heavily subsidised by the French Government, because of her prestige value. Despite the threat of strike action by the French seaman's union, she was withdrawn from service late in 1974 and was laid up at le Havre. It was reported in 1977 that the Russians might be interested in purchasing the ship.

1962/1964

SS SAVANNAH, 15585tG, was completed in 1962 by New York Shipbuilding Company for the United States Department of Commerce. She is a single-screw ship powered by two de Laval steam turbines, single-reduction-geared to the screw shaft. Her speed in service is 20 knots.

SAVANNAH is the world's first merchant ship in which the turbines are driven by steam generated by nuclear power, and the weight of her reactor and its shielding is over 2400 long tons, enriched uranium providing the energy.

The ship has very good facilities, including a swimming pool, and she has accommodation for 60 passengers in one class. She can carry a large amount of cargo. She is operated by *First Atomic Ship Transport Incorporated* and, after making a number of 'shakedown' cruises and being laid up temporarily as the result of strikes, in 1964 she commenced a passenger and cargo service between New York and Mediterranean ports. After running thus for three years she then made four voyages without passengers, and in early 1970 plans were made for her to be laid up. If she is laid up for a long time, as seems probable, the cost will be very considerable, as it would involve bringing the reactor to a state of complete decontamination.

SS SAVANNAH the American nuclear-powered merchant ship /Real Photographs

1964

SS SHALOM, 25320tG, was built for Israeli *Zim Lines* (Zim Israel Navigation Company) at Penhoët and entered service between Haifa and New York in 1964. She made intermediate calls at Naples, Genoa, Cannes, Barcelona, Lisbon and Ponta Delgado, an itinerary which extended the Haifa–New York schedule to twelve days. SHALOM was also used for Mediterranean cruises during the winter season.

She is a luxuriously appointed ship, fully air conditioned and fitted with stabilisers. Originally she carried 72 first class passengers and 887 tourist class. She cost about £7½m to build and before she entered

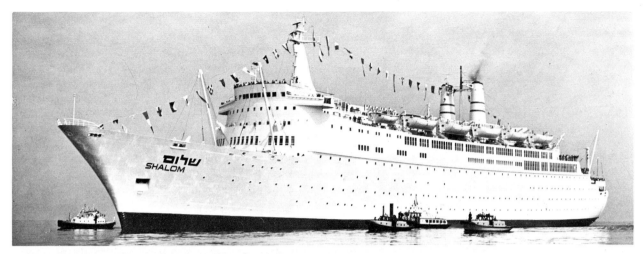

service a serious argument arose between the Israeli Ministry of Transport, who as representatives of the Israeli Government owned seventy-six per cent of the ship, and the Rabbinate Religious Party. The owners wished to provide both Kosher and non-Kosher food for the passengers. The Rabbinate insisted that only Kosher food should be served. The compromise decision was that mixed food should be served on cruises but that on voyages originating in Israel, Kosher food only should be provided.

SHALOM is a twin-screw ship with two Parsons turbines double-reduction-geared to each shaft. Three water-tube boilers supply steam at 740psi. Her speed in service is 19·5 knots.

By 1967 losses incurred in operating this ship had totalled more than £5½m and, although she 'broke even' on cruises, her North Atlantic voyages were

Top: SS SHALOM, renamed DORIC, she is now employed exclusively in cruising /*German Atlantic*

Above: SS HANSEATIC /*German Atlantic*

very poorly patronised. As a result *Zim Line*, with the approval of the Israeli Government, sold the ship in March 1967 for £6m to the *German-Atlantic Line*, who renamed her HANSEATIC as a replacement for their previous ship of that name (page 105). She operated between Hamburg, Southampton and New York as well as becoming a popular and well-patronised cruise liner.

In September 1973 she was sold to *Home Lines SA* and was renamed DORIC. She is now employed exclusively on cruising.

1965

The *Italia Line* sister ships SS MICHELANGELO, 45911tG, and SS RAFFAELLO, 45933tG, went into North Atlantic service in 1965 between Genoa and New York with calls at Naples and Cannes. MICHELANGELO was built by Ansaldo at Sestri and

RAFFAELLO by Cantieri Riuniti dell' Adriatico at Trieste.

They are twin-screw ships, each with two sets of cross-compound impulse-reaction turbines, double-

reduction-geared to the screw shafts, with four Foster Wheeler boilers supplying superheated steam at 782psi and 914°F. Each ship has a service speed of 26·5 knots, corresponding to a shaft speed of 169rpm and an output of 87000shp. On trials a sustained speed of 29·15 knots was reached by MICHELANGELO and 29·76 knots by RAFFAELLO, with short bursts in excess of 30 knots. The ships have bulbous bows and very beautiful hulls. The superstructures are of aluminium alloy. The appearance of these ships is distinctive, largely as a result of the unusual funnel design. Wind-tunnel tests showed that the larger the funnel diameter, the greater was the partial vacuum created behind it as it moved forward. This caused smoke, fumes and smuts to be sucked downwards on to the decks and even the provision of large smoke deflectors on the funnel tops could not altogether prevent this. The designers therefore decided on a

funnel design which used the minimum diameter uptake required for the boilers and surrounded it with a tubular structure which offered minimum wind resistance and therefore minimum 'suction effect', but which was sufficiently strong to support the large 'duck's foot' smoke deflectors on the funnel top (page180). The result has been highly successful.

MICHELANGELO and RAFFAELLO have identical hulls and machinery but the interior fittings and décor are different in each ship. Each liner is most elegant in its own way and each contains fine paintings and works of art. The public rooms are gracious and restful and the modern plastic garishness of some other modern

Above: MICHELANGELO entering Genoa /PR-W
Below: The beautiful lines of SS MICHELANGELO as seen from the air. RAFFAELLO is identical /*Italia*

liners has been completely avoided. A sense of spaciousness has been maintained throughout, even in the four-bedded tourist class cabins, while the first class lounge (salon) has the height and dignity usually only associated with older ships.

Each ship has luxurious first class accommodation for 535 passengers, with 550 in the cabin class and 690 in the tourist class. All cabins have private baths and facilities and even the passenger paying the lowest fare has a degree of comfort and luxury found in only a few other ships. The 720 officers and crew have accommodation in no way inferior to that of the passengers.

The ships are fully air conditioned and each has four Denny-Brown stabilisers.

Italia Line is one of a consortium of four large shipping companies comprising the Finmare Group which is partly, if not completely, state-owned. For prestige reasons, the government heavily subsidised MICHELANGELO and RAFFAELLO, first on the North Atlantic and then as cruise liners. Neither ship ever made a profit and in 1975 both were withdrawn and laid up. After talk of their purchase by Liechtenstein business men for use as cancer research clinics and later of their possible sale to Russian interests, both ships were finally disposed of to Iran in December 1976, to be used as floating hotels for the Iranian navy. The price paid for each ship was $17·8m and this sum included the costs of refit and delivery. The ships arrived in Iran about six months after date of purchase.

Below: SS ALEXANDR PUSHKIN arriving at Tilbury /PR-W
Bottom: SS ALEXANDR PUSHKIN—midships /PR-W

The Russian *Baltic Steamship Line* MV ALEXANDR PUSHKIN, 19861tG, was completed by the East German yard of V. E. B. Mathias-Thesen-Werft in 1965, and after making two cruises she inaugurated in 1966 a new service between Leningrad and Montreal, with calls at Helsinki, Copenhagen, London and Quebec. She has accommodation for 680 passengers in first class cabins and for about a further 500 in the tourist class. She is fully air conditioned and has four sister ships, IVAN FRANKO, TARAS SHEVCHENKO, SHOTA RUSTAVELI (at present on charter to *CTC*) and MIKHAIL LERMONTOV. All are widely used for cruising and for a 'round the World' service. They are advertised as 'ships for all weathers'; all are fitted with stabilisers and are air conditioned.

The five sisters are 20-knot twin-screw ships, each driven by two single-acting nine-cylinder MAN diesel motors.

MV SAGAFJORD, 24002tG, is the seventh North Atlantic passenger liner to be built for *Norwegian-America Line*. Like her immediate predecessors OSLOFJORD and BERGENSFJORD, she is a twin-screw diesel-engined vessel but has Sulzer engines instead of the Stork engines used in the previous ships. Her speed is 20 knots.

SAGAFJORD was completed in 1965 by Société des Forges et Chantiers de la Mediterranée, La Seyne, France, and she is a dual-purpose ship. As a transatlantic liner she carries 70 first class and 680 tourist class passengers between Norwegian ports, Copenhagen and New York, while as a cruise liner she carries 460 passengers in one class on Caribbean and round-the-world cruises. She is fitted with stabilisers and is fully air conditioned. A garage for twelve cars is provided in the ship.

Above: SS MIKHAIL LERMONTOV—the last of the five sister ships entered service in 1972 /PR-W
Below: MV SAGAFJORD. The photograph shows her entering the harbour at le Havre /PR-W

1966

MV KUNGSHOLM, 26678tG, is the fourth *Swedish-American Line* ship to carry the name. She was ultimately completed by John Brown, Clydebank, in the spring of 1966. Like her predecessor of the same name she was engaged on the company's Gothenburg–New York service, but was later mostly used as a cruise liner. She is fully air conditioned and has anti-roll stabilisers. Her two Götaverken diesel engines drive twin screws and give her a speed of 21 knots. On the North Atlantic her complement of passengers was 750 and of crew 355, but when cruising she carries 450 passengers and a crew of 430. She is a fine ship, luxuriously appointed, and she has a garage for thirty cars.

In 1975 she was sold to *Flagship Cruises Ltd.*, Liberia and registered in Bermuda. She retains her original name and cruises from US ports.

MV KUNGSHOLM is the largest and fastest ship ever to be owned by *Swedish America Line* /PR-W

1969

SS HAMBURG, 25022tG, is the largest passenger ship built in Germany since the end of World War II. She was completed in 1969 by Howaldtswerke-Deutsche Werft AG for the *German-Atlantic Line* (formerly *Hamburg-Atlantic Line*) and she was employed on cruising and on a regular transatlantic schedule between Hamburg and New York, in conjunction with HANSEATIC and with ships of *Holland-America Line*.

When cruising she carries about 600 passengers and when on transatlantic service about 800 in two classes. Her accommodation is air conditioned throughout and is well up to the high standards expected from the modern liner. Great emphasis is placed on providing a large amount of space for each passenger and all her cabins are particularly roomy. They are equipped with bath, toilet facilities, television, radio and a telephone.

Right: SS HAMBURG showing the unusual funnel design / Skyfotos

HAMBURG is a twin-screw ship and has two turbines (each a high-pressure and a low-pressure unit) double-reduction-geared to each screw shaft. Normally 23000shp is developed for a service speed of 23 knots. The astern turbines are located in the exhaust hood of the two low-pressure turbine casings. Steam is supplied by three Foster-Wheeler water-tube boilers at a pressure of 870psi and a superheat temperature of 968°F. The uptakes from these boilers are led up inside the single funnel casing but remain distinct and are splayed out at the top of the funnel. There they are surrounded by a flat platform and the whole arrangement, ugly as it may be, is said to be completely efficient in keeping fumes and smuts away from the passenger decks.

HAMBURG was built without Government aid, much of the money for her construction being raised by wealthy passengers who had regularly sailed in the company's other ships.

In 1973 the company's ship HANSEATIC was sold to *Home Lines*, being renamed DORIC, and HAMBURG was renamed HANSEATIC. She made only one cruise carrying the name before being sold in 1974 to the USSR. She now sails, usually on cruises from New York, as MAKSIM GORKIY (MAXIM GORKY).

The *Cunard Line* twin-screw steamship QUEEN ELIZABETH 2, 65863tG, was built by John Brown. The ship was launched by Her Majesty Queen Elizabeth on September 20th, 1967 and she left her builders' yard, six months behind schedule, on November 19th, 1969. Her construction was largely financed by a Government loan of £24m.

Above: SS HAMBURG at Southampton in 1973 /PR-W

Below: SS QUEEN ELIZABETH 2 at Southampton /PR-W

When the *Cunard Company* was considering a replacement for QUEEN MARY and QUEEN ELIZABETH, it was obvious that to be a profitable proposition such a replacement would have to be a dual-purpose ship, capable of express service on the North Atlantic during the summer months and suitable for luxury cruising during winter. A ship of the same size as the older 'Queens' would be impracticable, as it would be too large to transit the Panama Canal and to enter many of the ports and harbours included in the itineraries of the best cruise liners. Thus a ship was designed which was nearly 20000 tons gross less than QUEEN ELIZABETH and 800 tons gross less than the *CGT* liner FRANCE.

QUEEN ELIZABETH 2 now ranks as the second largest passenger ship in the world and the most powerful twin-screw liner ever built. She has a beautiful hull with a bulbous bow but her funnel, though functional, is very ugly. Much of her superstructure is fabricated from welded aluminium alloy and this has given rise to some troubles with split deck coverings. The ship is constructed to very high standards of safety and fire prevention. The official United States requirements in these respects have been fully implemented and non-combustible materials have been extensively used, though not quite to the same extent as in UNITED STATES (qv). She has a very comprehensive damage control system, operated from a continuously-manned centre located above the turbo-alternator room amidships. There are fifty-four remotely-controlled watertight doors.

QUEEN ELIZABETH 2 has a high standard of luxury and all the amenities to be expected in a modern liner. She is completely air conditioned and two sets of Denny-Brown-AEG fin-type stabilisers ensure her steadiness in even the worst Atlantic weather. Her passenger cabins and public rooms certainly achieve the object of her designers to be modern and smart

without ostentation. The elegance and serenity of the former 'Queens' is missing, but there is still a sense of spaciousness, even though in many places the deckheads appear low.

On transatlantic service the ship can carry 2025 passengers, nominally divided into 564 first class and 1461 tourist class, but these proportions can vary since much of the accommodation is interchangeable. There is however a complete deck of public rooms reserved for those passengers paying the highest fares. When cruising, 1400 passengers are carried in one class. Officers and crew number 906, considerably fewer than in the previous 'Queens' and the transatlantic passenger/crew ratio of 2·23 to 1 is much more economic than in the earlier ships.

The main engines of QUEEN ELIZABETH 2 are two sets of Pametrada cross-compound impulse-reaction turbines with astern blading on both the high-pressure and low-pressure rotors of each set. Each set drives a screw shaft through double-reduction-gearing and a total of 110000shp was developed on trials for a speed of 34·5 knots. For the ship's designated cruising speed of 28·5 knots, 94000shp is developed. The two screw propellers are of the six-bladed type and each is 19ft in diameter. Superheated steam at 850psi is supplied by three very efficient Foster Wheeler boilers, each of which has a much higher steam output than any previous marine boiler.

The maiden voyage of the QUEEN ELIZABETH 2 to New York had to be postponed from January 17th to May 2nd, 1969, on account of severe failures in both her high-pressure turbines. Many rotor blades were fractured, mainly as a result of resonant vibration set up in the blading by steam issuing from the steam nozzles. This is by no means an unknown phen-

SS QUEEN ELIZABETH 2 leaving Southampton /PR-W

omenon in turbine design, and in this case it was not unusual, as the power output of 55000shp from each set is the highest ever developed by a single unit in marine use.

The troubles were put right, but not before the mass media had done their best to denigrate British shipbuilding generally and British turbine design in particular. The ship is now popular and well patronised and makes a good profit for her owners.

In 1973 extra accommodation was added to the ship by the provision of 'penthouse' cabins on her upper deck. These are constructed of prefabricated aluminium and have made a small addition to the ship's gross tonnage, which is now 66850.

In 1974 QUEEN ELIZABETH 2 was again in trouble. On this occasion the fracture of an oil pipe contaminated the feed water to one of her boilers, the alarm system failed to operate and before the defect was noticed, a second boiler had also been badly contaminated and the third less so. The ship was completely immobilised and most of her services put out of action. After many of her 1630 passengers had been taken off by MV SEA VENTURE, the ship was towed to Hamilton, Bermuda, where temporary cleaning and repairs were carried out, enabling her to reach Southampton where final repairs were made.

Since 1969 Cunard has been owned by a London property firm, Trafalgar House Investments Ltd and the Cunard Chairman, Mr Victor Matthews, recently stated that during the first eight years of operation QUEEN ELIZABETH 2 had cost the company more than £10m as a result of failure of her main engines and boilers and of other mishaps. Despite this and the need to replace a high pressure turbine in 1977, the ship makes a handsome profit for her owners, especially from her world cruises and, no doubt, as a result of the absence of big-ship opposition on the North Atlantic since the withdrawal of FRANCE.

In 1977, the commercial facilities in the ship were augmented by the installation of satellite communications equipment, which provides a direct link with telephone and telex systems throughout the world.

1972

The Norwegian MV ROYAL VIKING STAR, 21488tG, left Southampton for her first transatlantic crossing to New York on September 2nd, 1972. She is one of the most luxurious and elegant liners of the postwar era. Built by Wartsilla in Finland, the elegance and restful good taste shown in her public rooms are a welcome change from some of the more brash décor of recent years and the ship is probably second only to FRANCE in this respect. ROYAL VIKING STAR is built for cruising and will work mostly from United States ports. She is of course, fully air conditioned and stabilised. She has four nine-cylinder Sulzer diesels developing 18000shp, geared to two shafts, and there are two controllable pitch propellers. Her service speed is 22·5 knots. A transverse thrust propeller is

MV ROYAL VIKING STAR leaving Southampton for New York 2nd September 1972 /PR-W

fitted in the bow and, like the main propulsion units, this can be controlled from the bridge.

MV ROYAL VIKING SEA and ROYAL VIKING SKY are now also in service and are sister ships of ROYAL VIKING STAR. They are all engaged in cruising but make transatlantic voyages from time to time.

1973

The building by Swan Hunter of the MV VISTAFJORD, 24292tG, for *Norwegian America Line* during 1970-1973 provided a welcome return to British shipbuilders of the construction of a luxury liner. Furthermore, the ship was most unusually completed some six weeks ahead of schedule, a feat which was acknowledged by the owners with a cash gift to the workers. However, this gesture precipitated the usual strike by those members of the yard who had not been included in the gift!

VISTAFJORD made her maiden voyage from Oslo and København to New York as a transatlantic liner, though she will be used mainly for cruising.

The performance and stability of SAGAFJORD decided the company to have the new ship built to the same hull form and dimensions. However, the aluminium superstructure was extended fore and aft and an extra deck added, which increased the passenger accommodation from 460 in the older ship to 550. To compensate for the additional top weight some 250 tons of additional permanent ballast were provided in VISTAFJORD.

The splendid private and public rooms are completely air conditioned and are constructed throughout of non-combustible materials. The décor is tasteful and restrained, giving an atmosphere of calm luxury. There are two swimming pools and a theatre/cinema; the dining room extends the whole breadth of the ship and can seat 670 persons at one sitting.

VISTAFJORD has twin screws driven by two turbocharged single acting nine-cylinder Sulzer engines, each of which develops 12000hp at 150rpm. Service speed is 20 knots, with a maximum of about 22·5 knots. A 1000hp Kamewa lateral thrust propeller is provided at the level of the forward collision bulkhead.

A beautiful ship and a credit to both builders and owners.

MV VISTAFJORD leaving København Fri-haven on her maiden voyage to New York, 23rd May 1973 /PR-W

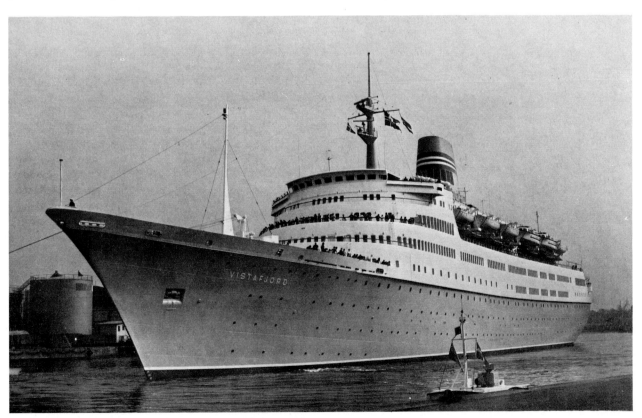

Appendix 1

SHIP DIMENSIONS

Original name on North Atlantic	Commencement of North Atlantic passenger service	Length to nearest foot	Breadth to nearest foot
ADRIATIC	1907	709	75
ALBANIA	1921	523	64
ALAUNIA	1913	520	64
ALAUNIA	1925	519	65
ALBERT BALLIN	1923	602	79
ALSATIAN	1914	571	72
ALEXANDR PUSHKIN	1965	578	78
AMERICAN BANKER	1924	437	58
AMERICA	1946	664	93
AMERIKA	1905	669	74
ANDANIA	1913	520	64
ANDREA DORIA	1953	654	90
AQUITANIA	1914	869	97
ARGUS	Never	565	68
ARKADIA	1958	590	84
AROSA SUN	1955	575	68
ATHENIA	1923	526	66
ATLANTIC	1958	564	76
AUGUSTUS	1927	666	83
AUGUSTUS	1957	680	87
AURANIA	Never	520	65
BALTIC	1904	709	76
BEAVERHILL	1941	503	62
BEAVERBRAE	1947	469	60
BELGENLAND	1921	670	78
BERGENSFJORD	1956	548	73
BERLIN	1925	549	69
BISMARCK (MAJESTIC)	1922	915	100
BREMEN	1929	899	102
BREMEN	1959	670	88
BRITTANIC	Never	852	94
BRITANNIC	1930	684	82
BLUE HEN STATE	1921	502	62
CALGARIC	1923	550	67
CALIFORNIA	1923	552	70
CALEDONIA	1905	500	58
CAMERONIA	1921	552	70
CARMANIA	1905	650	72
CARINTHIA	1956	608	80
CAROLINE (JACQUES CARTIER)	1912	413	52
CARONIA	1905	650	72
CARONIA	1949	665	91
CARPATHIA	1903	540	64
CEDRIC	1903	681	75
CELTIC	1901	681	75
CHAMPLAIN	1932	607	83
CINCINATTI	1909	582	65
COLUMBIA	1949	450	60
COLUMBUS	1923	750	83
CONTE BIANCAMANO	1925	651	76
CONTE DI SAVOIA	1932	786	96
CONTE ROSSO	1922	570	74
CORSICAN	1907	500	61
CRISTOFORO COLOMBO	1954	701	90
DE GRASSE	1924	552	71
DE KALB	1921	488	56
DEUTSCHLAND	1900	663	67
DEUTSCHLAND	1924	602	79
DORIC	1923	576	68

Original name on North Atlantic	Commencement of North Atlantic passenger service	Length to nearest foot	Breadth to nearest foot
DUCHESS OF BEDFORD	1928	582	75
DUCHESS OF YORK	1929	582	75
DUILIO	1922	602	76
EMPRESS OF AUSTRALIA	1927	590	75
EMPRESS OF BRITAIN	1931	733	98
EMPRESS OF BRITAIN	1956	640	85
EMPRESS OF CANADA	1929	582	75
EMPRESS OF CANADA	1961	650	87
EMPRESS OF ENGLAND	1955	640	85
EMPRESS OF IRELAND	1906	549	66
EMPRESS OF JAPAN	1930	640	84
EUROPA	1930	890	102
EXCALIBUR (I)	1931	450	62
EXCALIBUR (II)	1948	452	66
EXCAMBION (I)	1931	413	52
EXCAMBION (II)	1948	452	66
EXETER (I)	1931	413	52
EXETER (II)	1948	452	66
EXOCHORDA (I)	1931	413	52
EXOCHORDA (II)	1948	452	66
FLANDRE	1952	568	80
FRANCE	1912	689	76
FRANCE	1962	1035	111
FRANCONIA	1923	601	74
GEORGIC	1932	684	82
GIULIO CESARE	1956	681	87
GRIPSHOLM	1925	553	74
GRIPSHOLM	1957	632	82
GROOTE BEER	1952	440	62
HAMBURG	1926	602	79
HAMBURG	1969	638	87
HAVERFORD	1901	531	59
HOMERIC	1920	751	83
HOMERIC	1954	604	79
ILE DE FRANCE	1927	764	92
IMPERATOR (BERENGARIA)	1913	884	98
INDEPENDENCE	1950	638	90
ISRAEL	1955	454	65
IVERNIA	1900	582	65
IVERNIA	1955	608	80
JOHAN VAN OLDENBARNEVELT	1939	588	75
JUSTICIA	Never	740	86
JUTLANDIA	1946	437	61
KAISERIN AUGUST VICTORIA	1906	677	77
KAISER WILHELM DER GROSSE	1897	627	66
KAISER WILHELM II	1903	684	72
KRISTIANIAFJORD	1913	512	61
KRONPRINZESSIN CECILIE	1907	678	72
KRONPRINZ WILHELM	1901	637	66
KUNGSHOLM	1928	595	78
KUNGSHOLM	1953	588	77
KUNGSHOLM	1966	600	77
LAFAYETTE	1930	577	78
LAKE CHAMPLAIN	1900	446	52
LA LORRAINE	1900	563	60
LAPLAND	1909	606	70
LA PROVENCE	1906	602	65
LA SAVOIE	1901	563	60
LAURENTIC	1909	550	67

Original name on North Atlantic	Commencement of North Atlantic passenger service	Length to nearest foot	Breadth to nearest foot
LAURENTIC	1927	578	75
LEERDAM	1934	450	58
LEONARDO DA VINCI	1960	767	92
LETITIA	1925	526	66
LUSITANIA	1907	762	88
MAASDAM	1952	475	69
MANCHESTER MARINER	1955	466	60
MANHATTEN	1932	668	86
MAURETANIA	1907	762	88
MAURETANIA	1939	739	89
MEDIA	1947	518	70
MEGANTIC	1909	550	67
MICHELANGELO	1965	900	102
MILWAUKEE	1929	544	72
MINNEDOSA	1918	520	67
MINNEWASKA	1909	600	65
MINNEWASKA	1923	601	80
MONTCALM	1922	549	70
MONTCLARE	1922	549	70
MONTREAL	1921	476	55
MUNCHEN	1923	527	65
NELLY	1953	492	69
NEW YORK	1927	602	79
NIEUW AMSTERDAM	1906	600	69
NIEUW AMSTERDAM	1938	759	88
NOORDAM	1938	502	64
NORMANDIE	1935	981	118
NOVA SCOTIA	1947	423	61
OHIO	1923	591	72
OLYMPIA	1953	569	79
OLYMPIC	1911	852	92
ORBITA	1921	550	67
OSLOFJORD	1938	564	73
OSLOFJORD	1949	545	72
PARIS	1921	735	85
PARTHIA	1935	518	70
PILSUDSKI	1935	499	71
POTSDAM	1900	550	62
PRESIDENT GRANT	1907	599	68
PRESIDENT HARRISON	1924	502	62
PRINZESS IRENE	1903	524	60
PRINSES MARGRIET	1961	456	61
PRINZ FRIEDRICH WILHELM	1907	590	68
QUEEN ELIZABETH	1946	1031	119
QUEEN ELIZABETH 2	1969	963	105
QUEEN MARY	1936	1019	119
RAFFAELLO	1965	902	102
REGINA	1918	575	68
RELIANCE	1922	592	72
RESOLUTE	1922	596	72
REX	1932	833	97
ROCHAMBEAU	1911	559	64
ROMA	1926	666	83
ROTTERDAM	1908	650	77
ROTTERDAM	1959	749	94
ROYAL EDWARD	1910	526	60
RYNDAM	1951	475	69
SAGAFJORD	1966	620	80
SAMARIA	1922	601	74
SATURNIA	1928	631	80
SAVANNAH	1964	596	78
SAXONIA	1900	580	64
SAXONIA	1954	608	80
SHALOM	1964	627	81
SOBIESKI	1946	493	67
STATENDAM	1929	670	81
STATENDAM	1957	642	79
STAVANGERFJORD	1918	533	64
STOCKHOLM	1948	510	69
STRATHEDEN	1950	639	82
SYLVANIA	1957	608	80
TITANIC	1912	852	92
TRANSYLVANIA	1914	549	66
TRANSYLVANIA	1925	552	70
TUSCANIA	1922	552	70
TYRRHENIA	1922	553	70
UNITED STATES	1952	990	102
VATERLAND (LEVIATHAN)	1914	907	100
VICTORIAN	1905	520	60
VIRGINIAN	1905	520	60
VOLENDAM	1922	550	67
VULCANIA	1928	631	80
WASHINGTON	1933	668	86
WESTERDAM	1946	496	66
ZION	1956	454	65

The length is between perpendiculars

Appendix 2

THE BLUE RIBAND

The serious competition between shipping companies for their vessels to make the fastest North Atlantic crossings began in the 1850s and continued until the outbreak of World War II. In the postwar period, although the honour of being the fastest ship between Europe and America was held first by QUEEN MARY and finally by UNITED STATES, there was no element of competition, for the very high speed of which the latter ship was capable was attributable to military rather than commercial purposes.

A certain vagueness has often characterised the term 'Blue Riband of the North Atlantic'. Since 1850, however, the Blue Riband record holders have always sailed between Europe and the United States and ships on the Canadian service are not included. Even so, difficulties in interpretation have sometimes arisen, since the inevitable differences in points of arrival and departure have provided considerable variations in mileage run.

Again, while it is generally conceded that the holder of the Blue Riband has made the fastest times both eastbound and westbound, reference is still made in some places to the 'Blue Riband Eastbound' and the 'Blue Riband Westbound'.

Until 1935 the Blue Riband was purely an honour held by a ship until a faster ship improved on her timing. In 1935 Mr Harold Hales MP commissioned Henry Pidduck & Sons, Silversmiths, of Hanley to make a magnificent silver trophy standing nearly 4ft high and symbolic of the development of the transatlantic liner. This he presented to the *CGT*

NORMANDIE as being the then holder of the fastest eastbound and westbound passages in 1935. It was intended that the trophy should be held by the company whose ship held the record but it is not known whether in fact *United States Lines* do have possession at the present time.

In the following tables the best speeds attributed to individual ships are given, together with times, distances and the points between which the times were taken. The tables have been compiled from information given by the companies, various technical journals and published in various books. The figures given are those on which there is agreement between all sources of information.

FASTEST PASSAGES WESTBOUND

Year	Ship	Nationality	From	To	Distance nautical miles	Speed knots
1898	KAISER WILHELM DER GROSSE	German	Needles	Sandy Hook	3120	22·29
1900	DEUTSCHLAND	German	Cherbourg	Sandy Hook	3050	23·02
1902	KRONPRINZ WILHELM	German	Cherbourg	Sandy Hook	3047	23·09
1904	KAISER WILHELM II	German	Cherbourg	Sandy Hook	3068	23·12
1907	LUSITANIA	British	Queenstown	Ambrose	2780	23·99
1908	MAURETANIA	British	Queenstown	Ambrose	2889	24·86
1909	LUSITANIA	British	Daunts Rock	Sandy Hook	2784	25·85
1909	MAURETANIA	British	Daunts Rock	Sandy Hook	2784	26·06
1929	BREMEN	German	Cherbourg	Ambrose	3164	27·83
1930	EUROPA	German	Cherbourg	Ambrose	3157	27·91
1933	BREMEN	German	Cherbourg	Ambrose	3199	28·51
1933	REX	Italian	Gibraltar	Ambrose	3181	28·92
1935	NORMANDIE	French	Bishops Rock	Ambrose	2971	29·98
1936	QUEEN MARY	British	Bishops Rock	Ambrose	2907	30·14
1937	NORMANDIE	French	Bishops Rock	Ambrose	2906	30·58
1938	QUEEN MARY	British	Bishops Rock	Ambrose	2907	30·99
1952	UNITED STATES	USA	Bishops Rock	Ambrose	2906	34·51

FASTEST PASSAGES EASTBOUND

Year	Ship	Nationality	From	To	Distance nautical miles	Speed knots
1897	KAISER WILHELM DER GROSSE	German	Sandy Hook	Needles	3099	22·35
1900	DEUTSCHLAND	German	Sandy Hook	Eddystone	3085	22·46
1900	KAISER WILHELM DER GROSSE	German	Sandy Hook	Cherbourg	3184	22·80
1900	DEUTSCHLAND	German	Sandy Hook	Eddystone	2982	23·36
1906	KAISER WILHELM II	German	Sandy Hook	Eddystone	3014	23·58
1907	LUSITANIA	British	Ambrose	Queenstown	2807	23·61
1907	MAURETANIA	British	Ambrose	Queenstown	2807	23·69
1924	MAURETANIA	British	Ambrose	Cherbourg	3008	26·16
1929	BREMEN	German	Ambrose	Eddystone	3084	27·92
1935	NORMANDIE	French	Ambrose	Bishops Rock	3015	30·31
1936	QUEEN MARY	British	Ambrose	Bishops Rock	2939	30·63
1937	NORMANDIE	French	Ambrose	Bishops Rock	2978	30·99
1938	QUEEN MARY	British	Ambrose	Bishops Rock	2938	31·69
1953	UNITED STATES	USA	Ambrose	Bishops Rock	2942	35·59

Appendix 3
NORTH ATLANTIC FUNNELS

Just as the shape and design of the chimney could make or mar the beauty of a steam locomotive, so the funnel is of equal importance to the appearance of a ship. There are many instances in comparatively recent times where a ship has been given an additional dummy funnel purely for the sake of appearance, to improve the balance of the design.

Ever since the early days of the steamship the outer casing of the funnel has traditionally carried the owner's colours, and this gives it an added dignity.

Fashions in funnel design have changed radically in the past fifty years, even to the extent that the 'funnel' of some motor ships has nothing to do with the diesel exhaust but serves, on its outer surface, to carry the owner's colours while the space inside may be used for a variety of purposes, from a radio office to dogs kennels. The actual exhausts are usually to be found as insignificant uptakes somewhere near the stern of the ship.

The principal problem in the funnel design of the steamship is to provide an adequate and direct flue for the boilers while at the same time as far as possible ensuring that the smuts and fumes are kept clear of the decks and thus do not interfere with the comfort and enjoyment of passengers using these decks. The following illustrations show seven funnel designs which have appeared on the North Atlantic during the past seventy years.

Left: The first *Cunard* liner MAURETANIA had four beautifully proportioned funnels but no attempt at smoke deflection was made /NMM

Below: The third, 'dummy' funnels in the great liners MAJESTIC, BERENGARIA and LEVIATHAN have been erroneously described as engine room air takes. This sketch shows the construction of these funnels and the use to which they were put.

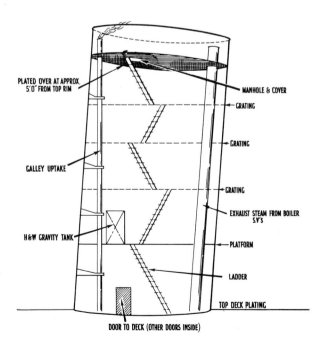

Above left: In the *United States Lines* UNITED STATES the elliptical funnels are surmounted by 'duck's foot' smoke deflectors and there are multiple louvres in the after part of the casing. The elliptical shape and the louvres are effective in reducing the partial vacuum and consequent down-draft or suction effect on the smoke as the ship moves forward /PR-W

Above: The *CGT* liner FRANCE has two elegantly streamlined funnels, each with two lateral 'fins'. The boiler uptakes are angled outwards near each funnel top and then led inside the fins, so that the smoke is voided on either side of the ship. Louvres in the funnel casings and in the under surfaces of the fins are effective in preventing smoke from being sucked downwards /PR-W

Left: The *Italia* liners MICHELANGELO and RAFFAELLO have unusual funnels. In order to keep the diameter of the funnels to a minimum and thus avoid the suction effect behind them, the casing has been replaced by a lattice work structure which offers very little air resistance but is adequate to support the large 'duck's foot' deflector plates which surmount each funnel. The *Italia Line* colours are carried on each funnel but are not very obvious /PR-W

The *Cunard Line* QUEEN ELIZABETH 2 has a single funnel surrounded by a small diameter casing. The boiler smoke and smuts are kept clear of the deck by virtue of the greatly reduced wind resistance of such a small-diameter funnel, and also by the help of two lateral deflectors. At the base of the funnel there is an inclined, angled trough which creates a strong updraught at the sides and back of the funnel proper. No attempt has been made to carry the *Cunard* colours conventionally though the funnel is painted black and the the interior of the wind trough is red. This arrangement is effective but ugly, and adds nothing to the dignity of this great ship /PR-W

The Russian liner MAKSIM GORKIY, formerly the German-Atlantic liner HAMBURG, has the individual uptakes from her boilers splayed out at the top and a large platform supported by them. This extraordinary arrangement is said to be very efficient in preventing the down draught of boiler fumes on to the upper decks /PR-W

Appendix 4

TRANSATLANTIC AIR-SEA SERVICES

The use of aircraft for the conveyance of mails, passengers and urgent freight across the Atlantic is responsible more than any other factor for the decline and near-extinction of the transatlantic passenger liner.

It is of interest to recall that before the long range air liner was developed a number of combined sea and air services were introduced to expedite the mail services between Europe and the United States.

Above: The first of these services was introduced in 1928 with the fitting of an aircraft catapult to the *CGT* liner ILE DE FRANCE, from which a biplane flying-boat was launched when the liner was about 400 miles from its destination. The aircraft carried mails and the saving in delivery time was about two days. This service ran into technical difficulties and was withdrawn, it is believed after about three months /NMM

Below: A second and more successful service was established by the *NDL* liner BREMEN in 1929, when a Heinkel 1717 float boat was catapulted from the ship 600 miles from New York and landed off the *NDL* pier at New York four hours later. This service was maintained during the summer months for several years /NMM

Above: In 1938 the Deutsche Lufthansa Company made a number of extended trials using a moored catapult ship as a halfway house for a direct service between Europe and America. The aircraft landed on the water near the ship and was lifted by crane to the catapult for servicing and relaunching. The aircraft used were Dornier type Do 18 flying boats powered by two 440hp diesel engines. These aircraft had a range 2600 miles at

130mph. The photograph shows the twin-screw MV SCHWABENLAND, 8183tG, fitted with catapult and moored off S. Miguel, Azores /PR-W

Below: The second photograph shows the Do 18 AEOLUS on the catapult of MV SCHWABENLAND /PR-W

Appendix 5

SOME TRANSATLANTIC TERMINALS

Above: Bremerhaven: the transatlantic quays /Port of Bremerhaven

Below: Hamburg: a small area of this great port, showing the terminal buildings and quays /Port of Hamburg

Above: Rotterdam: the *Holland-America Line* quay and terminal buildings /*Holland-America*

Below: Genoa: a part of this very compact harbour. The main terminal buildings serving transatlantic liners are shown left of centre with two liners alongside /*Italia*

Above: le Havre: a general view of the port /Port of le Havre

Left: Cherbourg: the transatlantic terminal can be seen to the right of centre /Port of Cherbourg

Top right: Liverpool: the landing stage, point of departure for many famous ships. The Liver Building is prominent slightly to right of centre. EMPRESS OF CANADA is at the landing stage /*Canadian Pacific*

Centre right: Southampton: the Ocean Dock and Terminal. The ship is QUEEN ELIZABETH 2 /PR-W

Bottom right: New York: QUEEN MARY, LIBERTE and UNITED STATES—three of the world's greatest ships at their piers /*Cunard*

Above: Boston: a view of the port from Custom House Tower 1912. *Cunard Line* CARMANIA leaving /*Cunard*

Below: Montreal: a view of the docks. This is the largest inland seaport in the world and is 1000 miles from the Atlantic Ocean. EMPRESS OF ENGLAND is seen leaving /*Canadian Pacific*

Appendix 6

INTERNATIONAL MERCANTILE MARINE COMPANY

The International Mercantile Marine Company (IMM) was formed in 1902 as the successor to the International Navigation Company of America, which owned the *American Line* and was the majority shareholder in the *Inman Line* and in the Belgian-America *Red Star Line* founded in 1872. IMM, which was headed by the American multi-millionaire Pierpont Morgan, became the most powerful influence in transatlantic shipping in the first twenty years of the twentieth century. Its ramifications and interests were many and complex. Perhaps its major operations were the purchase of the share capital of the mainly American owned *Atlantic Transport Line*, the British *Dominion* and *Leyland Lines* and, most important, the *White Star Line*. IMM also obtained substantial holdings in the German *Hamburg-Amerika* and *Norddeutscher Lloyd* Companies and in the Dutch *Holland-America*.

The policy of the IMM was generally to allow its constituent companies to operate individually, but there was considerable transfer of ships between *Red Star, Atlantic Transport* and the British companies. *Red Star Line* ships operated first under the Belgian and then under the British flag, while *Atlantic Transport Line* ships sailed under the British flag. IMM kept *White Star* as its principal constituent company, and when new ships were built and others were transferred within the group, *White Star* received and retained the best and its prestige was maintained.

Despite the size and influence of IMM, competition in the transatlantic trade was fierce and it was particularly affected by competition from *Cunard*, which had steadfastly avoided being drawn into the IMM network. Only two years after its formation IMM found itself in financial difficulty and the directors, headed by J. Pierpont Morgan, persuaded Bruce Ismay, son of T. K. Ismay and himself one of the British directors of IMM, to become its president.

Ismay, using his great knowledge and expertise, undoubtedly saved IMM from disaster, but at various times many of the constituent companies bought themselves out of the group or were bought out by other interests. As a result of the purchase of *White Star Line* by the *Royal Mail Steam Packet Company* in 1927, this important prestige company reverted entirely to British interests.

During the depression of the 1930s many shipping companies went out of business and the policy of the IMM was then to sell off all its European shipping interests. One of the most interesting of European sales by IMM was of its original company, *Red Star Line*, to the Hamburg shipowner Arnold Bernstein, who not only bought the remaining ships, PENNLAND and WESTERNLAND, but also the right to trade on the North Atlantic and elsewhere as *Red Star Line*.

The principal interests of the International Mercantile Marine Company are now in American companies and, probably, its most important holding is the virtual ownership of *United States Lines*.

Appendix 7

Shipbuilders mentioned in abbreviated form in the Text

Ansaldo, Genoa—Ansaldo, SA, Sestri Ponente, Genoa, Italy

Ansaldo, Sestri Ponente—Ansaldo, SA, Sestri Ponente, Genoa, Italy

Armstrong Whitworth—Sir W. G. Armstrong, Whitworth & Co Ltd, Newcastle-on-Tyne, England

Ateliers et Chantiers de France—Ateliers et Chantiers de France, Dunkirk, France

Barclay Curle—Barclay, Curle & Co Ltd, Glasgow, Scotland

Beardmore—Wm Beardmore & Co Ltd, Glasgow, Scotland

Bethlehem—Bethlehem Shipbuilding Corporation, Quincy, Mass

Bremer Vulkan—Bremer Vulkan, Vegesack, Germany

John Brown—John Brown & Co Ltd, Clydebank, Glasgow, Scotland

Cammell Laird—Cammell, Laird & Co Ltd, Birkenhead, England

Cantieri Navale, Triestino—Cantieri Navali Triestino, Monfalcone, Italy

Cantieri Riuniti dell' Adriatico—Cantieri Riuniti dell' Adriatico, Monfalcone, Italy

De Morwede—De Morwede, Harinxveld

De Schelde, Flushing—De Schelde Koninklijke Maatschappij, Flushing, Netherlands

Deutsche Werft—Deutsche Werft AG, Hamburg, Germany

Fairfield—Fairfield Shipbuilding & Engineering Co Ltd, Govan, Glasgow, Scotland

Götaverken—Götaverken, Gothenburg, Sweden

Harland & Wolff, Belfast—Harland & Wolff, Belfast, Northern Ireland

Hawthorn Leslie—R. & W. Hawthorn, Leslie & Co Ltd, Hebburn-on-Tyne, England

Henderson—James Henderson & Sons, Glasgow, Scotland

Howaldtswerke-Deutschewerft AG—Howaldtswerke AG, Kiel, Germany

Nakskov—Nakskov Skibsvaerft, Nakskov, Denmark

Nieuwe Waterweg—Nieuwe Waterweg, Schiedam, Netherlands

Netherlands Shipbuilding Company—Netherlands Dock & Shipbuilding Co, Amsterdam, Netherlands

New York Shipbuilding Co—New York Shipbuilding Corporation, Camden, NJ, USA

Penhoët—Chantiers de Penhoët, St Nazaire, France

Permanente Metals Corporation—Permanente Metals Corporation, Richmond, Calif, USA

Rotterdam Drydock Co—Rotterdamsche Droogdok, Maatschappij, Rotterdam, Netherlands

Schichau—F. Schichau, Danzig, Germany

Scotts Yard, Greenock—Scott's Shipbuilding & Engineering Co Ltd, Greenock, Scotland

P. Smit Jnr—P. Smit Jnr, Rotterdam, Netherlands

Société des Forges et Chantiers de la Mediterranée—Société des Forges et Chantiers de la Mediterranée, La Seyne, France

Alexander Stephen—Alexander Stephen, Linthouse, Glasgow, Scotland

Swan, Hunter—Swan, Hunter & Wigham Richardson, Wallsend-on-Tyne, England

Tecklenborg—Tecklenborg AG, Geestemunde

Vickers—Vickers-Armstrong Ltd, Barrow-in-Furness, England

Vulkan, Hamburg—AG Vulkan, Hamburg, Germany

Vulkan—AG Vulkan, Stettin, Germany

Weser—Weser Yard, Bremen, Germany

Wilton—Wilton-Fijenoord, Rotterdam

Workman-Clark—Workman, Clark & Co Ltd, Belfast, Northern Ireland

BIBLIOGRAPHY

During the past fifty years I have amassed a great number of notes and jottings about North Atlantic passenger ships. Much of the material of this book has been written from these notes, but I have been very happy to be able to check and to fill in the many gaps from the following books and journals in my library:

A CENTURY OF ATLANTIC TRAVEL *by Frank C. Bowen*

BRITISH PASSENGER LINERS OF THE FIVE OCEANS *by Vernon Gibb*

CANADIAN PACIFIC *by Musk*

THE DONALDSON LINE *by Dunnett*

FAMOUS LINERS AND THEIR STORY *by A. L. Cary*

THE FUTURE OF SHIPS *by Birt*

GIANT LINERS OF THE WORLD *by A. L. Cary*

HISTORY OF THE GREAT WAR—THE MERCHANT NAVY *by Hurd*

FROM LAKE AND RIVER TO DISTANT OCEANS *by Brostroms*

LLOYD'S REGISTER OF SHIPPING

MAIL LINERS OF THE WORLD *by A. L. Cary*

A SHORT HISTORY OF MARINE ENGINEERING *by Smith*

MAURETANIA *by Humfrey Jordan*

MERCHANT SHIPS *by Talbot-Booth*

NORDDEUTSCHER LLOYD *by Bessell*

NORTH ATLANTIC SEAWAY *by Bonsor*

NUCLEAR SHIP PROPULSION *by Pocock*

PASSENGER LINERS *by Laurence Dunn*

QUEEN ELIZABETH 2 *by Potter & Frost*

SHIPS OF THE HOLLAND-AMERICA LINE *by le Fleming*

SOME SHIP DISASTERS AND THEIR CAUSES *by Burnaby*

STEAM AT SEA *by Rowland*

STEAMERS OF THE PAST *by Isherwood*

THE VOYAGE OF THE DAMNED *by Thomas & Witts*

WESTERN OCEAN PASSENGER LINES AND LINERS *by Vernon Gibb*

WHITE STAR LINE *by Roy Anderson*

WILTON-FIJENOORD HISTORY *by P. J. Bouman*

Journals

ENGINEERING

MARINE ENGINEER AND NAVAL ARCHITECT

MARINE NEWS (THE WORLD SHIP SOCIETY)

MOTOR SHIP

SEA BREEZES

INDEX

ADMIRAL NAHKIMOV (1925) 88
ADRIATIC (1907) 19, 20, 21, 106, 176
AGAMEMNON (1903) 13
AJAX HMS 48
ALAUNIA (1913) 47, 176
ALAUNIA (1925) 86, 87, 176
ALBANIA (1921) 64, 176
ALBANY (1909) 39
ALBERT BALLIN (1923) 14. 79, 80, 89, 176
ALBERTA (1907) 38
ALBERTIC (1913) 62, 75, 76
ALESIA (1906) 61
ALEXANDR PUSHKIN (1965) 169, 170, 176
ALIYA (1913) 149
ALSATIAN (1913) 56, 176
AMELIA DE MELLO (1956) 149
AMERICA (1905) 25
AMERICA (1940) 127, 176
AMERICAN BANKER (1920) 83, 84, 176
AMERICA (1905) 21, 24, 25, 28, 41, 176
ANDANIA (1913) 47, 48, 176
ANDANIA (1922) 86
ANDREA DORIA (1953) 134, 145, 147, 153, 162, 176
ANGRO DO HEROISMO (1955) 149
ANTILLES (1952) 140, 141, 154
ANTONIA (1922) 86
AQUILA (1926) 91
AQUITANIA (1914) 7, 8, 9, 35, 50, 53, 54, 117, 176
ARABIC (1908) 36
ARAMAC (1948) 132
ARAWA (1907) 159
ARGENTINA 47
ARGUS HMS 74, 75, 176
ARKADIA (1931) 157, 158, 176
AROSA KULM (1920) 83, 84, 148
AROSA STAR (1931) 148
AROSA SUN (1930) 148, 176
ARTIFAX HMS (1924) 86
ASCANIA (1924) 86, 150
ATHENIA (1925) 81, 82, 176
ATLANTIC (1953) 159, 176
ATLAS (1951) 138
AUGUSTUS (1927) 91, 176
AUGUSTUS (1952) 147, 153, 176
AURANIA (1913) 47, 48, 176
AURANIA (1924) 86
AURELIA (1939) 133
AUSONIA (1922) 86
AUSTRALIS (1940) 127

B.2 25
BADGER MARINER (1953) 159
BALTIC (1904) 19, 20, 21, 176
BATORY (1936) 115
BEAVERBRAE (1939) 133, 176
BEAVERHILL (1928) 125, 176
BERENGARIA (1912) 7, 35, 49, 50, 52, 117, 119 176, 179
BELGENLAND (1914) 56, 57, 176
BELGIC (1914) 56
BERLIN (1908) 36
BERLIN (1925) 87, 89, 176
BERGENSFJORD (1913) 46, 47, 149
BERGENSFJORD (1956) 154, 170, 176
BISMARCK (1914) 51, 52, 60, 101, 176
BLUE HEN STATE (1921) 64, 66, 176
BORINQUEN (1931) 148
BRABANTIA (1920) 69
BRASIL (1905) 24
BREMEN (1900) 22, 35
BREMEN (1927) 61, 101, 102, 103, 104, 111, 117, 144, 145, 176, 178, 182
BREMEN (1939) 160, 161, 176
BRITTANIC (1914) 39, 44, 60, 176
BRITTANIC (1930) 105, 106, 107, 110, 176
BURZA 108

CAIRO (1907) 41
CALEDONIA (1905) 25, 176
CALEDONIA (1925) 66, 68, 69
CALEDONIA HMS (1914) 52
CALGARIAN (1913) 55, 56
CALGARIC (1918) 62, 75, 76, 176
CALIFORNIA (1921) 64, 66, 67, 69, 176
CAMERONIA (1921) 66, 67, 70, 176
CANTIGNY (1920) 83
CAP TRAFALGAR 27
CAPTAIN COOK (1925) 83
CARIBIA (1928) 97
CARIBIA (1948) 134
CARINTHIA (1925) 77
CARINTHIA (1956) 150, 152, 176

CARLA C (1952) 141
CARMANIA (1905) 25, 26, 27, 71, 176, 188
CARMANIA (1956) 150, 151, 152
CARNIVALE (1956) 155
CARONIA (1905) 25, 26, 27, 71, 176
CARONIA (1948) 133, 134, 176
CAROLINE (1908) 45, 176
CARPATHIA (1903) 22, 26, 176
CATIGNY (1920) 148
CEDRIC (1903) 19, 20, 24, 176
CELTIC (1901) 19, 20, 24, 176
CHAMPLAIN (1932) 110, 176
CHORAN MARU 17
CINCINATTI (1909) 40, 41, 176
CITY OF ATHENS (1920) 83
CITY OF ROME (1881) 6
CLEVELAND (1908) 41
COLUMBIA (1913) 135
COLUMBIA (1914) 57
COLUMBIA (1902) 25
COLUMBIA (1948) 134, 176
COLUMBUS (1923) 20
COLUMBUS (1923) 60, 61, 176
CONSTITUTION (1951) 136
CONTE BIANCAMANO (1925) 87, 176
CONTE GRANDE (1932) 87
CONTE ROSSO (1917) 75
CONTE ROSSO (1922) 75, 87, 90, 176
CONTE DI SAVOIA (1929) 102, 110, 111, 112, 176
CONTE VERDE (1923) 75, 87
CORAL RIVIERA (1956) 154
CORSE (1908) 45
CORSICAN (1907) 30, 176
COSTA RICA VICTORY (1944) 139
COVADONGA 9
COVINGTON 41
CRISTOFORO COLOMBO (1954) 8, 145, 147, 153, 162, 176
CURACAO HMS 119, 120

DAUPHIN 110
DE GRASSE (1924) 84, 85, 86, 99, 176
DE GRASSE (1956) 154
DE KALB (1904) 62, 176
DEUTSCHLAND (1900) 11, 13, 31, 176, 178
DEUTSCHLAND (1924) 14, 79, 80, 89, 176
DINTELDYK (1951) 138
DORIC (1923) 57, 77, 176
DORIC (1964) 167, 172
DROTTNINGHOLM (1905) 24
DUCHESS OF ATHOLL (1928) 98, 99
DUCHESS OF BEDFORD (1928) 98, 99, 176
DUCHESS OF RICHMOND (1929) 86, 98, 99
DUCHESS OF YORK (1929) 68, 98, 99, 176
DUILIO (1923) 73, 74, 176
DUTCHESS 110

EDAM (1921) 113, 114
EDMUND B ALEXANDER (1905) 24
EDWARD RUTLEDGE (1931) 110
EMPIRE BRENT (1925) 83
EMPIRE CLYDE (1921) 66
EMPIRE WAVENEY (1929) 101
EMPRESS OF AUSTRALIA (1913) 95
EMPRESS OF AUSTRALIA (1924) 85, 86, 95, 99, 176
EMPRESS OF BRITAIN (1906) 16, 29
EMPRESS OF BRITAIN (1931) 108, 176
EMPRESS OF BRITAIN (1956) 9, 142, 154, 155, 176
EMPRESS OF CANADA (1920) 99
EMPRESS OF CANADA (1929) 86, 99, 176, 186
EMPRESS OF CANADA (1961) 154, 155, 156, 176
EMPRESS OF CHINA (1907) 36
EMPRESS OF CHINA (1913) 95
EMPRESS OF ENGLAND (1957) 154, 155, 176, 188
EMPRESS OF FRANCE (1913) 55, 56
EMPRESS OF FRANCE (1928) 98, 99
EMPRESS OF INDIA (1907) 36
EMPRESS OF IRELAND (1906) 16, 29, 176
EMPRESS OF JAPAN (1930) 104, 176
EMPRESS OF SCOTLAND (1906) 24, 28, 29
EMPRESS OF SCOTLAND (1930) 104, 105
EUROPA (1906) 28, 35
EUROPA (1927) 61, 101, 102, 103, 104, 176, 178
EUROPA (1953) 144, 145, 160
EXCALIBUR (1931) 109, 176
EXCALIBUR (1944) 110, 176
EXCAMBION (1931) 109, 176
EXCAMBION (1944) 110, 176
EXETER (1931) 109, 176

EXETER (1944) 110, 176
EXOCHORDA (1931) 109, 176
EXOCHORDA (1944) 110, 176

FAIRLAND 152
FAIRSEA (1957) 150
FAIRWIND (1957) 150, 152
FEDOR SHALYAPIN (1956) 150
FELIX ROUSSEL (1930) 148
FLANDRE (1952) 85, 140, 141, 176
FLAVIA (1947) 132
FLORIDA (1905) 21
FLORIDE (1907) 45
FORFAR HMS (1922) 73
FORMIGNY 77
FORT ST GEORGE 44
FRANCE (1912) 30, 45, 46, 64, 93, 94, 176
FRANCE (1962) 8, 164, 165, 172, 174, 176, 180
FRANCE IV (1912) 46
FRANCIS DRAKE (1947) 131
FRANCIS Y SLANGER (1925) 97
FRANCONIA (1923) 77, 78, 150, 176
FRANCONIA (1956) 150, 152
FULVIA (1949) 136
FURANZO MARU (1927) 94
FURST BISMARCK (1890) 6, 96

GENERAL VON STEUBEN (1923) 78
GEORGE ANSON (1947) 131
GEORGE WASHINGTON (1907) 51
GEORGIC (1932) 105, 106, 107, 108, 110, 176
GEROLDSTEIN (1904) 159
GIGANTIC (1911) 42, 44
GREAT SEA (1951) 153
GRIPSHOLM (1925) 24, 88, 176
GRIPSHOLM (1957) 88, 157, 176
GROOTE BEER (1944) 139, 140, 176
GRUZIA (1939) 126
GUADALUPE 9
GUGLIELMO MARCONI (1929) 110, 111
GUILIO CAESARE (1922) 73, 90
GUILIO CAESARE (1941) 147, 153, 176

HAMBURG tug 134
HAMBURG (1926) 89, 90, 122, 162, 176
HAMBURG (1969) 171, 172, 176
HANSA (1900) 14
HANSA (1923) 80
HANSEATIC (1930) 104, 105, 122, 162
HANSEATIC (1964) 167, 171, 172
HANSEATIC (1969) 172
HARRY LEE (1931) 110
HAVERFORD (1901) 18, 19, 176
HAWKE HMS 44
HELIOPOLIS (1907) 41
HIGHFLYER HMS 12
HOMELAND (1905) 24
HOMERIC (1920) 60, 61, 176
HOMERIC (1931) 146, 176
HUASCARON (1931) 133

ILE DE FRANCE (1927) 46, 93, 94, 140, 146, 164, 176, 182
ILSTENSTEIN (1904) 159
IMPERATOR (1913) 25, 49, 50, 51, 60, 101, 176
IMPERIAL BAHAMA (1928) 98
INDEPENDENCE (1950) 136, 137, 176
ISRAEL (1955) 149, 150, 176
ITALIA (1905) 74
ITALIA (1928) 98
ITHACA (1956) 149
IVAN FRANKO 170
IVERNIA (1900) 14, 15, 22, 176
IVERNIA (1956) 150, 152, 176

JACQUES CARTIER (1908) 45, 176
JERUSALEM (1913) 47, 149
JOHANN HEINRICH BURCHARD (1920) 69
JOHAN VAN OLDENBARNEVELT (1930) 123, 176
JOHN ERICSSON (1928) 97
JOHN PENN (1931) 110
JOSEPH HUGHES (1931) 110
JURY DOLGURUKY (1926) 89
JUSTICIA (1914) 56, 176
JUTLANDIA (1934) 125, 126, 176

KAISER WILHELM DER GROSSE (1897) 6, 11, 12, 13, 31, 33, 176, 178
KAISER WILHELM II (1903) 11, 12, 13, 31, 176, 178
KAISERIN AUGUST VICTORIA (1906) 24, 28, 29, 176
KARLSRUHE (German Navy) 12

KARLSRUHE (1900) 22
KATOOMBA (1913) 135
KING GEORGE V 17
KONIG FRIEDERICH AUGUST (1960) 61
KONIGSTEIN (1907) 159
KRISTIANIAFJORD (1913) 46, 47, 59, 176
KRONPRINZ WILHELM (1901) 11, 12, 31, 176, 178
KRONPRINZESSIN CECILIE (1907) 11, 12, 13, 31, 176
KUNGSHOLM (1900) 15, 24
KUNGSHOLM (1928) 97, 176
KUNGSHOLM (1953) 144, 160, 176
KUNGSHOLM (1966) 171, 176

LACONIA (1922) 66, 71, 77
LAFAYETTE (1930) 105, 106, 110, 176
LAFAYETTE (1935) 117
LAKE CHAMPLAIN (1900) 16, 17, 176
LAKONIA (1930) 123
LA LORRAINE (1900) 17, 18, 29, 176
LA PROVENCE (1906) 29, 30, 176
LA SAVOIE (1900) 18, 29, 176
LA TOURAINE (1891) 45
LANCASTRIA (1922) 26, 66, 70
LAPLAND (1909) 38, 57, 176
LAURENTIC (1907) 7, 38, 39, 176
LAURENTIC (1927) 92, 177
LEERDAM (1921) 113, 114, 177
LEONARDO DA VINCI (submarine) 99
LEONARDO DA VINCI (1960) 8, 147, 153, 162, 163, 177
LEONID SOBINOV (1956) 150, 152
LETITIA (1912) 83
LETITIA (1925) 81, 82, 177
LEVIATHAN (1914) 50, 51, 127, 177, 179
LIBERTE (1927) 103, 104, 140, 164, 186
LIGURIA (1917) 60
LIMBURGIA (1920) 69
LOMBARDIA (1920) 70
LONG ISLAND USS (1940) 143
LORRAINE II (1900) 18
LUREGETHAN 92
LUSITANIA (1906) 11, 13, 26, 31, 32, 33, 45, 53, 177, 178

MAASDAM (1921) 113
MAASDAM (1952) 138, 139, 157, 177
MAJESTIC (1890) 6, 7, 21, 51
MAJESTIC (1914) 52, 179
MAMARI (1904) 159
MANCHESTER MARINER (1955) 149, 177
MANHATTAN (1932) 112, 113, 177
MARDI GRAS (1961) 155
MARIANNE IV (1944) 140
MARIPOSA (1931) 146
MARLOCH (1905) 23
MARNIX VAN ST ALDEGONDE (1930) 123
MARVALE (1907) 30
MATATUA (1904) 159
MAURETANIA (1907) 7, 11, 13, 26, 31, 32, 33, 34, 35, 45, 50, 53, 102, 117, 177, 178, 179
MAURETANIA (1939) 124, 125, 177
MAXSIM GORKIY/MAXIM GORKY (1969) 172, 181
MEDIA (1947) 119, 132, 177
MEGANTIC (1909) 39, 177
MELITA (1917) 59
MICHELANGELO (1965) 8, 147, 162, 163, 167, 168, 169, 177, 180,
MIDWAY USS 142
MIKHAIL LERMONTOV 170
MILWAUKEE (1929) 100, 101, 177
MINNEDOSA (1917) 59, 177
MINNETONKA (1924) 78, 79
MINNEWASKA (1909) 40, 177
MINNEWASKA (1923) 78, 79, 177
MOLTKE (1902) 74
MONARCH OF BERMUDA (1931) 157, 158
MONTCALM (1922) 73, 177
MONTCLARE (1922) 72, 73, 177
MONTICELLO (1903) 13
MONTEITH (1907) 36
MONTLAURIER (1907) 36
MONTNAIRN (1907) 36
MONTREAL (1906) 61, 177
MONTROSE (1922) 73
MONTROYAL (1906) 29
MORMACMAIL (1940) 143
MOUNT VERNON (1907) 13
MOUNT VERNON (1933) 13
MUNCHEN (1913) 76
MUNCHEN (1923) 62, 77, 78, 177

NAPIER STAR 92
NAVARINO (1957) 157

NEA HELLAS (1922) 68, 142
NELLY (1940) 143, 177
NEW AUSTRALIA (1931) 157, 158
NEWFOUNDLAND (1947) 131
NEW YORK (1922) 68, 142
NEW YORK (1927) 89, 90, 177
NIAGARA (1908) 45
NIEUW AMSTERDAM (1906) 27, 28, 177
NIEUW AMSTERDAM (1938) 120, 121, 161, 162, 177
NOORDAM (1900) 15, 24
NOORDAM (1938) 122, 177
NORMANDIE (1935) 94, 102, 103, 115, 116, 117, 119, 165, 177, 178
NOVA SCOTIA (1947) 131, 177
No. 252 (1940) 128
No. 534 (1936) 117
No. 552 (1938) 128

OCEAN MONARCH (1957) 155
OCEANIC (1899) 21
OCEANIC CONSTITUTION (1951) 137
OCEANIC INDEPENDENCE (1950) 137
OCEANIEN (1935) 123
OHIO (1913) 62, 76, 177
OLYMPIA (1953) 68, 142, 143, 177
OLYMPIC (1911) 19, 21, 39, 42, 43, 44, 50, 51, 60, 177
ORBITA (1915) 62, 63, 76, 177
ORCA (1918) 62, 75, 76
ORDUNA (1915) 62, 76
ORION 77
OROPESA (1915) 62
OSLOFJORD (1938) 122, 123, 177
OSLOFJORD (1949) 136, 154, 170, 177

PARIS (1921) 46, 64, 65, 93, 94, 104, 177
PARTHIA (1948) 132, 177
PASTEUR (1939) 145, 160, 161
PENNLAND (1918) 57, 58, 159
PESARO (1902) 75
PIEMONTE (1917) 60
PILSUDSKI (1935) 155, 177
PITTSBURGH 57
POCOHONTAS (1900) 21, 22
POTSDAM (1900) 51, 177
PRESIDENT GARFIELD (1921) 64, 65, 66
PRESIDENT GRANT (1903) 35, 177
PRESIDENT HARRISON (1920) 81, 177
PRESIDENT LINCOLN 35
PRESIDENT MADISON (1921) 66
PRINS WILLEM VAN ORANJE (1953) 163
PRINSES IRENE (1959) 163, 177
PRINSES MARGRIET (1961) 163, 164, 177
PRINZ EITEL FRIEDRICH (1904) 62, 63
PRINZ FRIEDRICH WILHELM (1907) 36, 177
PRINZESS IRENE (1900) 21, 22
PROTEA (1920) 83
PROVENCE II (1906) 30

QUEENS 110
QUEEN ANNA MARIA (1956) 9, 142, 155
QUEEN ELIZABETH (1940) 7, 119, 128, 129, 130, 164, 173, 177
QUEEN ELIZABETH 2 (1968) 7, 8, 9, 172, 174, 177, 181, 186
QUEEN MARY (1935) 7, 102, 115, 117, 118, 119, 120, 128, 129, 164, 173, 177, 178, 186

RAFFAELLO (1965) 8, 147, 162, 163, 167, 168, 169, 177, 180
REGINA (1918) 57, 58, 77, 177
REGINA MAGNA (1939) 145, 160, 161
RELIANCE (1920) 69, 70, 177
REMUERA (1948) 132
REPUBLIC (1903) 20, 21, 35, 51
RESCUE (1921) 66
RESOLUTE (1920) 69, 70, 177
REX (1929) 102, 110, 111, 112, 117, 177, 178
ROCHAMBEAU (1911) 42, 177
ROMA (1926) 90, 91, 177
ROTTERDAM (1908) 37, 177
ROTTERDAM (1959) 122, 161, 162, 177
ROYAL EDWARD (1907) 41, 177
ROYAL GEORGE (1907) 41
ROYAL VIKING SEA (1972) 175
ROYAL VIKING SKY (1972) 175
ROYAL VIKING STAR (1972) 174, 175
RUTHENIA (1900) 17
RYNDAM 15
RYNDAM (1951) 138, 157, 177

SABAUDIA 134
SAGAFJORD (1965) 170, 175, 177
SAMARIA (1922) 66, 71, 77, 150, 177
SAN GIUSTA (1890) 96

SATURNIA (1925) 96, 97, 177
SAVANNAH (1962) 166, 177
SAXONIA (1900) 14, 15, 22, 177
SAXONIA (1956) 150, 151, 177
SCHWABENLAND 183
SCOTLAND (1930) 104
SCOTIAN (1903) 35
SCOTSTOUN HMS 68
SCYTHIA (1921) 66, 71, 77, 150
SEA LUCK (1950) 137
SEA VENTURE cf. 174
SEAWISE UNIVERSITY (1936) 130
SERVIA (1903) 35
SEVEN SEAS (1940) 143, 144
SHALOM (1964) 149, 166, 167, 177
SHELBY cf. 110
SHOTA RUSTAVELI 170
SOBIESKI (1939) 126, 177
SOLGLIMT (1900) 15
SOVETSKY SOJUS/SOVIETSKY SOJUS (1923) 80
SPAARNDAM (1921) 113
SPARVIERO (1927) 91
ST LOUIS (1929) 101
ST PAUL (1895) 12
STATENDAM (1914) 56
STATENDAM (1924) 100, 122, 177
STATENDAM (1957) 156, 162, 177
STAVANGERFJORD (1915) 47, 58, 59, 177
STEFAN BATORY (1952) 138, 139
STEUBEN (1923) 78
STOCKHOLM (1900) 15, 16
STOCKHOLM (1948) 134, 135, 146, 177
STORSTADT 39
STRATHAIRD 116
STRATHALLAN (1937) 137
STRATHEDEN (1937) 137, 177
STRATHMORE (1937) 137
STRATHNAVER 116
SUFFREN (1919) 84
SYLVANIA (1956) 150, 152, 177

TAISEIYO MARU (1905) 26
TARAS SHEVCHENKO 170
TARSUS (1931) 110
TEUTONIC (1889) 21
TIRPITZ (1913) 69, 94, 95
TITANIC (1911) 19, 22, 39, 42, 43, 44, 177
TRANSYLVANIA (1914) 54, 55, 177
TRANSYLVANIA (1925) 66, 68, 69, 177
TUBER ROSE HMS 34
TUSCANIA (1915) 26, 66, 68, 69, 71
TUSCANIA (1922) 68, 142, 177
TYRRHENIA (1922) 66, 70, 177

U-20 33
U-30 82
U-32 108
U-56 69
U-99 73
U-103 44
U-178 99

UNITED STATES (1952) 119, 141, 142, 173, 177, 178, 180, 186
UNIVERSE (1939) 160
UNIVERSE CAMPUS (1935) 159

VATERLAND (1914) 51, 60, 101, 177
VEENDAM (1923) 71
VENEZUELA (1924) 86
VICEROY OF INDIA 77
VICTORIA LUISE (1900) 13
VICTORIAN (1905) 23, 55, 177
VILLE D'ANVERS (1920) 83
VIRGINIAN (1905) 23, 24, 55, 177
VISTAFJORD (1970) 175
VOLENDAM (1921) 71, 72, 177
VOLKERFREUNDSCHAFT (1948) 134
VOLTURNO 27
VON STEUBEN (1901) 12
VULCANIA (1928) 96, 97, 177

WAKEFIELD (1932) 113
WASHINGTON (1933) 112, 113, 177
WATERMAN (1951) 138
WAYLAND (1922) 86
WESTERDAM (1940) 130, 177
WESTERNLAND (1918) 57, 58, 77, 159
WEST POINT (1940) 127
WILLIAM O'SWALD (1920) 69
WOLFE HMS (1922) 73
WOLVERINE STATE (1920) 81

ZAANDAM (1938) 122
ZION (1956) 148, 150, 177
ZUIDERDAM (1940) 130